THE SWEDISH EXPERIMENT IN FAMILY POLITICS

THE SWEDISH EXPERIMENT IN FAMILY POLITICS

The Myrdals and the Interwar Population Crisis

Allan Carlson

Transaction Publishers
New Brunswick (U.S.A.) and London (U.K.)

Copyright © 1990 by Transaction Publishers.
New Brunswick, New Jersey 08903

Library of Congress Catalog Number: 89-5092
ISBN 0-88738-299-1 (cloth)
Printed in the United States of America

Library of Congress Cataloging-in-Publication Data

Carlson, Allan C.
    The Swedish experiment in family politics: the Myrdals and the interwar poplulation crisis/ Allan Carlson.
        Bibliography: p.   cm.
        Includes index.
        ISBN 0-88738-299-1
        1. Family policy—Sweden—History—20th century. 2. Family size-Sweden—History—20th century. 3. Myrdal, Gunar, 1898-1987.
    4. Myrdal, Alva Reimer, 1902-1982.   I. Title.
    HQ647.C37   1989
    304.6'34'09485—dc 20   89-5092
                                                                          CIP

To my parents

Contents

Acknowledgments

My work on the subject of the Myrdals and the origins of a Swedish family politics began as a dissertation project in the History Department of Ohio University. I need thank my major professor, Carl G. Gustavson, for his guidance and encouragement during that phase of the project.

My research work in Sweden enjoyed the full support of the staff of the Labor Movement Archive. Stellan Andersson, archivist for the Myrdal collections, deserves special note, along with Sven Bodin and Eva Karlsson. I am grateful to the Steering Committee of the Social Democratic Labor party and to the Social Democratic Parliamentary Group for granting permission to review restricted materials. Ann-Katrin Hatje, herself a scholar on this subject, guided my exploration of materials at the Swedish National Archive. My colleagues at the Rockford Institute, notably Bryce Christensen and Thomas Fleming, helped me to formulate my understanding of the true meaning and current relevance of the Swedish experiment. Heidi Bradford coordinated the typing chores.

I owe immeasurable gratitude to my wife, Elizabeth, who gave assistance and support in every phase of the project and who kept spurring me on when the doldrums set in. Finally, I need to thank my parents, who convinced me that it all might be worthwhile and to whom I dedicate this volume.

Introduction

Swedish debate over "the population question" of the 1930s represents the first decisive infusion of modern social science research into
the shaping of public policy. Armed with a new kind of statistical analysis, Alva and Gunnar Myrdal used the sharp decline in the Swedish
birth rate to justify a fresh phase of social reform, an unprecedented
intervention of democratic government into hitherto private questions
of gender and sexuality, and a new vision of the individual's and the
family's relationship to the central state. Using persuasive reasoning
and political muscle, the Myrdals successfully wrested the population
issue away from Swedish conservatives and nationalists and turned it
toward the service of socialist goals. In a remarkable four-year period,
they implemented a large share of their ideological program and
helped transform the nature of the Swedish domestic state. As an intel-
lectual-political feat, their achievement knows few parallels. As a
model for the use of social science in political debate, their work set an
important and widely copied precedent that continues both to inspire
and bedevil modern policy-making.

Sweden stands, today, as a widely touted example of modern family
policy, a system that recognizes the social transformations made necessary by the commitment to gender equality and the full industrialization of social life. American policy analysts, in particular, turn to Sweden as the purest model for a regime of day care, progressive
schooling, paid paternal leave, children's allowances, and a child-oriented health system, which reconciles the need for human reproduction with the drive for gender equality. In both overall vision and program specifics, the origins of this Swedish model lay in the ideology
and social science of the Myrdals. But ironically, the Myrdals themselves looked to the United States in the interwar period as their labora-

tory source for both a new, activist social science and provocative policy ideas. Their use of survey research, demographic statistics, and sociological analysis lent a new power and force to political argumentation that swept aside traditionalist sentiments. Similarly, the dark side of modern Sweden—seen in the subsequent dissolution of social bonds—derives in part from the inherent, but then little understood, weaknesses of the social science data they used.

The Myrdals' experience also casts a strong light on the question of the individual's role in political change. Is each actor largely a reflection of broad social and intellectual currents that are irresistible in any broad sense of time? Or can individuals, acting as agents of their own will, redirect the path of a community or nation through the force of ideas?

Most recent interpreters of the Swedish population debate of the 1930s see the Myrdals primarily as popularizers of already extant policy ideas, in service to historically irresistible shifts in social organization. Historian Ann-Katrin Hatje, for example, finds the Myrdals mere borrowers of existing political theories, with, if anything, too little appreciation for the changing roles of women and sexuality, which were driven in turn by social and economic evolution. Ann-Sofie Kälvemark, in her assessment of the effects of the pronatalist policies adopted in the 1930s, describes considerable confusion over goals, means, and results, suggesting that historical trends moved in spite of ideas and policy. In his provocative analysis of family decline in modern Sweden, sociologist David Poponoe gives primary emphasis to socioeconomic currents that have produced what he calls "the postnuclear family." While cautious, he nonetheless shows the Myrdals' involvement as essentially an interesting ripple on a tidal wave of historical change.[1]

However, close analysis of the Myrdals as historical actors reveals a different picture: In a fundamental way, their application of intellectual muscle and political and institutional skills altered the course of their society. Not the social trends they decried, nor the policies they sought, nor the results they achieved were the immutable workings of history. Rather, they used the power of ideas to redirect Sweden in radically new ways. In their pursuit of social revolution they foreclosed other options and possibilities and so served as progenitors of the postfamily welfare state.

The Myrdals' entry into the Swedish debate and the scope of their influence should also be seen in the context of European-wide angst over demographic developments in the interwar years, 1919–39. Differential population pressures came to obsess contemporary politics. Throughout large sections of Eastern Europe, for example, birth rates remained relatively high. Poland, Slovakia, Yugoslavia, Rumania, Greece, and Italy all confronted large numbers of landless rural peasants and an industrial sector that seemed incapable of offering relief. Considerable attention focused on crafting solutions to this apparent "overpopulation."[2] The problem was compounded by the significant minority populations found in the restructured postwar nations of Central and Eastern Europe, ethnic groups often exhibiting very different, and politically explosive, levels of fertility.[3]

Meanwhile, an altogether different problem confronted the nations of Western and Central Europe, the British Commonwealth, and North America: a sharp and apparently accelerating decline in fertility and the growing specter of "depopulation." The development of new demographic measures in this period, particularly the net reproduction rate, focused attention on the diminishing number of children. Beginning in the late nineteenth century and expanding rapidly after 1918, a visible pronatalist movement emerged throughout Western Europe intent on giving political affirmation to marriage, family creation, and high fertility.

While varying in emphasis and intensity from land to land, pronatalist writers and organizations shared common motivations. At root level, pronatalism rested on nationalist, even "tribal," emotions. After a century and a half of uninterrupted population expansion and evident racial vigor, the specter of a declining and aging population, an influx of "colored" immigrants, miscegenation, and the loss of national and racial distinctiveness seemed a grave and humbling threat to many Europeans. Much of the pronatalist literature from the period dealt explicitly with the white race's decline and eventual submersion by expanding black and yellow peoples. Apprehension and fear were common emotions.[4]

A related theme was concern over the geopolitical implications of an aging and shrinking population. For German and Scandinavian authors, the threat arose from the rapidly growing Slavic nations to the east. For imperial Britain and France, their ability to hold onto transoceanic empires in the face of growing native populations came increasingly into question. France also looked at the perceived demographic threat across the German border.[5]

A third shared motivation was economic. In contrast to the neo-Malthusians, who projected an increase in average living standard from a declining population, European pronatalists argued that in an aging population, social welfare and medical costs would swell and fall on an ever shrinking number of economically active people. They also noted that older people tended to consume less, which resulted in lower demand, less capital formation, and a generally contracting economy. The modern European economy, they argued, was predicated on a growing population. Declining numbers would mean economic crisis, a thesis drawing particular attention after 1929.[6]

Analyses of the cause of the birth decline also had common characteristics. Most interwar European pronatalists saw the root cause of the birth decline as a decay in the spiritual nature of Western man. This product of the bourgeois ethic was seen in the middle class's upward striving spirit, drive for excessive luxury, individualistic egoism, and unwillingness to sacrifice for children. Neo-Malthusian propaganda in favor of contraception as an antipoverty tool also drew regular scorn, as did women's emancipation. Analysts saw poverty, the lack of housing, unemployment, and the breakdown of the extended family as sometimes important, but merely secondary, causes.[7]

Turning to specific policies, pronatalists called on the state to reward those exercising social responsibility and to penalize the unmarried and childless. They opposed the employment of married women and supported policies aimed at keeping or returning women to the traditional role of mother in the home. They distrusted or actually deplored all things urban, while supporting the establishment of "garden suburbs" and the reinvigoration of the rural or agrarian sector. Pronatalists usually opposed voluntary sterilization of the genetically healthy. They supported laws banning sex education, the sale or use of contraceptives, and abortion. Positive social policy measures regularly included creating or raising family tax deductions; the imposition of a special "bachelor" tax on the unmarried or childless; the implementation of maternity bonuses; cash loans to newlyweds; payments to families with three or more children; wages or family allowances differentiated according to number of children; the use of certain honorary inducements, such as medals, for the mothers of many children; special housing programs for large families; and the use of propaganda emphasizing the value of family life and children to the nation.

In France and Belgium, pronatalism had both democratic and Catholic casts. Associations of large families, commonly affiliated with Catholic parishes, coalesced by 1920 into powerful national lobbies seeking an array of tax, financial, and welfare benefits for the parents of many children. Catholic leaders drew encouragements from the papal encyclicals *Rerum Novarum* and *Quadragesimo Anno*, which affirmed state efforts to redistribute income in favor of large families. The movement's proudest achievements were comprehensive family allowance systems, constructed at first on a voluntary, industry-by-industry basis but nationalized during the 1930s and transformed into broad family benefit plans.[8] Fascist Italy drew pronatalism into its proclaimed struggle against hedonism and for the renaissance of the spiritual force in Western man. The state imposed a heavy tax surcharge on bachelors and offered large families free transportation, utility rebates, employment preference, maternity clinics, guaranteed maternity leave for working mothers, eight-day honeymoons with double-pay, and a fledgling family allowance program.[9]

Pronatalist concerns marked Weimar Germany (the constitution of 1919, for example, contains several positive references to "family" and "large families"), and the democratic regime gave tax and other preferences to couples with five or more children. Between 1928 and 1933, though, the German birthrate plunged again and pronatalist voices grew frantic, adding to the mood of pessimism that dominated Germany in these years. Shortly after the national socialists took power in 1933, Interior Minister Wilhelm Frick called for the reconstruction of Germany's whole political system from a population perspective. The most famous of the German innovations was the June 1933 marriage loan act, which offered one thousand Deutsche Marks to newly married "racially acceptable" couples, for the purchase of furniture and household goods, with one-fourth of the principal forgiven for each child born.[10]

In England, meanwhile, pronatalist sentiments among committed imperialists clashed with concern over eugenics and the variation in birthrate between social classes. While the privately organized National Birth Rate Commission, in its 1916 report, lamented population stagnation as "injurious" to the national interest, others gave attention to the "the extinction of the upper classes" and the promiscuous overbreeding of "the lower orders."[11] Serious British debate over the issues of a "living wage" and children's allowances rarely touched on the pronatalist theme, being viewed instead as a component of welfare policy.[12]

The birth question generated intellectual anxiety and policy action in many other European states,[13] including Switzerland, Austria, the Netherlands, Estonia, Latvia, Hungary, Spain, and Bulgaria. Related fears haunted Canada, Australia, and the United States.[14] European peoples everywhere, it seemed by the mid-1930s, were poised above the abyss of demographic ruin.

Into this volatile mix stepped Alva and Gunnar Mydral in 1934, with a unique approach to the population issue. With other pronatalists from the period the Myrdals shared concerns for maintaining racial or ethnic homogeneity, for national defense, and for the negative psychological and economic effects of depopulation. They declared an open goal of raising Swedish fertility by 40 percent and advocated massive state incentives in favor of marriage and fertility.

Yet in other ways, the Myrdals broke ranks with pronatalist sentiments. Concerning cause, they dismissed concern about "the spiritual sickness of Western man" as anachronistic and instead focused on recent changes in the material circumstances of families that reduced the desire for children. They embraced "women's emancipation" and other feminist themes with enthusiasm, casting the homemaker as an outdated parasite. While other pronatalists sought to reconstruct rural or semirural habitats for families, the Myrdals celebrated city living as the inevitable and desirable future. In a still sharper break, they advocated state-run sex education and freely available contraceptives as necessary to a successful population program. While continental pronatalists looked back wistfully to better times, the Myrdals called for a forced march into modernity as the only hope for families and children. Ideologically, they sought nothing less than to reconcile pronatalism and nationalism with neo-Malthusianism, socialism, and feminism.

Representing what might be called an intellectual political biography, this volume looks at the influence of personal ideology on social science and of self-proclaimed social scientists on public policy. It places the Myrdals' work within a dual context: as a distinct response to a European-wide problem and as an integral force in the emergence of the modern Swedish welfare state. The volume chronicles the origin, clear expression, political implementation, and long-term influence of a unique set of ideas, created, borrowed, and adapted by two individuals. Short of revolution or war, our century can show no better example of the power of ideas and human will in altering the course of a nation.

Chapter 1 provides an overview of the Swedish demographic, intellectual, and political mix into which the Myrdals projected their work. Chapter 2 traces the origin of the Myrdals' intellectual scheme, through an analysis of the influences that shaped their minds and careers prior to 1934. The new ideas themselves and the argumentation that sustained them are summarized in chapter 3. The next chapter describes the policy debate that exploded in Sweden during 1934–35. Chapter 5 details the extraordinary intellectual influence that the Myrdals exercised over the Population Commission of 1935 and related governmental and private organizations. Chapter 6 traces the political reactions and the development of new policies that marked the 1936–38 period. A final chapter offers conclusions about the ability of ideas bound to modern social science to influence human events and suggests how the Swedish debate of the 1930s may be replicated in the American domestic policy debate of the 1990s.

Notes

1. See Ann-Katrin Hatje, *Befolkningsfrågan och välfärden: Debatten om familjepolitik och nativitetsökning under 1930-och 1940-talen* (Stockholm: Allmänna Förlaget, 1914); Ann-Sofie Kälvemark, *More Children of Better Quality? Aspects of Swedish Population Policy in the 1930's* (Uppsala: Historiska institutionen, 1980); and David Popenoe, *Disturbing the Nest: Family Change and Decline in Modern Society* (New York: Aldine de Gruyter, 1988).
2. J. D. Black, "The Problem of Surplus Agricultural Population," *International Journal of Agrarian Affairs* 1 (1939): 5–90; Josef Poniatowski, "Le probleme du sur peuplement dans l'agriculture polonaise," *L'est Européaen agricole* 5 (April 1936): 21–60; and Oscar Jazzi, "The Economic Crisis in the Danubian States," *Social Research* 2 (February 1935): 98–116.
3. See Eugene M. Kulischer, *Europe on the Move: War and Population Change, 1917–1947* (New York: Columbia University Press, 1948); and Institut National de la Statistique et des etudes economiques, *Les Transferts internationals de populations* (Paris: Presses Universitaires de France, 1946).
4. Examples of pronatalist literature predicated on racial fears include

Henri Decugis, *Le destin des races blanches* (Paris: Librairie de France, 1936); Fernand Boverat, *Le race blanche en danger de mort* (Paris: Alliance nationale pour l'accroissement de la population francaise, 1938); Friedrich Burgdörfer, *Volk Ohne Jugend* (Berlin-Grunewald: Kurt Vowinckel Verlag, 1932); F. Burgdörfer, *Sterben die weissen Volker? Die Zukunft der weissen und farbiger Volker im Lichte der Biologiske Statistik* (Munich: Georg D. W. Callwey Verlag, 1934), pp. 49–71; Roderich von Ungern-Sternberg, *De Sorge Europas* (Berlin: Verlag von George Stilfe, 1936); and Otto Helmut, *Volk in Gefahr* (Munich: J. F. Lehmanns Verlag, 1930).

5. See Hans Weigert, *Generals and Geographers: The Twilight of Geopolitics* (New York: Oxford University Press, 1942); Roderich von Ungern-Sternberg, "Die biologisch-demographische Lage und die Weltgeltung Westeuropas," *Jahrbücher für Nationalökonomie und Statistic* 149 (February 1939): 160–78; Robert P. Meade, "Population Trends and the Future of European Democracies," *South Atlantic Quarterly* 37 (July 1938): 229–38; Karl Loesch, *Die aussen-politischen Wirkungen des Geburtenrückganges dargelegt am Beispiel der Französen* (Berlin: Junkder und Dunnhaupt, 1938); Anton Reithinger, *Why France Lost the War: A Biological and Economic Survey* (New York: Veritas Press, 1940); Pierre Nobecourt, "Le Denatalite francaise," *Revue des questions de defense nationale* 1 (June–August 1939): 213–35, 241–51; "The Birth Rate and the Empire," *Round Table* 106 (March 1937): 308–18; Ernst Schultze, "Bevölkerungssorgen des britische Weltreichs," *Reichs-Gesundheitsblatt* 14 (6 December 1939): 1001–12; Paul de Valliere, "Natalite et defense nationale," *Revue militaire suisse* 85 (December 1940): pp. 501–509.

6. On the debate over the relationship between population decline and economics see A. Loveday et al., *The World's Economic Future* (London: George Allen and Unwin, 1937); Louis I. Dublin, *The Population Problem and World Depression* (New York: Foreign Policy Association, 1936); William Adams, *A Financial Officer's Concern in the Probable Decline of Population* (London: Institute of Municipal Treasurers and Accountants, 1939); W. B. Reddaway, *The Economics of a Declining Population* (New York: Macmillan, 1939); Georg Schönbrunn, *Die Bevölkerungsbewegnung der Gegenwart und ihr Einfluss auf die sozialen und wirtschaftlichen Verhaltnisse der Statten Mittel-Europas* (Vienna: Selbst-Verlag, 1935); John Maynard Keynes, "Some Economic Consequences of a Declining Population," *Eugenics Review* 29 (April 1937): 13–18; Roderich von Ungern-Sternberg, *Biologie und Ökonomie* (Berlin: Schoetz, 1936); Fernando Gazzeti, *Economica del declino demographico: Premessa alla politica demografica* (Rome: Mediterranea, 1938); Fritz Huhle, "Ist Frankreichs Nationalwirtschaft durch den Geburtenrückgang dedraht?," *Jahrbücher für Nationalökonomie und Statistic* 15 (February 1940): 186–211; Johan Akerman, "Bevolkerungswellen und Wechsellagen," *Schmoller's Jahrbüch* 61 (February 1937): 91–98; August Lösch, "Population Cycles as a Cause of Economic Cy-

cles," *Quarterly Journal of Economics* 51 (August 1937): 649–62; "Le Probbleme de la natalite," *Bulletin de la Chambre de commerce de Paris* 46 (8 July 1939): 652–85; and Henri Brenier, "De Quelques Consequences economiques prochaines de la denatalite en France et en Europe," *Congres international de la population*, Vol. 7 (Paris: Hermann et Cie, 1937), pp. 118–26.

7. See Max Von Gruber, *Ursachen und Bekampfung des Geburtenrückgangs im Deutschen Reich* (Munich: J. F. Lehmann Verlag, 1914), pp. 1–6, 55–69, 73–76; Fritz [Friedrich] Burgdörfer, *Das Bevölkerungsproblem: Seine Erfassung durch Familien Statistik und Familienpolitik: Mit besonders Berücksichtigung der Deutschen Reformplane und der Französischen Leistungen* (Munich: Verlag von A. Buchholz, 1917), pp. v–x, 1–46; Roderich von Ungern-Sternberg, "Die Ursachen des Geburtenrückgangs im Welteuropäischen Kulturkris wahrend des 19. und 20. Jahrhunderts," *Archiv für Bevölkerungswissenschaft und Bevölkerungspolitik* 8 (January 1939): 1–19; Fernand Boverat, *L'Effrondrement de la natalite* (Paris: Alliance nationale contra la depopulation, 1935); and V. M. Palmieri, *Denatalita* (Milan: S.P.E.M., 1937).

8. The literature on the French depopulation scare is vast. Major works include Jacques Bertillon, *La depopulation de la France* (Paris: F. Alcan, 1911); Joseph J. Spengler, *France Faces Depopulation* (Durham, N.C.: Duke University Press, 1938); Robert Talmy, *Histoire du Mouvement familial en France, 1896–1939*, Vols. 1 and 2 (Paris: Union Nationale des Caisses d'Allocations Familiales, 1962); and Jean Pinte, *Les Allocations familiales—Origines regime legal* (Paris: Librarie de Recueil Sirey, 1935). On Belgium see E. Dembour, *La Question de la population* (Brussels: Ligue des Familles Nombreuses de Belgique, 1933); and Valere Fallon, *Famille et population* (Tournoi: Casterman, 1942).

9. See Benito Mussolini, *La politica demografica* (Rome: Pinciana, 1937); Filippo Robatti, *Il problems demografico sul piano dell'impero* (Torino: La Stella di San Domenico, 1937); and Orazio di Marco, *La legislazione fascista per l'incremento demografico e l'assistenza sociale* (Campobasso: DiNunzio e Santorelli, 1938).

10. See Max Reuscher, *Der Kampf gegen den Geburtenrückgang früher und heute* (Stettin: Ostsee-Druckerei und Verlag, 1935); Siegfried Boschan, *Nationalsozialistische Rassen- und Familiengesetzgebung, praktische Rechtsanwendung und Auswirkungen auf Rechtspflege Verwatung und Wirtschaft* (Berlin: Deutscher Rechtsverlag, 1937); Elisabeth Nutt, *Die Bevölkerungspolitische Auswirkungen des Ehestandsdsdarlehens* (Berlin: Pfau, 1940); and Frank H. Hankins, "German Policies for Increasing Births," *American Journal of Sociology* 42 (March 1937): 630-52.

11. James Marchant, *Birth Rate and Empire* (London: Williams and Norgate, 1917); National Council on Public Morals, National Birth Rate Commission, *The Declining Birth Rate: Its National and International Significance* (London: Chapman and Hall, 1916); W. C. D. and C. D.

Whetkam, "The Extinction of the Upper Classes," *Nineteenth Century* (July 1909): 97–108; and R. B. Catell, *The Fight for Our National Intelligence* (London: D. S. King and Son, 1937).

12. G. D. H. Cole, *The Next Ten Years in British Social and Economic Policy* (London: Macmillan, 1929), pp. 183–99; and Eleanor F. Rathbone, *The Case for Family Allowances* (Harmondsworth: Penguin Books, 1940).

13. The best survey of interwar pronatalist movements remains the classic D. V. Glass, *Population Policies and Movements in Europe* (Oxford: Clarendon Press, 1940).

14. Literature on the nativity crisis affecting the Commonwealth nations included A. E. Mauder, *Alarming Australia* (Sydney, London: Angus and Robertson, 1939); H. I. Sinclair, *Population: New Zealand's Problem* (Dunedin: Gordon and Gotch, 1944); and A. N. MacKenzie, "Problems of Population and Persons," *Canadian Defense Quarterly* 14 (October 1937): 84–92.

Eugenicists dominated the debate in the United States. Relevant works included Henry Pratt Fairchild, *People: The Quantity and Quality of the Population* (New York: Henry Holt, 1938); Ernest Kulka, *The Causes of the Declining Birth Rate* (Cold Harbor, N.Y.: Eugenics Research Association, 1932); J. C. Litzenberg, "Presidential Address: Challenge of the Falling Birthrate," *American Journal of Obstetrics and Gynecology* 27 (March 1934): 317–29; and Joseph J. Spengler, "Population Policy in the United States: The Larger Crisis in American Culture," *Vital Speeches* (1 January 1941).

1

The Social and Ideological Setting

The Myrdals' new approach to the population issue appeared on an already crowded Swedish stage following sixty years of intensifying debate over the political meaning of demographic change.

Vast economic changes formed part of the picture. Early nineteenth-century Sweden had witnessed the breakdown of the old agrarian system through the enclosure of "open field" villages. Often labeled, with some accuracy, "the fortified poor house," Sweden also experienced in this peiod a stagnation in real wages and a visible rise in rural pauperism. Yet the groundwork of a new economic order was already being laid. Parliamentary acts of 1846 and 1864 dissolved the guild system and simplified regulations on industry. The Poor Law of 1847 transformed poor relief from charitable alms into a community-guided system. So began Sweden's age of bourgeois liberalism, running from about 1850 to 1930.

Responding to a general upswing in European economic activity in the 1850–70 period, expansion in Sweden started with the lumber industry, followed by growth in the ironworks. It was not until the 1870s, though, that the "breakthrough" of industrialization actually occurred, marked by familiar patterns of rural depopulation, urbanization, and massive emigration. At the same time, business interests and bourgeois sensibilities came to dominate the nation's urban culture. As late as 1870 the agrarian sector still accounted for a relatively stable 72.4 percent of Sweden's population. By 1880, that figure had dropped to 67.9 percent. Thereafter, agriculture experienced a continuous absolute decline in numbers. By 1910, the rural population had fallen below 50 percent of the total.[1]

Migratory movements, particularly among the younger age groups, turned toward the cities and to North America. In 1900, 21.5 percent

1

of Sweden's population was urban. By 1935, that figure had risen to 34 percent.[2] While emigration to North America began in the 1840s, massive members were not involved until the middle 1860s. In the whole 1840–1930 period some 1.1 million Swedes—roughly one-fourth of the nation's total population—migrated to North America, with the peak years occurring in 1866–74, 1878–84, 1886–93, 1902–1907, and 1924–26.[3]

Fueling this massive movement of Swedish people was an accelerating increase in numbers. Sweden's population doubled between 1720 and 1840 and doubled again by 1930. Long-term crude birth- and death rates showed minimal fluctuation prior to 1800, yet a century of relative peace after 1700 had resulted in fewer catastrophic increases in the death rate and allowed a steady rise in population size. Sweden's crude death rate began an absolute decline after 1800, falling from an annual average of 28.4 per 1,000 persons in 1801–10 to 21.7 in 1851–60, 15.5 in 1901–1905, and 12.1 in 1926–30. Meanwhile, following the classic pattern of the demographic transition, Sweden's birthrate remained relatively stable, rising from 30.9 per 1,000 persons in the 1801–10 period to 34.6 in the 1821–30 period and still as high as 29.1 in 1881–90.

After 1890, though, Sweden's crude birthrate began a decline paralleling the earlier decline in mortality. It fell to an average of 26.1 in 1901–1905, to 21.2 in 1916–20, and to 15.9 in the 1926–30 period. In 1933, Sweden's crude birthrate reached 13.8, the lowest peacetime figure recorded for any modern nation. The absolute number of births, which had risen from a yearly average of 51,900 in 1721–40 to 135,800 in 1881–90, fell back to 87,400 for 1930–35.

Observers in 1934 could also look back over significant changes in Sweden's marriage, married fertility, illegitimacy, and infant mortality rates. For example, reflecting a pattern common to much of northwestern Europe, Sweden's marriage rate fell by half between the 1750s and the 1870s, with a figure stabilizing at approximately sixty per one thousand by 1900. The marital fertility rate (births per 1,000 married women, ages fifteen to forty five) stable as late as 1900, fell from 274 in that year to only 114 in 1933, a 60 percent decline in a mere three decades. Meanwhile, the illegitimacy rate (births per one thousand unmarried women, ages fifteen to forty five), climbed from eleven in 1750 to forty five in 1912, when a decline set in, falling back to twenty-three by 1933.[4]

Observers expressed particular concern over Sweden's striking retreat from marriage. While in 1830, 25 percent of men under age twenty five and 48 percent between twenty-five and thirty were married, the figures for 1880 were only 8 and 40 percent respectively. Similar, although less sharp, declines could be found among the female population. There was agreement that the enclosure of village land and the emergence of small, individual farm holdings played important roles in delaying marriages before 1850. Thereafter, the onset of emigration and industrialization in Sweden, with a resulting increase in mobility and an unfavorable rural-urban sex ratio, further limited and delayed marriage.

The climb in the nation's illegitimacy rate between 1750 and 1912 had a more readily obvious source. In some parts of agrarian Sweden, a highly structured system of mores had controlled the courtship and mating of the young while still allowing for some premarital sexual experimentation. Known as *frieri*—or "night courting"—this practice virtually ensured that if pregnancy occurred, the male partner would be known and marriage would almost always follow. As the old village system disintegrated after 1850, though, sexual relationships within courtship involved increased risk. The decline in the unmarried fertility rate after 1912 seemed largely the result of a spread in knowledge about and use of illegal contraceptives.

Other social developments in late nineteenth-century Sweden helped set the stage for the Myrdals' unique initiative in population politics. Dominated in 1800 by traditional forces of nobility, king, and state clergy and sporting a rigid class system, the old kingdom of Sweden succumbed to the impact of new ideas and popular political movements. To begin with, the massive migration of Swedes to North America after 1845 stimulated in turn a powerful flow of attitudes and ideas back across the Atlantic that destabilized traditional patterns of living. Letters from the United States to the homeland, countless *Amerikaböker*, or "America books," that preached the virtues of a free and wealthy new land, and the influence of those emigrants who returned after a decade or two in the United States with American clothes, mannerisms, and contempt for the old ways—these corroded the influence of traditional folk culture. From the 1840s until the end of the 1920s, progressive American ideas and life patterns held an almost mythical image among Swedish peasants and workers. Children, it was said, "grow up in order to emigrate." As one observer wrote in 1907:

> Many have been to America and have returned—that you surmise as you travel along the roads, by the clothing and the panama hats of the men in the fields, looking just as they did on the farms in Minnesota. Many, both young and old, are learning English so that it will be easier for them when they "go over" to America. Everything tends to be a preparation for emigration. That is the purpose of education, and it is easier to borrow money for a ticket to America than for one to Stockholm.[5]

This movement of people extended to the importation of ideologies and popular movements. For example, the powerful Mission Covenant movement in Sweden took institutional form only in 1878, through the organization of the Swedish Mission Conference. Nine years earlier, though, their counterparts in the United States had organized as the Swedish Evangelical Lutheran Missionary Association of Chicago, and the American movement had sent numerous preachers back to Sweden to proselytize on behalf of the Mission movement and encourage the later break. Similarly, while growing religious adversion to alcohol had native Swedish roots, the institutionalized prohibition movement was born in Swedish America, where the Good Templar Order organized in the mid-1870s. This group crossed the Atlantic in 1879, and the first of hundreds of Good Templar community houses were built in rural Sweden. By 1907, there were two hundred thousand Swedish members in the American born International Order of Good Templars, all actively campaigning to halt the sale of beer, wine, and spirits.[6]

Second, these "folk movements"—as the "free church," temperance, and trade union activities have been collectively labeled—independently disrupted traditional Sweden, leaving an opening for new visions of life and truth. As historian Sven Lundkvist has explained, they served as vehicles for the displacement of "vertical loyalties" rooted in *Gemeinschaft*, or inherited society, by "horizontal loyalties" common to the modern *Gesellschaft* model.[7] These successful collective protests represented fundamental challenges to traditional loyalties, and their success introduced new living patterns for both urban and rural workers. Indeed, by 1920 these movements claimed 830,000 active adult members, with frequent cross-fertilization. In cities, union halls served as the focus of both recreation and indoctrination, while in rural locales the Good Templar halls became the center of community life, offering lectures, dances, and amusements as substitutes for intoxicants.

The folk movements also helped to politicize Swedish society in an altogether new way. Each of them looked at the old Swedish kingdom as immoral, in need of regeneration through a new morality. In turn, each offered an alternate "moral system" that demanded political reforms. Working within the political parties, the temperance and free church movements proved dramatically successful in electing their candidates to the Second Chamber of the Riksdag, or Swedish Parliament. By 1911, one-fourth of its members were "free church" and nearly two-thirds were "teetotallers." The trade unions, meanwhile, dominated the rapidly growing Social Democratic party. The temperance movement, through its successful achievement of a "local veto" by plebiscite over alcohol sales, also introduced universal suffrage and direct democracy to Swedish life.[8]

Third, the great upsurge in religious enthusiasm that marked the middle decades of the nineteenth century degenerated by 1900 into an advanced case of secularization. Rebelling against the impersonal theology and class-ridden nature of the state church, "readers" had begun holding illegal Bible studies and hymn sings in the 1830s and 1840s. Despite (or perhaps because of) scattered arrests, these informal conventicles swelled in number and divided into varied dissenting sects. In 1873, they finally squeezed from the Riksdag a law granting religious freedom in Sweden. Reenergized then by the temperance cause, the free churches continued to grow in size and activity for another thirty-five years, reaching a membership peak in about 1910. However, the state church continued to claim the loyalties of the large majority of Swedes, and as early as the 1880s observers noted signs of religious exhaustion and growing indifference. Forced now to win, rather than merely conscript, adherents, the state church quickly adjusted doctrines in line with fashionable liberal tenets, and its leaders altered hymnals, prayer books, and catechisms to meet demands of the pietists. But the strategies did not seem to work. Even in rural areas historically conservative and fervent in devotion to the Lutheran faith, observers reported growing religious indifference, a development often attributed to the materialism imported from the United States. The secular trend continued into the twentieth century, with weekly attendance at Communion falling from 17 percent of the population in 1890 to only 5.6 percent in 1927.[9]

Finally, the effects of revolutions in both industrial and agrarian production began to erode the natural economy of the intergenerational Swedish family. While regional variations were considerable, the extended family had remained a common phase of traditional Swedish life, particularly among the landholding peasants. According to one study of two mid–nineteenth-century parishes, nearly two-thirds of all households went through an extended phase where three generations lived within the same dwelling (although at any given time only one-third of households would be found to be extended). Children also remained economic assets within these families and preservation of the land to posterity an accepted obligation.[10]

By 1890, though, there were signs of shifts away from extended family bonds and from attachment to the land. For example, the number of extended families had fallen sharply by that year: 52 percent of peasant widows were then living alone compared to only 25 percent a century before. This move away from intergenerational living patterns was probably due, in part, to the growing use of *undantag*, an informal retirement system where a peasant couple yielded its holding to a son or nephew on the pledge of independent maintenance for the rest of their days. In addition, the spread of the *statare* system—a form of sharecropping—also could help account for the decline, as the proportion of independent landowners fell. Of equal importance, though, may have been a breakdown in veneration toward the soil, as the old peasant custom of passing on the farm, intact, to a single son succumbed to the claims of other children for some share of the family inheritance. Loss of the land at auction and migration of the entire family to the cities or the United States were the common results.[11]

By the early 1930s, intellectual controversy swirled over the cause of the decline in Sweden's marital fertility. The fall of Sweden's birthrate at a more rapid pace than in any other European country[12] could be partly explained by Sweden's abnormally low marriage rate and partly by the swift pace of industrialization after 1870. Yet Sweden had remained neutral during World War I and so had avoided the most severe economic and social dislocations of the period. Similarly, the Great Depression had a relatively modest impact in Sweden, compared to other Western European lands. Nonetheless, the nation stood in 1933 at the very bottom of the international demographic pile.

Such changes stirred policy debates. Early nineteenth-century population movements had generated strong interest within academic circles, with attention centered on the growing mass of rootless "surplus" agrarian workers. The theories of Thomas Malthus correspondingly found a receptive audience. After 1850, though, the Malthusian thesis ebbed. The studies that did emerge, such as C. E. Ljungberg's *Sveriges befolkningsförhållanden* (1857), simply repeated old arguments.[13] Neo-Malthusianism[14] emerged in Sweden in the late 1870s, conditioned by the massive flow of rural youth to the cities and the United States, visibly rising illegitimacy, and a severe business recession. Breaking with the pessimism and religious moralism of Malthus, neo-Malthusians argued that the rational control of fertility through artificial birth control could slow population growth. The initial impulse came from Great Britain, as the English movement became an international force through the publicity surrounding the 1876 trial of Charles Bradlaugh and Annie Besant, charged with reprinting a tract on birth control. The Malthusian League, organized the following year, served as a vehicle for the translation and publication of basic neo-Malthusian literature.

The key figure in adapting this message to Sweden was a young student of economics at Uppsala University, Knut Wicksell. His general social and political views were rooted in the liberalism of John Stuart Mill. Wicksell's interest in the population question came in 1878, after reading an anonymously authored booklet (actually written by George Drysdale), recently translated into Swedish, titled *Samhällslärans grunddag (The elements of social science)*. It exerted a profound and lasting influence on his perception of social problems. There are also indications that Wicksell may have read Drysdale's *The Population Question* and Annie Besant's *The Law of Population* prior to early 1880. Additional influences came from a group of German socialist authors, particularly Karl Kautsky, who sought to reconcile socialism to the modified Malthusian message.[15]

The actual "breakthrough" of neo-Malthusianism in Sweden can be precisely dated as 19 February 1880, when Wicksell gave a lecture at an Uppsala temperance meeting on the causes of alcoholism. In arguing that poverty, not irreligion or immorality, turned men to drink, he raised the ancillary question of why Sweden had such a high average age for marriage and concluded that the problem again was poverty. Wicksell argued, however, that there existed a cure for poverty, one sufficiently effective to meet the evil it challenged and one already proven successful in France: a voluntary limitation of number of children.

Wicksell differentiated between absolute and relative overpopulation. Where the former was difficult to determine, the latter existed at any time that an economy was unable to meet a people's needs. In pointing to Malthus's "positive checks" in the birth question, Wicksell argued that no woman ought to bear more than two or three children. An average of 2.5 children per marriage would allow for a "healthy population increase" and would enable more marriages to occur without resulting in an overly large population.[16]

The lecture came as a "bombshell" within the closed academic atmosphere of Uppsala. One report said that student opinion was "agitated as seldom before"; another saw the lecture as a "fresh wind in a stale atmosphere." University authorities threatened Wicksell with expulsion. Yet within a month he gave the same lecture to a packed Uppsala auditorium. He also sponsored the translation into Swedish of another Drysdale pamphlet[17] which further developed the argument linking poverty to excessive number of children. Scholar A. G. Högborn's recollections of his Uppsala years traces the radical changes that occurred there after 1880 to two sources: Arnoldson's motion on religious freedom in 1882 and Wicksell's lecture on alcoholism, poverty, and population. These events, Högborn concluded, marked the dividing line between the university's two epochs.[18]

Over the next several decades, Wicksell continued his campaign for the legalization of birth control, assisted in particular by a colleague at Uppsala, Hjalmar Öhrvall. While Wicksell's message grew more explicit, it remained constant. Critical social problems such as poverty, alcoholism, and prostitution derived from relative overpopulation. The simple solution was the voluntary limitation of family size through the use of contraceptives. In his later economic work Wicksell built on the musings of Mill and developed a theory of "optimum population" representing the ideal balance between human numbers and a land's renewable resources.[19]

As Wicksell stirred up neo-Malthusian sentiment in intellectual and radical circles, conservative voices also emerged arguing the pronatalist case. Typical was historian Pontus Fahlbeck, who termed the two-child system the cause of the fall of Greece and Rome. The European peoples were on the same road, he warned, relative to the "colored peoples" of the world. Neo-Malthusianism, Fahlbeck concluded, represented national suicide.[20]

Shortly after the turn of the century, Swedish demographers concluded that the decline in marital fertility rate was permanent, which linked Sweden to a general trend among the "cultured peoples." Gustav Sundbärg, section chief of the Swedish Central Bureau of Statistics, traced the decline to 1888 and suggested that the nation was entering a wholly new and troubling demographic era.[21]

The investigation by a worried Riksdag into the causes of the continuing flow of Swedes to North America produced an abundance of information on prevailing social conditions. The body's principal 1913 report concluded that emigration was caused by economic distress, which added further fuel to the neo-Malthusian argument. Conservative critics, such as Fahlbeck, replied that a poor use of resources—not overpopulation—lay behind these apparent social problems.[22]

Swedish radicalism's close yet unofficial linkage to neo-Malthusianism was further strengthened by the agitation of Hinke Bergegren, leader of the syndicalist-tinged Social Democratic Youth Union. In a famous lecture, "Love without Children," first presented to a women's group in 1910, Bergegren startled bourgeois Sweden and delighted young radicals with his open advocacy of female liberation, premarital sex, and birth control, including an explicit discussion of the available means of contraception.

Pointing to the destitute woman jailed by "Christian Sweden" for trying to feed her many children through petty theft, and to the desperate woman with numerous children and an unemployed husband who finds herself pregnant again, Bergegren found a solution to such problems in love without children. He rejected both free love and holy marriage, attacking instead the double standard applied to men and women concerning premarital sex. Women, he charged, had a sex drive equal to that of men, which deserved equal recognition.

Bergegren warned sexual partners not to set children lightheartedly into the world. High infant mortality rates and the possibility of genetic defects should weigh heavily in the decision to bear them. He acknowledged that love for children could be a warm and wonderful thing and a complement to parents' love for each other. Unmarried mothers, he quickly added, should enjoy all the legal protections afforded married mothers, while the abortion law should be more understandable and less harsh. Above all, Bergegren argued that it was better, under existing social conditions, for women, both married and unmarried, to utilize contraceptives: ". . . the most important of all questions in the great sex problem is: precautionary measures . . . precautionary measures . . . precautionary measures. . . ."

On the "population question" Bergegren made no apologies. He noted that the poorer a social class was, the more children it had. The largest number of Swedish children were born into dark, unhealthy, overcrowded urban apartments. He rejected the old arguments that contraception was against God's word, sinful, unnatural, or biologically harmful, and he reminded his audience that birth control was not abortion. He then launched into an explicit discussion of birth control techniques, including the rhythm method, coitus interruptus, and the condom, diaphragm, pessary, and douche. Bergegren particularly recommended the condom and diaphragm for the control over the sex act that they gave to women. Concluding, he stated that "love without children . . . is better than children without love."[23]

Other radical neo-Malthusians pressed the case. In *Poverty and Children* (*Fattigdom och barnalstring*), Anton Nyström stressed that children's welfare should be the guiding principle for parental decisions on procreation. He pointed to evidence showing the linkage between number of children in a family and poverty, overcrowded housing, high infant and maternal mortality rates, and disease. He denied that social anomalies were the only cause of poverty; when one peered beneath the surface, it was clear that the poor had too many children. The solution, he concluded, lay in the use of birth control. The delay and reduction in the total number of children would make for happier marriages and would reduce the social burden of the poor. Birth control was, in fact, good "preventive" social policy: "As one seeks in medicine not only to remedy sicknesses, but also—with widening knowledge of their causes—to expand the possibility of preventing them, so should those dealing with poor relief not only give comfort to the needy, but also seek by rational means to prevent need where possible."[24]

Meanwhile, other socialists remained attached to the classic Marxist dismissal of "overpopulation" as a fraudulent concept.[25] Rickard Sandler, who later served in Social Democratic governments as prime minister and foreign minister, wrote in 1911 that the cause of poverty and emigration from Sweden was not overpopulation, but rather unequal income distribution and inadequate social organization. Sweden's abundant natural resources, he concluded, would support a much larger population.[26]

Otto Grimlund, writing in *Tiden* (the Social Democratic political monthly, particularly influential among younger intellectuals), analyzed recent data on the French population. He concluded that the decline in the French birthrate derived from the injustices of capitalism. When socialism was established, he continued, children would grow up in secure homes, with parental love and social support. Every child in the family would be welcomed as a potential worker who would make society still richer and happier and more chaste, pure, and noble. Under existing circumstances, he was unsure whether population stagnation was in the working class's interest. On the one hand, it was the great masses that would lead the proletariat to victory; on the other, raising too many children would reduce the working class's endurance and power.[27]

In response to the growing fervor of the neo-Malthusians and in the name of Christian decency, the Conservative government, under the initiative of prime minister Arvid Lindman, approved two measures in 1910–11: the so-called "anti–birth control" laws. The first added paragraph 13 to chapter 18 of the Swedish penal code forbade the exhibition or public showing of objects intended for "unchaste use" or to prevent the consequences of the sexual act. The second change revised chapter 8 of the Law of Freedom of the Press by prohibiting the advertising, offering, or mention of these objects in publications and other communications.[28]

Over the next two decades, the population debate in Sweden segmented into five distinct messages.

Neo-Malthusians

Rebuffed by the anti–birth control laws, these activists stepped up their agitation, with notable success on the political left. A Swedish Malthusian League organized in 1911. The National Association for Sex Education (*Riksförbundet för sexuellupplysning*) emerged several years later and had forty thousand members by 1933.

John Andersson, a socialist from Göteborg, carried the neo-Malthusian message to its radical extreme. The working class, he said, was locked in a bitter, compassionless class strugle. A great number of children was a hindrance to workers' power and to the freedom of the labor movement. Men with large families were often those who served as strike breakers for the enemy capitalists: "It was in many cases their hungry children's cry for food which drove them to become traitors against the working class."

Poverty, Andersson continued, impelled workers to agitate on the population question. Parents had no right to bear children into the suffering that awaited them under existing conditions. Within the working class, he charged, children did not bring happiness to their parents. More children meant more mouths to feed and bodies to clothe and more persons crowded into dirty, dark, unhealthy urban tenements. The infant mortality rate remained high among workers. He pointed specifically to the use of cheap female labor by industry, the mockery of unenforced child labor laws, and the high mortality rate among the poor compared to the wealthy. "Capitalism, with its plundering system, murders masses of our children." Capitalists encouraged a high birthrate, Andersson stated, to swell the "reserve army" of unemployed with expendable industrial slaves. It also sought more children who could serve as taxpayers and cannon fodder to support imperialistic ambitions and the current world war.

Andersson rejected the call from "certain German socialists" for more working-class children to serve as soldiers of the revolution. Such an action would merely press the working class further down. Only through "a smaller number of children could workers, both men and women, raise themselves to fully conscious individuals . . . and energetic socialists."[29]

Others used more traditional neo-Malthusian arguments. Hjalmar Öhrvall warned that Sweden could not repeat the doubling of its population experienced in the nineteenth century. Rather, a constant number, balanced against the land's resources, should be the goal. He saw world peace as the probable result of lower population growth, as civilized nations no longer battled for their place in the sun. Ohrvall blasted as hypocrites those in the upper class who argued against birth control for nationalistic and economic reasons while using it themselves. He welcomed the nativity decline already apparent in Sweden as a "satisfying" development.[30]

Knut Wicksell until his death in 1926 continued actively to propagandize for the neo-Malthusian movement and to solidify its linkage to Swedish socialism. In lectures before the Neo-Malthusian Society and the radical *Clartesektion* at Lund University he reiterated the three central goals: to allow parents to provide better for their own children by controlling their own fertility; to bring population size into a better relationship with Sweden's own natural resources; and to battle prostitution and other "sexual deviations" in order to allow all individuals to live healthy, natural, and happy lives. He noted that the second goal required broader actions, including a rationalization of the sex laws and the socializing of all sectors of the economy that tended toward monopoly. "But on the other hand," he continued, "all of these reform efforts become powerless, a shot in the air, if a reasonable solution to the population question is not brought about at the same time."[31]

More generally, Wicksell welcomed the nativity decline throughout Western Europe, believing that it would mean improved living standards for everyone, particularly those at lower income levels, and a positive step toward world peace. Where growing populations looked across their borders for more land and resources, a stable or declining population would be better able to achieve a balance with its own resources. Indeed, Wicksell continued, Western Europe currently had a "highly artificial economic life," built on an exchange of its industrial products for the raw materials and food of the transoceanic nations. As these lands developed their own industrial plants, Western Europe would be thrown back on its own resources. A nativity decline, he insisted, was necessary to bring an oversized population back into balance.

This argument, he said, certainly held true for Sweden, which was overly dependent on the import of raw materials and foodstuffs. A lower birthrate and a declining population represented essential adjustments to economic realities. Wicksell expressed gratitude that the anti–birth control laws had failed in their purpose, and he praised Hinke Bergegren for his propaganda work among the laboring class. Together, Wicksell stated, they had prevented the procreation of a new one-hundred-thousand-man reserve army of unemployed.[32]

Wicksell also entered the abortion debate, arguing that under current conditions abortion was sometimes necessary. Saying that it was impossible for society to choose between "necessary" and "unnecessary" abortions, he advocated turning the question over to the individuals involved by allowing for abortion during the first three months of pregnancy.[33]

Similar arguments dominated debate among younger socialist intellectuals. G. Westin Silverstolpe, writing in *Tiden*, argued that the recent restrictions clamped down by immigrant-receiving lands such as the United States represented a turning point for Europe. He warned his readers that the population of Western Europe had extended itself beyond the "optimum level." The birth decline, he implied, was a welcome and necessary adjustment to this reality.[34]

In his book *Folkmängd och välstånd*, Silverstolpe stated the problem more clearly: "If the immigration lands are full, then it appears as clear as day that the emigration lands are overly crowded." He argued that the birthrate decline had already begun to stabilize economic, social, and political relationships in Europe. He called for a repeal of Sweden's anti–birth control laws to allow people access to contraceptives for "population policy" reasons.[35]

Frans Severin, again in *Tiden*, repeated the Wicksellian argument that as old colonies were transformed by industrialization and no longer needed European-produced goods, Europe's population must be adjusted to better balance that continent's own resources. He praised the positive effects of the birthrate decline on the working class's spiritual and economic condition.[36] Economist Sven Brisman, before a 1925 meeting of the *National ekonomiska föreningen* in Stockholm, argued that Sweden—with a population of 6 million—was "certainly" above its optimum population. He felt that further emigration and a diminished birthrate could only work to raise the average living standard.[37] Bertil Mogård analyzed the Malthusian question from the perspective of availability of agricultural land. He termed the experience of the nineteenth century—when Europe was able to sustain a high population growth rate through the breakthrough of industrialization and the availability of virgin land in the Americas and Australia—as a special case. Under current conditions he welcomed the nativity decline.[38]

Other prominent socialist voices concurred. Nils Karleby, a young radical of wide influence, included a discussion of the Malthusian question in his major work, *Socialism Faces Reality* (*Socialismen inför verkligheten*). While concerned largely with the migration question, Karleby acknowledged that the threat of overpopulation continued to "color" the troubles of his century.[39] Eva Wigforss, in adapting G. D. H. Cole's proposed "family wage" to Swedish conditions, asked whether a "family wage" might result in more births. She argued that the French and Italian experiences had shown that nativity was not so easily stimulated. It was possible, she admitted, that an allowance rising in relation to number of children might still increase fertility. As such, she concluded, it would represent an undesirable side effect of the plan.[40]

Neo-Malthusian influences penetrated into the center of the Social Democratic party. Ernst Wigforss, husband to Eva and finance minister for several socialist-led governments in the 1920s and 1930s, drafted a manuscript in 1930 on the relationship between wages, prosperity, and population predicated on the "optimum population" idea.[41]

Marxist Pronatalists

While neo-Malthusian ideas were clearly gaining ground in socialist circles, the older view of Malthus as a handmaiden of capitalism retained a few Swedish advocates. P. J. Welinder, repeating the arguments advanced by Marx, rejected the "common opinion" that the only solution for the working class lay in a radical cut in population. He noted that at the same time that industry spewed forth luxury goods and farmers complained about overproduction, the working class was lectured on overpopulation. Welinder charged that Malthus's disciples had again tricked the working class into believing that their own labors were for nothing and that they were the cause of their own misery:

> I have accepted the socialist way of viewing things because I have found in it a life-affirming principle. I have understood it as an aspiration to assert humanity's sovereignty over everything alive, the recognition of human dignity as the highest value, not humanity's disappearance. If I have been mistaken, if socialism is synonymous with race-suicide, then I would be compelled to battle against this movement.[42]

Rejecting the Malthusian economic theories, Welinder argued that the earth's material resources were not limited but abundant and that the work and effort of each living generation added onto the material and scientific inheritance passed to the future. The cause of poverty and misery was not overpopulation, but capitalistic productive relationships that denied the working class the fruits of its labor. Belgium had twenty-nine times the population density of the United States, he explained, yet workers in both countries were exploited equally. He pointed to the virtual cessation of population growth in Europe after 1914 and asked if the working class was any better off as a result.

Welinder affirmed the value of birth control and planned parenthood, yet rejected the "mindless" life-denying propaganda of the neo-Malthusians. Motherhood was not martyrdom but a natural function with its own satisfaction. The sex act provided only momentary pleasure; the real and lasting joys, he concluded, came with children.[43]

Conservative Pronatalists

Mixing Christian, "mercantilist," racial, and nationalistic arguments, Swedish conservatives raised a vocal and visible pronatalist case before the neo-Malthusian challenge. The anti−birth control laws of 1910–11 were the most prominent result. Conservatives in the Riksdag also introduced proposals for a special bachelor tax in 1892, 1893, 1908, 1915, and 1916. The latter motion, for example, called for a special income tax on the unmarried, childless couples, and those with only one or two children. It cited Sweden's rich natural resources and the social, economic, and "national" need for a growing, healthy working population and warned of the serious consequences of current declines in marriage frequency and birthrate. Fortunately, the motion continued, a number of large Swedish families were still to be found among the agrarian population, social units needing protection.[44]

With the Swedish birthrate continuing its decline after 1920, the so-called "bourgeois"[45] economists intensified their critique of the neo-Malthusians. David Davidson, in a 1926 article in *Aftonbladet*, attacked the "optimum population" theory. It was unhealthy, Davidson charged, for the most advanced racial groups to limit their procreation while other, more primitive peoples continued to grow. The increasing numbers of the latter would, in time, become a threat to the integrity and wealth of the former. Eli Heckscher, in a series of newspaper articles for *Svensk tidskrift*, assaulted both the economic logic and the moral basis of neo-Malthusianism. The use of child limitation techniques, he claimed, was based too often on lust and hedonism. Heckscher defended family values and sacrifice for children.[46] J. Guinchard and G. Silén, adapting the new net reproduction rate to Swedish data, discovered an NRR for Sweden in 1926 of only 0.95 (1.00 meant zero growth). For Stockholm their figure was a shocking 0.389.[47] Economist Bertil Ohlin, a subsequent leader of the Swedish Liberal party, warned in a 1929 speech before the Copenhagen Student Union of the consequences of declining Scandinavian birthrates.[48]

Religious conservatives called for moral renewal. Torsten Bohlin, writing for the Swedish Christian Student Movement, cited the extreme decline in births as a symptom of the modern sexual problem. While noting certain economic hindrances to marriage, he found the real problem at a deeper level: "No institution needs to be transformed. . . . It is the people within the institutions who need to be changed." Young people had lost their sense of purpose. Bohlin blamed this fracturing of the Christian world view on movies, modern literature, and a rationalistic view of life. Only when approached from a Christian perspective could sexuality be raised above animal instinct.[49]

By the early 1930s, conservative writers were hesitantly exploring public policy options in the birth question. While emphasizing the reality of the crisis and affirming fertility, they were generally reluctant to advocate social reforms that would draw the state into the matrix of the family. Small, targeted solutions were preferred. The dean of conservative economy, Gustav Cassel, turned his attention to the problems associated with the shifting age structure of the population. Given the projected doubling of the "over sixty-five" age category in Sweden by 1975, he advocated an increase in the retirement age from sixty-five to seventy.[50] Concerning the fall in the Swedish birthrate, he affirmed traditional family values and pointed out that the young must learn the lesson of "delayed gratification"—that one must work first and enjoy the fruits of that work later.[51] In a subsequent article, Cassel noted the European-wide nature of the nativity decline and advocated caution concerning a hasty turn to costly social policies. Instead, he argued for attention to long-term capital formation as a means of stimulating greater production.[52]

F. J. Linders, in his 1930 work *Our Population Problem (Vårt befolkningsproblem)*, argued that Sweden only had a problem of relative overpopulation, concentrated among students, aspiring young professionals, and artists in the large cities. He pointed to the real long-term problems found in the birth decline and predicted an "immigrant problem" in Sweden some fifteen years down the road. As an alternative, he called for economic and employment policies that would increase saving, raise investment, create jobs, and produce fewer luxury goods. In addition, he endorsed a voluntary "family wage" economy: "The goal ought to be that those married with children do not have a lower [living] standard than those who are unmarried or married and childless in the same social position. The valuation of labor ought to be after the principle: equal work, equal living standard, not after the principle: equal work, equal pay, as the foolish [Socialist] party slogan proclaims.[53]

In *Civilisations dilemma* (1934), Ivar Trägårdh called for a response from Europe's politicians that would shape conditions more conducive to families, children, and motherhood. This attention to quantity, he added, must not obscure concern for quality and social policy should also seek to raise the spiritual and genetic health of the population. He advocated eugenic measures that would diminish births among those social elements whose children could only be a burden on society.[54]

Conservative interest in providing tax relief to large families reappeared in 1931, when Arvid Lindmann, supported by fifty-eight other Riksdag members in the Second Chamber, proposed the creation of a special family tax deduction. The parliamentary motion noted that the sinking Swedish birthrate had given this problem a serious nature: "It is high time that we abandon the negative or indifferent position, which has distinguished Swedish population policy in this area, and instead seek through positive measures to promote family creation and to ease the large family's burden in respect to taxes."[55] The proposal emphasized that the new tax deduction would have the advantage of encouraging births among the wealthier classes, which had been hit particularly hard by the birth decline.

Race-hygiene Theorists

Still bolder, more far-reaching ideas on the "quality" problem were developed in this period by a group best termed *race-hygiene theorists*. Overlapping to some degree with both conservative and socialist approaches, their perspective was unique in its focus on eugenics and "racial health" and in its use of scientific evidence as a guide to policy.

Geneticist Nils von Hofsten, for instance, in his basic study on the science of genetics pressed from the eugenic perspective for an equalization of living standards between large and small families. He argued that it was essential to remove the social and economic handicaps that discouraged the "child rich" family.[56]

H. Lundborg, professor of biology and genetics at Uppsala University, argued that "a people of good race is an indispensible necessity so that a high culture shall rise in a land." He despaired over the declining fertility found among the better situated classes and chastized "the empty pram policy" of the 0-, 1-, or 2-child systems. Lundborg affirmed, however, the continuing racial vitality and importance of the Swedish farming class, which he termed a national treasure that ought not to be squandered: "Much more than before, we must work for the lineage and the race. It is genetic research and race-biology which have shown the way."[57]

Expanding this discussion in his 1934 work, *The Western Nations in Danger (Västerlandet i fara)*, Lundborg drew heavily on such German writers as Friedrich Burgdörfer, Otto Helmut, and Oswald Spengler. Affirming a "racially sound human material" as the basis of a people's wealth, he attacked the logic behind the two-child system. Symptoms of decline affecting the populations of the West included the rapid growth of large cities and the quantitative and qualitative decline of the farming class; the disintegration of family bonds within the city; greater "freedom" for women and their rejection of motherhood; abortion; the influx of "parasitic immigrants" from other lands; rampant, selfish individualism; moral and religious decline; a growing gap between rich and poor; a rise in chronic, degenerative diseases; the use of drugs such as alcohol, tobacco, morphine, and cocaine; and the loss of love of country. Crafting a program of response, Lundborg argued that the government should discourage large cities through its regulation of industry, trade, and banking. Schools should emphasize rural, agrarian-oriented subjects and discourage industrial and intellectual pursuits. Pointing to the 1932 program of the German Society for Race Hygiene, Lundborg called for a defense of the "valuable" genetic stock of all social classes, tax relief for large families, tax penalities for the unmarried and childless, a cash support payment to large families, the use of family allowances within the wage structure, incentives to family formation at an early age (particularly among academics), and a ban on the sterilization of healthy persons. The whole of life, Lundborg concluded, must be given a race-hygienic context.[58]

Biologist Folke Borg, also arguing from the race-hygienic perspective, advanced a decidedly more radical version. In a series of lectures and articles between 1931 and 1934,[59] he stated that while neo-Malthusianism had been a natural reaction to developments in the nineteenth century, it had now clearly gone too far. One could, in fact, talk of "the white race's suicide." In response, Borg proposed a series of positive race-hygiene measures, with a progressive political slant. They included increased support for the agrarian population, housing policies that would encourage procreation, family income tax deductions of such a size that those with four or more children would be completely tax-free, tax incentives to marriage, financial assistance to large families such as rent subsidies and lower utility rates, free schoolbooks, a special child support payment for civil servants, measures that would encourage early marriage among professionals, equal wages, and the right to employment for women tied to the elimination of marriage or pregnancy penalities. Borg also advocated improved training in sex hygiene, school training in housework, child care, parenting education, subsidized maternity care for all mothers, and an energetic battle against "race-hygiene" sicknesses such as tuberculosis and veneral disease.

He termed the anti−birth control laws a classic example of bad policy, for they resulted in more births only among the least desirable elements of the population. The state, he believed, should welcome only wanted children. While abortion was "fetus murder," he said that it should be allowed on medical, race-hygiene, and ethical (rape and incest) indications. He concluded with the warning that a modern nation that ignored the laws of biology and failed to take both positive and negative race-hygiene measures could only disappear.[60]

Biologist Lorentz Bolin developed a similar progressive policy framework in his 1933 work, *Biology and Society* (*Biologin och samhället*). In a section on racial hygiene, he turned to the question of fertility decline, which he saw as a component of general racial degeneration. While negative race-hygiene measures, such as sterilization, were helpful in reversing this trend, he placed much greater faith in positive measures designed to cope with the causes of declining nativity. Children, he argued, were not only a private but a social responsibility. Society at present actually economically rewarded the childless and penalized large families.

On the Malthusian question, Bolin noted that the neo-Malthusians had taken Malthus's law of population and altered it into an advocacy for small families or childless marriages. He doubted that Malthus would have approved of this change. Yet in a key section, Bolin added that racial hygiene and neo-Malthusianism need not stand in opposition. "Racial hygiene does not aim at some sort of overpopulation. There is no quantity without quality that is in its interest." It was not to society's benefit, for example, that the "worst" elements be relied on to assure its future existence. "A decline in their nativity is from all perspectives desirable."

As a more general guide to policy, he stated that children ought not cause an economic burden for a family. His briefly mentioned remedies included better housing, creation of "race-hygienic garden cities," cooperative day-care centers and nurseries, and family allowances built into the wage structure.[61]

Feminists

The growing Swedish feminist movement represented another focus of argumentation on the birth question, as liberals, Social Democrats, and communists united on questions of the anti–birth control laws and abortion.

Representative of the liberal wing was Kerstin Hasselgren, who sat in the First Chamber of the Riksdag in the 1928–34 period and led the Liberal Women's National Union (*Frissinade kvinnors riksförbund*) campaign to repeal the birth control laws. She asked how one could expect parents to exercise a responsible parenthood while denying them the means for the rational limitation of children. Too often, Hasselgren argued, social pressures left women only with the abortion option. In a 1929 Riksdag bill also sponsored by Social Democrats Agda Östlund and Olivia Nordgren, Hasselgren proposed a royal commission to study sexual questions, including sex education, repeal of the anti–birth control laws, and reform of the abortion law. On the latter point, Hasselgren—while opposed to abortion as a birth control technique—advocated its legalization on the basis of "social-medical" indications.[62]

The more radical feminist approach to the abortion question could be found in the popular translated work of Martha Ruben-Wolf. She argued that "the ruling class within all capitalist states needs cannon-fodder for their imperialistic wars together with an industrial reserve army, with whose help they can smother the demands of the working class." Only in Russia, she noted, was abortion free. Yet Russia had no "birth crisis," with the birthrate there still above forty per one thousand and a "birth surplus" every year of 3 to 4 million. While birth control would not solve all problems of the working class—only the expropriation of the means of production could finally eliminate the exploitation of humans by other humans—the rationalization of sex life and voluntary parenthood were necessary components of the coming revolution.[63]

Although neo-Malthusianism seemed triumphant on the left by the mid-1920s, the implications of the accelerating birth decline began to mellow what Tage Erlander once called his generation's "instinctive adversion" to population policies.[64] A search for new answers beyond neo-Malthusianism commenced. An important work in stimulating the shift of emphasis was a 1926 article by statistician Sven D. Wicksell (son of Knut) appearing in *Ekonomisk tidskrift*. Titled "Sweden's Future Population under Various Assumptions," it presented five projections, based on varied levels of nativity, mortality, and migration. His first, and most likely, projection assumed no net migration, a stabilization of the absolute number of births at one hundred thousand per year, and a stabilization of mortality at the existing level. On this basis Wicksell projected a decelerating rate of population increase, a maximum population of 6,348,000 in 1955, and an aging, shrinking population thereafter, finally stabilizing at 5.78 million in the twenty-first century.[65]

In an article for *Tiden* published the same year, Wicksell presented a statistical summary of population movements in Sweden since the mid-nineteenth century. He drew particular attention to the decline in nativity since 1880. Shrinking family size, he believed, was the result of developing economic tendencies, tied to changes in the attitudes of women, the entry of married women into the labor market, and a low infant mortality rate. He projected a further decline in the number of births, with the principal consequence being an accelerating aging of the population.[66]

In his 1931 critique of population theory, Wicksell discussed and rejected the "optimum population" theories of the neo-Malthusians. While believing that such a level must exist, he termed it impossible to identify, noting that one could not experiment with population size. In a decided break with his own father's work, Wicksell described the danger inherent in Western Europe's nativity decline occurring before similar population changes developed among the Slavic and Asiatic races. Such a differential, he warned, would result in new migratory movements. Wicksell concluded that, given his ability to control reproduction rationally, Western man had entered a new epoch in history. The social pessimism of Darwin was gone. The "cultural pessimistic" question was now: "Are civilized men able to reproduce sufficiently to prevent their decline or disappearance?"[67]

Other contributors to *Tiden* raised new questions about the population problem. Gillis Aspegren presented a survey of the earlier population debate, emphasizing inadequate socialist attempts to confront the Malthusian problem.[68] Axel Höjer attacked the contradictory results of the 1911 anti–birth control laws, emphasizing that despite their passage, Sweden's birthrate had plummeted to the lowest figure in the world, while venereal disease and permanent sterility grew more common.[69] Demographer Gustaf Alegård in a series of articles sought to lay the statistical and factual basis for the emerging debate on the population question. Two articles compared Swedish population movements to those found in the rest of the world, giving emphasis to the startling decline in Swedish fertility.[70] Two others presented statistical analyses of the nativity declines in Germany and France and questioned the validity of Malthusian reasoning.[71] An additional article defended the questionnaire used in the 1930 Swedish census, which sought information on family size, number of births, and income. Alegård argued that the "burning nature" of the nativity question made it imperative for demographers and social scientists to have better "family data" to understand the causes for the spread of child limitation.[72]

In a special *Tiden* publication, Gunnar Dahlberg laid out Sweden's "population problem" with unusual frankness. After describing the nativity decline in detail, Dahlberg noted that the growth rates experienced by Sweden in the nineteenth century legitimated fears of overpopulation and would justify welcoming the now evident decline in nativity. "On the other hand," he continued, "it is now clear that if this decline continues to proceed, it means that Sweden finally shall be empty of people." While suspicious of French attempts to raise fertility through cash payments, he acknowledged that an extreme situation might justify such measures in Sweden. He saw little chance of alleviating the population decline through immigration, for the peoples most like Swedes in Europe and North America were also experiencing birthrate declines, while the importation of cheap Asian or African labor would create more problems than it solved. Dahlberg concluded by warning that the nativity question could not be separated from other social relationships. Yet the time to effect change in developing downward trends might prove uncomfortably short.[73]

This new openness among radical intellectuals on the population question merged the problem of the declining birthrate into developing Social Democratic ideological trends.[74] Prior to 1925, for example, the Swedish Social Democrats retained the official goals of expropriation of the means of production and hostility to the economic interests of rural Sweden. By the early 1930s, however, these orientations had given way to policies of retaining private ownership of industry in union with close governmental regulation, economic planning, and centralized direction and price supports for farm products. Earlier, imprecise visions of a socialized societal structure also gave way in the 1920–33 period to establishment of several components of the modern welfare state.

The new Social Democratic reform line absorbed an older, locally run relief-oriented system,[75] yet fused to it central control, the socialist principles of equality, economic democracy, security, "the maintenance of human dignity," and a peculiar version of nationalism. Central theoretical figures in this work were Nils Karleby, Rickard Lindstrom, and Per Albin Hansson.[76]

Karleby, a young economist and student of Eli Heckscher and Gösta Bagge, was the charismatic leader of a group of radical intellectuals in the early 1920s. Before his untimely death in 1927, he played the leading role in crafting a distinctly new Social Democratic reform program. Karleby, his admirers said, bridged the continental ideology that the Social Democrats preached before audiences and the practical social and economic problems facing Sweden. At the same time, his analysis showed that the distinctions between the Social Democrats and the bourgeois parties need not be blotted out in the process.[77]

Karleby's major work, *Socialism Faces Reality,* appeared in 1926 and became the "bible" of youthful Social Democrats. Tracing the corruption of the French Revolution's call for "liberty, equality, and fraternity" by an individualistic society, Karleby reemphasized Swedish socialism's roots in the Enlightenment philosophy of the eighteenth century. Rejecting Marx, his principal argument was for a reorientation of socialist doctrine on a human, rather than scientific, economic basis. This humanistic base and the movement's commitment to democratic means, he charged, needed affirmation in the party's program.[78]

Rickard Lindstrom, chairman of the Social Democratic Youth League, authored an influential commentary on the Social Democrats' setback in the 1928 election. He strongly criticized the trade union movement for having ignored the farm workers and the concerns of the landholding peasants. The Social Democrats should lay aside their antiquated attachment to class analysis and recognize how the conflicts of economic groups and interests actually crossed party lines. Lindstrom called for less attention to the distinctions between social classes and construction instead of a "people's party" where the Social Democrats pursued a program based on common sense.

Lindstrom's arguments lay behind the famed 1933 "crisis agreement," or "cow trade," where the Social Democrats entered a parliamentary coalition with the hitherto "right wing" Agrarian party. Crafted in the atmosphere of the economic depression, the deal required the Social Democrats to abandon their customary support of free trade and consumer interests, in favor of price supports for Swedish-grown farm products and the long-despised excise tax on margarine. The Agrarian party, with its roots in the conservative anticapitalism and antisocialism of the far right, had also mellowed during the decade-long agrarian depression of the 1920s. Increasingly it had turned away from a broad defense of traditionalism and toward the politics of interest. In the mood of the early 1930s, with international trade generally in retreat and internationalism itself discredited, the Agrarians joined with the Social Democrats in a popular-front–styled alliance. They embraced the idea of national autarchy and a common turn to state management of the economy to the mutual benefit of workers and peasants. At a more symbolic level, the alliance represented an amalgam of socialism with agrarian nationalism, a common development in the period, which proved to be a potent brew even in democratic Sweden.[79]

Building on these themes, Per Albin Hansson began to construct his vision of Folkhemmet ("the people's home"), a linguistic move that extended warm sentiments of the hearth to the nation at large. Hansson gave it early expression during the Riksdag's 1928 budget debate:

> The home's foundation is community and concern. The good home does not know privilege or the feeling of being slighted, no pets and no step children . . . In the good home, equality, considerateness, cooperation, and helpfulness hold sway. Applied to the great people's—and citizen's—home, this should mean the demolition of all social and economic ranks, which now divide citizens into privileged and slighted, into rulers and dependents, into rich and poor, propertied and impoverished, exploiters and the exploited.[80]

Hansson charged that while a form of equality existed in political rights, social relationships were still burdened by class. "If Swedish society is to become the people's home," he continued, "class differences must be laid aside, social welfare developed, economic equalization secured where workers are provided a share in the management of the economy, [and] democracy realized and applied both socially and economically."[81]

While on the one hand a relatively vague formulation, Hansson's Folkhem approach also proved to be an original and politically clever doctrine that supported a flexible policy umbrella under which the Swedish welfare state would be built in the 1930s and 1940s. Folkhemmet sentimentalized otherwise radical policy formulations. It also legitimized a form of nationalism as a foundation for the Swedish social welfare state. Most important, it took the bourgeois family and transformed it into a metaphor for the socialized, centrally directed state. The population policies advocated by Alva and Gunnar Myrdal after 1934 found ample space under that umbrella.

The Myrdals drew together the two developing intellectual strands described in this chapter. To begin with, their work was in line with recent developments in Sweden's population debate. In light of a continuing decline in the national birthrate during the 1920s, the old arguments suddenly appeared insufficient. Accordingly, Social Democratic theorists, once comfortably advocating their own version of noe-Malthusianism, were open to new approaches. Second, the Myrdals' proposed population program offered a fresh, compelling, profamily blueprint for an expanded Swedish welfare state, to be built on nationalistic themes.

The Social Democrats came to power in Sweden with a functional coalition at the very moment when Sweden's "population crisis" reached its most severe level. With exquisite timing, the Myrdals offered the party a wildly popular, politically effective, scientifically justified response to what had been seen as an unsolvable problem, and they went on to reshape their nation.

Notes

1. For the most well known survey of this subject, see Eli F. Heckscher, *Svenskt arbete och liv. Från medeltiden till nutiden* (Stockholm: Albert Bonniers Förlag, 1941). On demographic developments see particularly

pp. 171–84, 240ff, 281ff, and 362–64. An English translation is available: *An Economic History of Sweden* (Cambridge: M.I.T. Press, 1954). See also Karin Koch, "Nymalthusianismens genombrott i Sverige," *Studier i ekonomin och historia tillägnade Eli F. Heckscher på 65-årsdagen den 29 november 1944* (Uppsala: Almqvist and Wiksell, 1945), pp. 79–80; Carl-Erik Quensel, "Landbygdens avfolkning och flykten från jordbruket," *Ekonomisk tidskrift* 42 (September 1940): 137–54; and Erland von Hofsten, *Hur den svenska landsbygden avfolkas* (Stockholm: Albert Bonniers Förlag, 1940).

2. See Jane Moore, *Cityward Migration: Swedish Data* (Chicago: University of Chicago Press, 1938); Staff of the Institute for Social Science at Stockholm University, *Population Movements and Industrialization, Swedish Counties, 1895–1930* (Stockholm: Norstedt, 1941); Gösta Ahlberg, *Befolkningsutvecklingen och urbaniseringen i Sverige, 1911–50* (Stockholm: Stockholms Kommunalförvaltning, 1953).

3. See Florence Edith Janson, *The Background of Swedish Immigration, 1840–1930* (Chicago: University of Chicago Press, 1931); and A. Friedrich, "Schwedens Geburtenmangel und Auswandererschwund," *Archiv für Wanderungswesen und Auslandkunde* 1 (Autumn 1942): 93–96.

4. The literature on Swedish population movements is extensive. In addition to the sources cited above see Ernst J. Hoijer, *Svensk befolkningsutveckling genom tiderna* (Stockholm: Svenska Bokförlaget, 1959); Gustav Sundbärg, *Bevolkerungsstatistik Schwedens, 1750–1900, Einige hauptresultate* (Stockholm: P. A. Norstedt och Söner, 1907); Erland Hofsten and Hans Lundstrom, *Swedish Population History: Main Trends from 1750 to 1970* (Stockholm: National Central Bureau of Statistics, 1976); Statistiska Centralbyrån, *Historisk statistik för Sverige. Part II: Befolkning andra upplagen, 1720–1967* (Stockholm: Statistiska centralbyrån, 1969); Eva Bernhardt, *Trends and Variations in Swedish Fertility: A Cohort Study* (Stockholm: Statistiska centralbyrån, 1971); Sven Wicksell, *Ur befolkningsläran* (Stockholm: Albert Bonniers Förlag, 1931), particularly pp. 13–58; Norman B. Ryder, "The Influence of Declining Mortality on Swedish Reproductivity," *Current Research in Human Fertility* (New York: Milbank Memorial Fund, 1955), pp. 65–81; and Carl Erik Quensel, *Den äktenskapliga fruktsamheten i Sveriges städer 1911–1953 efter äktenskapets varaktighet och hustruns ålder* (Lund: Statistiska Institutionen, 1956).

5. Gerhard Magnusson quoted in Florence Edith Janson, *The Background of Swedish Immigration, 1840–1930* (1934; New York: Arno Press and the New York Times, 1970), p. 434.

6. Janson, *The Background of Swedish Immigration*, pp. 208–09, 219.

7. Sven Lundkvist, *Folkrörelserna i det svenska samhället, 1850–1920* (Stockholm: Almquist and Wiksell, 1977).

8. Ibid., p. 299; and Sven Lundqvist, "Popular Movements and Reforms, 1900–1920," in Steven Koblik, ed., *Sweden's Development from Poverty to Affluence, 1750–1970* (Minneapolis: University of Minnesota Press,

1975), pp. 180–93.

9. Janson, *The Background of Swedish Immigration*, pp. 213–19; and Göran Gustafsson, *Religionen i Sverige: Ett sociologiskt perspektiv* (Stockholm: Norstedts Tryckeri, 1981), p. 41.

10. See Ingrid Eriksson and John Rogers, *Rural Labor and Population Change: Social and Demographic Developments in East-Central Sweden During the Nineteenth Century* (Stockholm: Almqvist and Wiksell, 1978), pp. 161–66.

11. Ibid., pp. 167–71.

12. Only Austria experienced a decline in its birthrate more rapidly than Sweden, yet Austria's severe dislocation and "loss of purpose" during and after World War I would seem to make it something of a special case. See Ivar Iverus, *Versuch einer Darstellung der Zusammenhanges Zwischen Bevölkerungsentwicklung, Familienpolitik und öffentlichen meinung in Sweden* (Helsinkikir: Japaino o.y. Sana, 1953), pp. 20–21.

13. See Karin Koch, "Nymalthusianismens genombrott i Sverige," *Studier in ekonomie och historia tillägnade Eli F. Heckscher på årsdagen den 24 November 1944* (Uppsala: Almqvist and Wiksell, 1945), pp. 84–88.

14. The term *neo-Malthusian* was coined by S. van Houten, vice president of the International Malthusian League, in 1879 and used to convey an optimistic faith in the power of human reason to use contraceptives to control fertility. See D. V. Glass, *Population Policies and Movements in Europe* (Oxford: Clarendon Press, 1940), note IAA, p. 425, and pp. 30–46. Also: F. H. Amphlett Micklewright, "The Rise and Decline of English Malthusianism," *Population Studies* 15, no. 1 (1961–62): 32–51.

15. Torsten Gårdlund, *Knut Wicksell: Rebell i det nya riket* (Stockholm; Albert Bonniers Förlag, 1956), p. 46; and Koch, "Nymalthusianismens genombrott i Sverige," p. 84. Karl Kautsky's major works included *Der Einfluss der Volksmehrung auf der Fortschritt der Gesellschaft* (Vienna: Boch and Harbuck, 1880) and *Vermehrung und Entwicklung* (Stuttgart: J. H. Dietz Nachf, 1910).

16. "What are the most serious causes of alcoholism and how can they be removed?" As later reprinted in brochure form: Knut Wicksell, *Några ord om samhällsolyckornas viktigäste orsak och botemedel med särskilt afseende på dryckenskapen* (Uppsala: n.p., 1880).

17. Charles R. Drysdale, *Om fattigdom såsom orsak till förtidig död samt nödvändigheten af nativtetens inskränkning* (Uppsala: Esaias Edqvist, 1880).

18. See Gårdlund, *Knut Wicksell*, pp. 49–54 and 68–69; Koch, "Nymalthusianismens genombrott i Sverige," pp. 75–76; and Georg Borgström, *Malthus om befolkningsfrågan* (Stockholm: LT's Förlag, 1969), p. 215.

19. Knut Wicksell, *De sexuela frågorna: Granskning af hrr Emil Svensens, Bjornstjerne Bjornsons samt professor Seved Ribbings brochyrer* (Stockholm: Kungholms Bokhandel, 1890), particularly pp. 56 and 68; and Wicksell, *Föreläsningar i nationalekonomi* (Lund: Gleerup, 1928).

20. From Gustaf Alegård, *Befolkningsfrågan genom tiderna* (Stockholm: Al-

bert Bonniers Förlag, 1926), pp. 69–70.
21. Sundbärg, *Bevolkerungsstatistik Schwedens*, pp. 40–41 and 47–48.
22. See Alegård, *Befolkningsfrågan genom tiderna*, pp. 71–75.
23. Hinke Bergegren, *Kärlek utan barn* (Stockholm: Ungsocialistiska Partiets Förlag, 1910), pp. 8–17, 30–31, and 48.
24. Anton Nystrom, *Fattigdom och barnalstring* (Stockholm: Björck and Börjessen, 1911), p. 15. Emphasis in original.
25. See Karl Marx and Friedrich Engels, *Marx and Engels on Malthus*, ed. Ronald Week (London: Lawrence and Wishart, 1953).
26. Richard Sandler, *Samhället sådant det är* (Stockholm: Frams Förlag, 1911), pp. 6–11, 27–38, and 51–86.
27. Otto Grimlund, "Några ord i befolkningsfrågan," *Tiden* 4 (1912): 272–77.
28. See Ulf Cervin, "Kris i befolkningsfrågan," in *1900-talet: Vår tids historia i ord och bild* (Helsingbort: Bokfrämjandet, 1975), p. 46.
29. John Andersson, *Barnalstringsfrågan och arbetarklassen* (Gothenburg: John Andersson Förlag, 1916), pp. 6, 19, and 31.
30. Hjalmar Öhrvall, *I vår befolkningsfrågan* (Stockholm: Albert Bonniers Förlag, 1917), particularly pp. 11–12, 20–21, and 24–26.
31. Reprinted as Knut Wicksell, "Befolkningsfrågans nuvarande lage," *Tiden* 16 (June 1924): 193–208.
32. Wicksell, "Befolkningsfrågans nuvarande lage" pp. 195–200. This pamphlet was also reprinted as *Barnalstringsfrågan: Föredrag, hållet vid nymalthusianska sällskapet* (Stockholm: Federatives Förlag, 1925).
33. Knut Wicksell, *Fosterfördrivning: Några reflektioner till en aktuell rättsfråga* (Stockholm: Bokförlaget Brand, 1927) pp. 5 and 7–8.
34. See G. Westin Silverstolpe, "Malthus och nutidens nationalekonomi," *Tiden* 19 (January 1927): 11–20.
35. G. Westin Silverstolpe, *Folkmängd och välstånd* (Stockholm: Bokförlaget Brand, 1926).
36. See Frans Severin, "Fackföreningsrörelsen och befolkningsfrågan," *Tiden* 19 (June 1927): 206 and 216–17.
37. In Alegård, *Befolkningsfrågan genom tiderna*, p. 85.
38. Bertil Mogård, "Folkökning och försörjning," *Tiden* 19 (June 1927): 218–23.
39. Nils Karleby, *Socialismen inför verkligheten: Studie över socialdemokratisk åskådning och nutidspolitik* (Stockholm: Tidens Förlag, 1926), pp. 271–72.
40. Eva Wigforss, *Arbetsinkomst och familjförsörjning* (Stockholm: P. A. Norstedt och Söners Förlag, 1929), pp. 6–7, 9–12, 18, 25, and 55–56. Other works on the "family wage" from the 1920s include Eva Wigforss, *Familje försörjning för industrinsarbetare* Fackföreningsrörelsen pamphlet no. 25 (1925); and Ella Anker, *Modralön, familjetillägg* (Stockholm: Stockholms fackliga kvinnliga samorganization, 1929).
41. Unnumbered manuscript, dated 4 February 1930, in EVW (Eva

Wigforss Collection), Arbetarrörelsens Arkiv, boxes 68–69.

42. P. J. Welinder, *Fattigdom och folkökning* (Gothenburg: Arbetarekurirens Förlag, 1928), p. 4.

43. Ibid., particularly pp. 14–15, 26, 37–39.

44. Quoted in Alegård, *Befolkningsfrågan genom tiderna*, p. 76.

45. The term *bourgeois* (*borgerliga* in Swedish) holds a special political meaning here, describing those politicians and economists to the right of the Social Democrats. It includes conservatives, "Manchester" liberals, and Agrarian party advocates, yet excludes the extreme right influenced or dominated by fascism or ultra-nationalism.

46. Both cited in Alegård, *Befolkningsfrågan genom tiderna*, pp. 79–80 and 85–86.

47. J. Guinchard and G. Silén, *En befolknings generationsreproduktions förmåga* (Stockholm: K. L. Beckmans Boktryckeri, 1929).

48. Bertil Bohlin, *Memoarer: Ung man blir politiker* (Stockholm: Albert Bonniers Förlag, 1972), p. 132.

49. Torsten Bohlin, *Äktenskapets kris och förnyelse* (Stockholm: Sveriges Kristliga Studentrörelsens Bokförlag, 1934), p. 18.

50. Gustav Cassel, *Liv eller död* (Stockholm: Albert Bonniers Förlag, 1935), pp. 181–83, from a 13 August 1930 article titled "Aktivitet och livslängd."

51. Ibid., pp. 186 and 189 from a 22 February 1931 article titled "Fattigdomens avskäffande."

52. Ibid., pp. 191–96, from a 25 August 1933 article, "Nativitet och social politik."

53. F. J. Linders, *Vårt befolkningsproblem* (Stockholm: P. A. Norstedt and Söner, 1930), p. 21.

54. Ivar Trägårdh, *Civilisations dilemma och andra biologiska skisser* (Stockholm: Holger Schildts Förlag, 1934), pp. 28–29 and 56–64.

55. 1931 Riksdag motion no. 160. *Riksdags protokoll. Bihang 1931 (30): Motion-andra kammaren*, pp. 7–8.

56. Nils von Hofsten, *Arftlighetslärans grunder. II: Människan.* (Stockholm: Albert Bonniers Förlag, 1931).

57. H. Lundborg, *Befolkningsfrågan ur rashygienisk synpunkt: Den svenska bondeklassens betydelse* (Sala: Sala-Postens Boktryekeri, 1928), pp. 3 and 7.

58. H. Lundborg, *Västerlandet i fara: Befolkningsfrågor i biologisk och rashygienisk betydsning* (Gothenberg: Ernest V. Hansson Förlag, 1934), pp. 29–31, 36–39, and 50–55.

59. Collected and rewritten as Folke Borg, *Ett döende folk: synpunkter i befolkningsfrågan* (Stockholm: Hugo Gebers Förlag, 1935), pp. 21 and 81–100.

60. Borg, *Ett döende folk,* (See Above) pp. 102–108 and 120. The close parallels between Borg's proposed program and that developed by Alva and Gunnar Myrdal will become apparent in the following chapters. While the lectures on which Borg based this book were presented in the

1931–34 period, the volume was not published until 1935 and consequently appeared after the Myrdals' *Kris i befolkningsfrågan*. While Borg does not mention the Myrdals' work directly, he does make an indirect reference to its effect (p. 51) and lists *Kris i befolkningsfrågan* in his appendix. The question arises concerning the degree to which the Myrdals may have influenced Borg or Borg the Myrdals or whether their approaches emerged independently. There is no direct evidence supporting any of these possibilities, although—as shown in chapters 2 and 3— the Myrdals' basic approach had roots in their earlier work in social and economic policy. On the other hand, the "qualitative" aspects of *Kris i befolkningsfrågan* clearly draw on components of Borg's race-hygiene theory.

61. Lorentz Bolin, *Biologin och samhället: biologins ekonomiska och sociala betydelse* (Stockholm: Koopertiva Förbundets Bokförlag, 1933), pp. 197–303.

62. Ingrid Gärde Widemar, "I politiken," in Ruth Hamrin-Thorell, et al., *Kerstin Hasselgren: En Vänstudie* (Stockholm: P. A. Norstedt and Söner, 1968), pp. 136–38.

63. Martha Ruben-Wolf, *Fosterfördrivning eller förebyggande åtgärder* (Stockholm: Förlagsaktiebolaget Arbetarkultur, 1931), pp. 10–11.

64. Tage Erlander, *1940–1949* (Stockholm: Tidens Förlag, 1973), p. 182.

65. From Sven D. Wicksell, "Sveriges framtida befolkning under olika forutsättningar," *Ekonomisk tidskrift* 28, no. 4–5 (1926): 100–11.

66. Sven D. Wicksell, "Folkmängden och dess förändringar," *Tiden* 18 (December 1926): 324–29 and 332–34.

67. Wicksell, *Ur befolkningsläran*, pp. 65–69 and 73.

68. Gillis Aspegren, "Befolkningsteorin: Historik," *Tiden* 18 (1926): 155–67.

69. Axel Höjer, "Den s.k. preventivlagens otidsenlighet," *Tiden* 19 (March 1927): 79–84.

70. See his statement of purpose in Gustaf Alegård, "Befolkningsförhållandena i olika länder," *Tiden* 19 (November 1927): 407; and Gustaf Alegård, "Befolkningsförhållandena i olika länder—II," *Tiden* 19 (December 1927): 464–75.

71. See Gustaf Alegård, "Folkökning och Krigsfara," *Tiden* 20 (March 1928): 104–106 and Alegård, "Tysklands nativitetsfråga," *Tiden* 22 (December 1930): 611 and and 616–17.

72. Gustaf Alegård, "Folkökning och familjestatistik," *Tiden* 23 (September 1931): 420–25.

73. Gunnar Dahlberg, *Sverges befolkningsproblem*, Offprint by *Tiden* 5 (Stockholm: Tidents Förlag, 1930), pp. 7 and 10–13.

74. Before turning to a description of these political trends, some background information on the political landscape in Sweden during the 1930s might be useful. The Social Democratic Workers party (SAP) emerged in 1889 during the period of heavy Swedish industrialization. With its base in the trade unions, the party maintained a remarkable discipline.

Early in the twentieth century, party and union leadership was formalized with the creation of the Landsorganization (LO), the union of unions; the party would henceforth serve only as the political expression of the labor movement. Rhetorically radical and revisionist in political approach, the Social Democrats, under the leadership of Hjalmar Branting, committed themselves early on to achieving power through agitation and democratic means rather than revolution. However, socialization of the means of production remained a part of the party's program into the 1920s. Red flags, May Day rallies, and revolutionary rhetoric were other evident components of the party's political approach. In the 1889–1922 period, the Social Democrats subordinated their program to the Swedish liberal goal of achieving the "democratic revolution." The party then turned to questions of social and economic reconstruction.

The Swedish Liberal party emerged out of the nineteenth-century struggle for democratic governance and universal suffrage. Liberal groups in the Riksdag united between 1900 and 1902 to form the party. For the next two decades the Liberals led the constitutional battle against royal power, inherited privilege, and restricted suffrage. After 1922, the party turned to the prohibition issue, yet proved unable to carry its earlier fervor over to social and economic questions. The party split in 1923 over prohibition (a national referendum in 1922 defeated a prohibition proposal: 925,000 against, 889,000 for). It was not reunited again until 1934 as Folkpartiet, "the People's party."

Both the Conservative and Agrarian parties emerged around 1900 out of debate on "free trade versus protection" for agricultural production. The Conservatives formed in 1904 a "general elector's federation" to finance and organize electoral campaigns. Yet the formal organization of a party did not occur until 1934, when Conservatives in both chambers elected a common leader for the Rikdagshögern (the Parliamentary Right). The party stood for old Swedish and Christian social values, the protection of Swedish industry through high tariffs, and the liberty of the individual, particularly relative to labor unions.

The youth wing of the conservative movement, *Sveriges nationella ungdomsförbund*, proved highly receptive to fascist and national socialist influences. The neo-fascist group split from the party in 1935, taking with them three Riksdag members who called themselves *Nationellagruppen*, or the National Group. All three were defeated in the 1936 election.

The Swedish Agrarian party (Bondeförbundet) was formally organized in 1921 through the union of several farmers' political organizations. During the 1920s, the party shifted its emphasis from support of large landowners to the protection of middle-sized and small farmers.   On the extreme left, the Social Democratic youth movement, under the influence of Hinke Bergegren, had long shown syndicalist tendencies. The "left" Social Democrats split with the party in 1917 and split again in 1921. The majority in this second split became a section of the Communist International; the minority rejoined the Social Democrats in 1933. The Communist party divided in 1924; the majority in this split rejoined the Social Democrats in 1926. The minority remained faithful to the International until 1929, when still another split occurred. The majority this time, while remaining "Marxist," renounced the dictatorship of the proletariat. Under the leadership of journalist Karl Kilbom, this group joined forces with several ex–Social Democratic Riksdag members and called themselves the Socialist party (*Socialistiska partiet*). This party divided again in 1937, with Kilbom leading a majority back into the Social Democratic ranks. The remaining members of the communist party (Komintern partiet) continued to elect members to the Riksdag through the 1930s.

The Swedish national socialists exhibited some strength after Adolph Hitler came to power in Germany. They drew 26,570 votes in the 1936 election and 19,738 votes in 1938, although they never succeeded in placing a member in the Riksdag.

75. While social welfare remained primarily a local matter until the late 1930s, the roots of the centralized Swedish welfare state reach further back in time. As early as 1750, the government provided a doctor for every Swedish province. An 1891 law sanctioned the existence of voluntary mutual sickness benefit funds and provided a small state grant for administrative costs. Mental hospitals had long been a state responsibility. In the nineteenth century, some maternity compensation was provided through benefit funds; after 1913, state subsidies were paid to such funds for female members. In 1931, the Riksdag voted a twenty-eight-kronor bonus to every mother below a certain income limit. A 1917 law equalized the legal status of legitimate and illegitimate children. The Riksdag approved its first housing legislation in 1904, establishing a state loan fund for the building of privately owned homes, farm or nonfarm, outside city limits, followed by a new law in 1919. A 1917 act placed all decisions on rent, selection of tenants, and security of contracts in the hands of local commissions. However, with the repeal of this law in 1923, a national tenants' organization (*Hyresgästernas sparkasse-och byggnadsförening* or HSB) was organized and soon became a national housing movement. The state created a fund for secondary housing credit in 1917 that had financed the construction of some thirty thousand units by 1930. The cooperative housing movement, dating back to the 1880s, continued slow expansion. An agrarian price support system was established in the 1920s. A 1901 law established a compulsory workmen's compensation scheme, substantially reorganized in 1916 and again in 1929.

76. On the general ideological development of Swedish Social Democracy see Herbert Tingsten, *The Swedish Social Democrats: Their Ideological Development*, trans. Greta Frankel and Patricia Howard Rosen (Totowa, N.J.: Bedminster Press, 1973); Frans Severin, *The Ideological Development of Swedish Social Democracy* (Stockholm: SAP, 1955); and Leif

Lewin, *Planhushållningsdebatten* (Stockholm: Political Science Association, 1967).

77. See the epilogue by Tage Erlander and Bjorn von Syndow to the 1976 facsimile edition of Nils Karleby, *Socialism inför verkligheten: studien över socialdemokratisk åskådning och nutidspolitik* (Kristianstad: Kristianstads Boktryckeri, 1976), p. 285.
78. Ibid., pp. 301–309; and Jan Lindhagen, *Socialdemokratins program: I rörelsens tid 1890–1930* (Stockholm: Tidens Förlag, 1972).
79. See Sven Anders Soderpalm, "The Crisis Agreement and the Social Democratic Road to Power," in Koblik, *Sweden's Development from Poverty to Affluence*, pp. 258–77.
80. Quoted in Bo Sodersten, "Per Albin och den socialistiska reformismen," in Gunnar Frederickson et al., *Per Albin linjen* (Stockholm: Bokförlaget PAN/Norstedts, 1970), p. 102.
81. In Sodersten, "Per Albin och den socialistiska reformismen," p. 103.

2

Wellsprings of a New Approach

The origins of the Myrdals' new Social Democratic line on the population question lay in their grappling over the implications of social science for ideology and policy in the 1929–34 period. More broadly, it grew out of the early lives of this unusually influential married couple.

Born 6 December 1898 in Gustafs Parish, Kopparberg, Karl Gunnar Myrdal spent his early childhood in the bucolic poverty of historic Dalarna. His father, Carl Adolf Petersson, worked on the construction of railway depots. Shortly thereafter, the family moved to Stockholm, where Petersson continued in construction.

At an early age Myrdal exhibited a superior mind. While attending the gymnasium, he fell under the influence of teacher John Lindquist, who directed his student toward the philosophy of the Enlightenment. Myrdal read extensively from the French and English utopian socialists, who, "different from Marx, were planners in the great tradition of Enlightenment philosophy." Their work instilled in Myrdal faith in a rational approach to problems and an egalitarian social policy. "The common trust in progress could prevail in this line of thought," he later stated. He also reported an early interest in the works of Max Weber.[1]

In 1918 Myrdal entered the University of Stockholm, Sweden's "new" institution of higher learning with a reputation for innovative science-oriented studies and quickly gained a reputation for achievement. He received his law degree in 1923. A year later, he married a student he had met five years before during a bicycle trip in the country, Alva Reimer.

Alva was born to Albert and Lowa Reimer in Uppsala on 31 January 1902. Her father was a master builder with strong labor-union and

Social Democratic ties, an ideological orientation that he passed on to his daughter. Alva's mother was a housewife with a reported talent for millinery work. Despite difficulties, Alva received an extensive education, uncommon for a young girl in early twentieth-century Sweden, for which her father was largely responsible. At age seventeen, with the gymnasium in Eskilstuna closed to girls, Alva participated in a study course privately organized by interested parents for ten young women. In mid-1922 she entered the University of Stockholm, and she received her FIL. KAND. degree in 1924 in the history of religion, Scandinavian languages, and the history of literature.[2]

The meeting of Gunnar and Alva in 1919 began a long, extraordinary partnership. The emotional bond that developed between the Myrdals must be appreciated before understanding the discussions, tensions, and care that went into their collaborative work and the influence each had on the other in their independent projects. Egon Glesinger, an American student of economics, first met Gunnar Myrdal at the Institut Universitaire de Hautes Études internationales in Geneva in late 1930. He reported that the entire research institute was then wrapped in tension, as Myrdal awaited news from the hospital of his wife, who had just suffered a miscarriage: "It was . . . during these weeks before I even knew Gunnar, that I sensed the place of Alva in his life."[3] In the early years of their marriage, Alva appeared to place her career, both through circumstance and design, behind her husband's. Yet while she acted as the traditional wife and mother in the latter 1920s, friends recognized at an early point that she was the more aggressive and the stronger of the two. She had a major effect on the direction of her husband's work, particularly encouraging his move into multidisciplinary social research.[4]

After receiving his law degree, Gunnar Myrdal established a legal practice in the picture book village of Mariefred, but soon found this career unsatisfactory. At Alva's urging, he returned to the university and began studies in economics under Sweden's prominent economist Gustav Cassel.[5]

In the 1920s, Cassel exerted a strong influence on a whole generation of emerging Swedish economists and politicians. Nils Wohlin, Gösta Bagge, Bertil Ohlin, and Myrdal were each students of his, and each went on to serve as a leader of a different political party. Alva and Gunnar Myrdal developed close personal relationships with Cassel and his wife, Johanna. In his letters from the 1930s, Myrdal addressed most of his correspondents as "Broder" (Brother) but continued to address "Professor Cassel" alone in the formal style. Myrdal described Cassel in 1931 as "extremely intelligent, a genius in his field. Even without much insight in modern institutional and sociological approaches, he is, as the true scholar, generous in his personal attitude towards every sort of earnest and intelligent scientific work."[6] The virtual father-son relationship that developed between Cassel and Myrdal survived even their sharp clash in late 1934 over the population question.[7]

The Myrdals made their first home in Stockholm in an apartment at Roslagstorg. A small group of friends met there every week in the middle 1920s, including Alf Johansson, then a student of social history, Fritz Thorén, a student of natural science, Pierre Guinchard, a student of economics, and Marta Fredrikson, a schoolteacher. They discussed economic and social-political issues, often well into the night. Johansson later recalled that Alva Myrdal's contributions were particularly clear, original, and influential.[8]

Gunnar published his dissertation in April 1927. Titled *Prisbildningsproblemet och föranderligheten*, it was based on the classical price theory of the economists Knut Wicksell and Cassel. Gunnar's significant modification was to place price changes over time within a new "dynamic" framework.[9] Significantly, financial support for the project came from the Laura Spelman Rockefeller Foundation, the first of several research grants that the young Myrdals received from this source. The same year, Gunnar obtained an appointment at the University of Stockholm as docent in political economy. The couple's first child, Jan, arrived at the same time.

During her last year at the university, Alva had grown interested in psychological studies and entered the relatively new field of social psychology. While on an extended research trip to England in 1925, she studied an aspect of this approach, developed by I. A. Richards, called Literary Criticism. He viewed literature from the point of view of how it was experienced by the reader. His theory of aesthetics studied the consumption of art, rather than artists or the production of art, seeking indications as to what lay behind "artistic taste" and how people in different social groups reacted to artistic impulses. In autumn of 1928, she also participated in a seminar at the University of Stockholm conducted by Prof. Bertil Hammer on "psychology and education," where she prepared a paper on Freud's theory of dreams.[10]

In spring of 1928, Gunnar Myrdal presented a series of important lectures dealing with the influence of politics in the development of classical economic theory at the University of Stockholm. These essays were reworked and published in 1929 under the title *Vetenskap och politik i nationalekonomien.*[11] This book had a powerful impact on the new generation of Swedish economists emerging from the universities. Myrdal's effort to see through the fallacies and political content of classical liberal economic doctrine shook earlier certainties and opened the gates to new economic theories and political experimentation. The influence his personal struggle over the book had on all his later work, not least on *Kris i befolkningsfrågan*, is difficult to overestimate.[12]

What began as a frontal attack on the economic dogma of the "old generation" of economists—from Malthus, Ricardo, and Mill to Marshall, Cassel, and Knut Wicksell—gradually became an effort to understand economic doctrines as a coherent, growing body of thought, closely integrated into the setting of contemporary ideas and aspirations. Most modern economic doctrines should not be seen as scientific, Myrdal warned, but as theories conceived in days when teleological meaning and "a normative purpose" were openly part of economic thinking. He posited that the political speculation that had permeated the theories of the classical economists from the very beginning had crystallized around three main foci—the ideas of value, freedom, and social economy: "These three notions, variously combined, have given economic doctrines their political content."

In the chapters that followed, Myrdal dissected classical economic doctrine, exposing its hidden value premises, social assumptions, and lack of scientific objectivity and logical coherence. He did not criticize opinions of economists as personal political belief, but only where they purported to be scientific. In his final chapter, he discussed how economics could be rendered useful again without becoming a theory of objective politics. In essence, he revived the concept of "political economy" and drew its relationship to a "modern, psychologically oriented sociology."

Myrdal argued that economists must not obscure normative principles by introducing them as "concepts." All definitions are tools constructed to analyze reality; they are "instrumental" and not justified in their own right. He affirmed that economists must define their concepts clearly and use them in a logically correct manner: "The perpetual game of hide-and-seek in economics consists in concealing the norm in the concept. It is thus imperative to eradicate not only the explicit principles but above all the valuations tacitly implied by the basic concepts."[13]

Myrdal noted that in most questions of economic policy there existed conflicts of interest, phenomena long ignored by the classical economists who believed in social harmony. Such conflicts should not be concealed by talk of *a priori* principles that misused the scientific method to obscure or conceal them. He argued that one of the main tasks of applied economics was to examine and dissect the "complex interplay of interests" in matters such as price.

Injecting his own Enlightenment type of faith in the future, the author turned to the political struggle and to the institutional setup—"the legal order and customs, habits and conventions which are sanctioned or tolerated by that legal order"—where that struggle took place. He found the scope for discovering economic interests greatly enlarged if one accepted the possibility of institutional change: "*All institutional factors* which determine the structure of the market, indeed the whole economic system including its tax and social legislation, *can be changed*, if *those interested in the change have enough political power*." He argued that inquiry into economic interests should treat *institutional arrangements* as a *variable* and should examine the extent to which groups were powerful enough to bring about changes and should trace the repercussions of possible changes throughout the price system. Social life, simply put, was the illogical result of human choices; at any moment we could decide whether to maintain or change it.[14]

The problem of isolating interests went beyond pure economics. Human activity was not solely motivated by economic interests. "[P]eople are also interested in social objectives," Myrdal insisted. "They believe in ideals to which they want their society to conform." He concluded that a "technology of economics" should not be built on economic interests, but on social attitudes. The analysis of attitudes became a problem of social psychology, and "since we are concerned with social groups, it is a problem of the social psychology of the character of groups. The technology of economics is a branch of modern, psychologically oriented sociology."[15]

Myrdal doubted that this active new sociology would provide a firm foundation for "the technology of economics" in the near future. In the interim, he suggested two requirements to ensure that economics not end up as metaphysics: (1) always formulate value premises in explicit, concrete terms and relate them to the actual valuations of social groups; and (2) give attention to the above mentioned problems of social psychology when formulating relevant economic attitudes. He concluded: "Only if economists are modest in their claims and renounce all pretensions to postulate universal laws and norms can they promote effectively their practical objectives, viz., to keep political arguments rational . . . to base them on as complete and as correct a knowledge of the facts as possible."[16]

As originally presented, the lecture series on which Myrdal based *Vetenskap och politik* contained a critique of the "optimum population" theory of the classical economists.[17] His original outline for the book gave the title for the sixth chapter as "Befolkningsfrågan" (The population question),[18] and his first draft contained a sketch for a chapter-length discussion of the population quantity question.[19] In his final draft, however, he dropped the chapter from the book, relegating the population question to footnotes and a few brief comments. As he later explained to Ernst Wigforss, "I had begun my earlier book with a critique of population theories, but when it came to the sticking point, I decided that population doctrine was actually so badly presented in economics that I could not give the matter its own chapter in a serious book".[20]

This early draft of the "lost chapter" of *Vetenskap och politik* represents Myrdal's earliest extant treatment of population theory. In it, he stated that the point of departure in "optimum population" theory had been "den liberala önskemaximum"—namely, the greatest possible good for the greatest possible number. He noted that the utilitarianism of John Stuart Mill, as interpreted by Sidgwick and Edgeworth, posited an optimal population formula, a mathematical product measuring the number of individuals in a particular economy and their average happiness.

Myrdal dismissed these optimum population theories as irrelevant. Strictly mathematical and economic formulations, he argued, were incapable of accurately measuring human happiness:

> Think how sagacious the theoretician must be, who would compute an optimum population and therefore give consideration to social man's intimate happiness and allowance to a person's partiality for solitude, to peo-

ple's joy in having children, to women's reluctance to give birth themselves and to people's moralistic and personal decisions to adopt measures to prevent conception.[21]

He noted certain political factors that would need to be taken into calculation: defense needs; the pressure of competing populations; and the "race-hygenic" viewpoint. Given these considerations and changes over time, Myrdal dismissed as impossible any attempt to determine an "optimum" level of population and added:

> [I]t is not my intention to propagandize [here] against neo-Malthusianism or against some special political conception of population. My desire is only that economists as scientists humbly ought to acknowledge that we know altogether too little about these endless, far reaching matters, and for the remaining have nothing special as a basis that could establish some value premises which have a claim to represent some majority opinion or otherwise has some reason to be taken as a useful hypothesis.[22]

While refusing at this time either to support or oppose neo-Malthusianism, Myrdal did posit one intriguing possible social dilemma: ". . . imagine that an individual—or let us say all individuals as members of society—on the basis of political values desire a large number of people for their nation, but for their own part, do not desire to bear any children at all."[23] As later adapted, this focus on the dissonance between collective and personal interestes in the birth of children would be fully explored by the Myrdals and would form the basic thrust behind their pronatalist program.

Vetenskap och politik represented a significant step in Gunnar Myrdal's development as a social scientist. In this work, he moved from a singular emphasis on economics toward a multidisciplinary involvement in economics, political science, social psychology, and sociology. He ruthlessly criticized the subjectivity he identified in the classical and neo-classical economists and formed the basis for his more "objective" approach to social and economic research: a commitment to clearly formulated value statements, the distinction between stated opinions and actual attitudes, and the emphasis on the relationship between economic and institutional changes. He also gave here early attention to the complexities of population theory, formulating many of the questions to be answered in his later work.[24]

Another indication of Myrdal's budding interest in demographics came in October 1928 when he proposed to direct "intensive research" from an economic viewpoint into the "population-statistical material" at the Swedish Central Statistical Bureau, with financial support from the Laura Spelman Rockefeller Memorial Fund. He specifically hoped to explore "how these demographic factors reacted to differences and to changes in the economic measurements of wages, unemployment, production, etc., together with how they in certain cases determine these quantities."[25] Other scraps and notes from the same period reflect an early interest in the effects of economic change on the institution of the family.[26] Myrdal also wrote several early essays dealing with the dynamics of Sweden's social structure[27] and a short study of Sweden's growing agrarian problem.[28]

However, prior to the autumn of 1929 and despite some early interest in social-economic and institutional problems, both Alva and Gunnar Myrdal remained "academics" in the strict sense of the word. Gunnar's work was principally centered on theoretical economics, Alva's on the social psychology of literature and aesthetics. Both were insulated by university life, and neither gave active attention to politics. Alva Myrdal, despite her Social Democratic inclinations, did not claim membership in the party. Gunnar Myrdal's roots lay in rural Sweden, where he developed an informal linkage to the policy concerns of the Agrarian party; he was actually asked to run as a Bondeförbund candidate to the Riksdag in the late 1920s.[29]

Their political awakening came as both received Rockefeller Foundation fellowships to study in the United States during the 1929–30 academic year.[30] They were part of a significant, albeit little known, Rockefeller program designed to bring young, promising European social scientists to the United States for a year of flexible study and travel. The effect on the Myrdals was large; more broadly, it represented a new phase in the flow of ideas from the Untied States to Sweden, as the Myrdals imbibed the spirit of scientific progressivism. Specifically, the American trip stimulated Alva's concentration on children's politics, collective child care, and the family. Gunnar Myrdal found his involvement in the politics of population strengthened during the same visit. Leaving Sweden in September 1929 as detached intellectuals, they returned a year later committed to political action and to radical reform of the Swedish social order on the basis of a scientific sociology.

Their trip began with a summer stopover in England, where they completed old projects and Alva began reading in the theory of pedagogy. In a letter to Prof. Bertil Hammer, Alva Myrdal reported her enthusiasm for the educational theories of the Scottish philosophers, who she felt had anticipated a good share of modern psychological concepts. She noted that her eyes had been opened to the "close relationship between pedagogy and the great social problems." An attached draft plan for her master's thesis (*Licentiauppsats*) cited "the school as a substitute for the family" and the need for school reforms better to meet children's psychological needs.[31]

In the United States, the Laura Spelman Rockefeller Foundation directed Alva Myrdal into study of the "socialization of the child" and "child psychology." New theories of child development and preschool care were then being developed in the United States, most notably at the Child Development Institute at Columbia University and the Institute of Human Relations at Yale. She traveled to these sites, as well as to the Child Welfare Institute at the University of Minnesota and operating experimental preschools in Toronto, Winnetka (Illinois), and Washington, D.C., which had Rockefeller Foundation support. The latter two, in particular, impressed her.[32]

In this period, Alva also read extensively on the interaction of psychoanalysis and pedagogy and on the relationship between the school and the family. She took extensive notes on studies such as J. C. Flugel's *The Psycho-Analysis Study of the Family* (London, 1921), G. H. Green's *Psychoanalysis of the Classroom* (London, 1921), and W. Lay's *The Child's Unconscious Mind* (London, 1919). She developed a strong interest in the American experimental schools' preparation of their students for family life and parenthood, in their encouragement of "open" study, and in the close association between parents and the schools. The concept of "parent education" particularly intrigued her.[33] She established contact with a number of American sociologists, most notably W. I. Thomas and Dorothy Thomas, authors of *The Child in America*. Sociologist William O. Ogburn impressed on her his view of the importance of recent changes in the structure of the family and its progressive "loss of function." Ogburn taught that institutions such as the school, industry, and the state had grown at the family's expense, with the latter institution retreating primarily toward the "personality function." Myrdal also met and studied under prominent European psychologists residing in the United States, including Alfred Adler and Charlotte Bühler.[34]

Gunnar Myrdal's Rockefeller fellowship program was less structured. As Gösta Bagge, the foundation's principal coordinator in Sweden, reported, Gunnar Myrdal spent most of his time traveling in order "to gain insight" into new approaches and methods in his field and to make contact with American scholars.[35]

Gunnar Myrdal spent most of the year at Columbia University, the University of Chicago, and the Library of Congress. Contact with American sociologists restimulated earlier interest in demographic indicators. In a letter to Cassel, he noted that his dissertation provided him with a basis in modern economic theory and that the research for *Vetenskap och politik* gave him a historical perspective on the development of economic theory. He added:

> But after this I am likely never in my life to write anything again on general economics. I have learned what I want to learn here. Demographic questions interest me, not primarily the purely scientific [sic] but because they in a central way possibly can tell us something about the deeper connections in the last decades' developments in Sweden; also about what is determining our people's present social and economic life.[36]

He cited his disillusionment with theoretical studies and pledged: "I will concern myself with something which has a more direct connection with human life."[37]

At the Library of Congress, Myrdal turned his attention more specifically to shifting demographic patterns: "I think increasingly that my research should make a deep, comprehensive sociological study of Sweden's industrialization from a population perspective and business-cycle perspective."[38] From the University of Chicago Myrdal wrote Bagge: "Generally over here I am in contact with sociologists who now have taken in hand the deeper population question in this country." He noted his pleasure in meeting Ogburn and added: "Alva and I have also quite thoroughly set ourselves . . . into the multifaceted demographic-sociological study of the Chicago population . . . which is directed by Burgess" and emphasized changing family functions. He resolved to return to Sweden and begin intensive study of the Swedish population.[39] Myrdal also made the acquaintance of W. I. Thomas and Dorothy Thomas, which blossomed into long personal and professional relationships, involving Gunnar's assistance to the latter in her important work on Swedish migration statistics.[40]

Of course, the 1929–30 academic year also represented the beginning of the Great Depression. The specter of economic collapse, growing unemployment, and aggravated poverty made a deep impression on the Myrdals. They expressed surprise that the richest country in the world—a symbol of the future, democracy, egalitarianism, and scientific progress—could at the same time be so backward and tolerate urban slums, "near starvation," and seemingly uncontrolled crime. They pointed to the brilliant ineffectiveness of American intellectuals, who wrote clever, articulate, and "muckraking" analyses of the American situation but who seemed incapable of positive political action.[41]

In 1930, Gunnar Myrdal gave up his docentur at the University of Stockholm and accepted, at Cassel's urging, a better-paying, more prestigious position at the *Institut universitare de hautes Etudes Internationales* in Geneva, teaching international economics. Drawing additional Rockefeller Foundation money funneled through Gösta Bagge, Gunnar Myrdal intensified his demographic research project. He sought to identify the relations between population movements—births, deaths, and migration—and other social and economic changes that made up industrialization. He concentrated on the dynamics behind the transfer of people from agriculture to industry and from rural to urban districts.[42] By early 1931, Myrdal was planning on a massive two-volume study, the first volume containing the compiled statistics and the second offering his analysis and interpretations. He contemplated a collaborative research effort on Swedish migration in conjunction with W. I. and Dorothy Thomas. Myrdal also developed an international reputation in demography and accepted, then rescinded, a request to present a paper on internal migrations in Sweden to the International Congress of Rome (on population) in 1931. However, he soon found that his heavy teaching load gave him insufficient time to pursue his research, and by March he was looking for a different arrangement.[43]

Alva Myrdal continued her studies in psychology at the Jean Jacques Rousseau Institut in Geneva, giving special attention to Piaget's theories on early childhood development. A miscarriage and complications in late 1930 placed her life in actual danger for a brief period. She was active again by February 1931 and rejoined her husband in a series of regular intense discussions with other expatriates in Geneva, notably Bertil Ohlin, who was working then for the League of Nations, and

Frances and Jacob Viner from the United States. On 25 April 1931, Alva Myrdal gave her first public lecture at the Nordic People's High School in Geneva, on "social policy for children and youth." She outlined a program of social reform to provide greater governmental support for families and children.[44]

In early 1931, Alva and Gunnar Myrdal first attempted to interpret the cause, meaning, and implications of Sweden's declining fertility rate in a pair of articles titled "The Population Question from the Social Policy Perspective" ("Befolkningsfrågan från socialpolitik synpunkt"). In these articles (the texts of which are lost), the Myrdals sought to pull together Gunnar's unused critique of the demographic theories of the classical economists and his research into Sweden's vital statistics with Alva's budding interest in the institution of the family, child psychology, early childhood development, and the relationship of government to the family. They used the unifying themes of nativity decline and social-political response. This pair of articles formed the skeleton on which their population book, *Kris i befolkningsfrågan*, would later be built. But they were, at this stage, incomplete, "a kind of artificial amalgam." The two authors, in fact, still argued over certain fundamental questions, including the desirability of seeking a higher birthrate and the shape of an effective countervailing social policy.[45]

In May 1931, Gunnar Myrdal submitted the two manuscripts to Ernst Wigforss, editor of *Tiden*, for publication. Wigforss's negative reply came quickly. He cited the great length of the manuscript and the small size of *Tiden* as the reason for his rejection.[46] The Myrdals, returning to Stockholm in June, laid the manuscript and the population theme aside for another three years.

In this period, their respective interests and careers diverged considerably, drawing together again only with the authorship of *Kris i befolkningsfrågan* in mid-1934. Gunnar returned to the University of Stockholm and focused on economics and agrarian and housing policy. Alva Myrdal projected her new interests in early childhood development, parent education, and the family onto the Swedish situation and became active in the women's movement.

The common and important external links they shared were several groups of people who met on a regular basis to discuss social and political questions. One included friends from the 1920s, such as Pierre Guinchard and Alf Johannson. Their discussions now dealt less with theory and more with political action. Some twenty graduate students in economics met biweekly in the Myrdals' apartment on Kungsholmsstrand to discuss economic problems into the early morning hours "while consuming lots of aquavit and whiskey."[47] The most influential new personal contacts for the Myrdals, though, were with a group of radical architects and industrial designers.

The origins of radical "functionalism" in modern Swedish design can be traced, in one sense, to certain elements of Sweden's own folk art.[48] The ideological element came from socialist Ellen Key's *Skönhet i hemmen* (1897) and *Skönhet för alla* (1899), where she argued for simple, sanitary, affordable, and machine-produced household goods. *Hemutställningen* (the Home Exposition) of 1917 featured the work of a new generation of Swedish designers, including Erik Wettergren, Elsa Gullberg, Carl Bergsten, and Gregor Paulsson. The influence of *Deutsches Werkbunds*, a center for modern German design, was evident.[49]

Meanwhile, the democratic wave that swept over the Europeans after World War I opened a new era of architectural experimentation. By the mid-1920s, numerous projects were on their way in Berlin, Frankfurt, Amsterdam, and other cities. Within Sweden, the Riksdag's 1920 Social Housing Investigation set new standards for building materials, which were subsequently refined by Eskil Sundahl for the Swedish cooperative housing movement, HSB. Le Corbusier's *Pavillon de l'espirit nouveau* at the 1925 World Exposition in Paris and the 1927 Stuttgart exposition exerted a strong influence on Swedish architects. Sven Wallander, chief architect for HSB, made numerous visits to continental Europe and became a driving force behind the introduction of functional design in furniture, appliances, and housing in Sweden. He was particularly impressed by the housing complexes constructed in Vienna's "Red" commune, which provided collective child care and sought to remove the "poor relief" aura around day-care centers.[50]

In 1928, designer-architect Uno Åhrén organized a study circle for architectural students on the relationship between functionalism and social policy, with Alf Johansson as leader and the Myrdals as regular participants. Social policy became an increasingly important focus of their approach to design.[51]

This group of architects and town planners—including Åhrén, Gunnar Asplund, Walter Gahn, Sven Markelius, Gregor Paulsson, and Eskil Sundahl—helped to organize the Stockholm Exposition of 1930.

It featured displays of rational, "social" design in housing, furniture, and household utensils—all expressions of what came to be called "Swedish modern." The exposition marked a break with past Swedish architectural tradition, particularly in the degree to which it linked design to ideology. The event offered an entire functionalist city representing a vision of a new democratic society and culture.[52] The book published in conjunction with this event—*Acceptera*—stands as a major document of modern Swedish social history.

The premise posed by the authors of *Acceptera* was their effort to avoid choosing between the individual and the mass, between the personal and the general, between quality and quantity, by providing for both quantity and quality and both the mass and the individual. They rejected current social policy, which sought to solve social questions "as though one should remedy the symptoms of sickness, not the sicknesses themselves."[53] They talked of industrialized Europe, or "A-Europe," as a vast, complex organism characterized by specialization and centralization, where all component cells were dependent on one another. This "A-Europe" formed a great circle from Stockholm to Florence and from Glasgow to Budapest, and it stood in sharp contrast to the old, pastoral world. They argued that Swedish culture faced a radical imperative to adapt to this new Europe or become a useless relic.[54]

In housing they derided current architectural forms as inefficient and uneconomical and noted that they now had the materials and ability to build larger, lighter, cheaper, and more rational structures than even ten years before. They saw how a "radical understanding" of the need for quality had already given rise to new concepts of construction, to a divergence from tradition, even to a totally different kind of aesthetic. They saw their combination of the radical, rational, and hygienic extending also to furniture, light fixtures, tableware, glassware, and even doorknobs: " . . . we will create things which we can fix ourselves and which function well and beautifully."[55]

They viewed the disappearance of handcrafts and the growth of industry as inevitable, the only way to provide affordable items of high quality for the coming generation: "We must accept these developments as an honest basis . . . for our work." Their theory of art was summed up in the words "art is order." They projected "[f]ree, independent, living art work in place of sweetly pretty, gushing, valueless decoration; in place of 'elegance.'"[56]

The designers saw themselves as the vanguards of a new cultural period, where art and architecture would leave the small town ideal forever and turn to the industrial city. In this way, functional architecture would become the very substance of the city. "Accept [*Acceptera*] the aforementioned reality," they declared; "only through that do we have the chance to govern, to have the power to change things and shape a culture which is a flexible instrument for life." Rejecting the old, pastoral Europe, their goals as planners, organizers, rationalists, and artists were "the reorganization of the world's economy and the improvement and stabilization of the individual's living conditions," as the means to a richer human existence.[57]

In *Acceptera*, Sweden's designers presented a vision of architecture and social policy that bound together the concepts of quality and quantity, implied a "preventive" as opposed to a symptom-oriented social policy, advocated rational planning, and involved a positive, bold, optimistic embrace of the industrial, urban future. The Myrdals' close association with these designers, particularly with Åhrén and Markelius, had significant impact on their perception of social policy changes that would find expression in their work on family and population.[58]

At the University of Stockholm, Gunnar Myrdal resumed active participation in the social science research project operating under the leadership of Bagge. Building on an earlier 1925 grant designed to encourage the study of sociology among the humanities faculty, the Rockefeller Foundation had recently pledged new financing of thirty thousand dollars through 1936.

Bagge described the project as an investigation into the factors underlying social developments in Sweden during the 1830–1929 period. At a humanities faculty meeting in May 1931, Bagge, Gunnar Myrdal, and five others were elected to serve on the committee directing research. Bagge—founder and director of the university's school of social work, Conservative party politician, and student of Cassel— was the driving force behind the project.[59]

The collected work of the *Socialvetenskapliga institutet* represents an impressive compilation of statistical material. Generally, it formed the data base for the work and recommendations of a number of social investigative commissions in Sweden during the 1930s, including the Population Commission of 1935. The institute also embodied a spirit of optimism and certitude, conveyed through a confident blend of numbers, scientific rhetoric, and faith in reason. In these senses, the project proved to be an important stimulant in the building of the modern Swedish welfare state.[60] More specifically, it produced a lively interchange of ideas between Myrdal and other participants and, in the subsidized work of Karl Arvid Edin, would provide the Myrdals with the statistical support necessary to give their major population thesis scientific validity.

Through an arrangement with a British publishing house, the studies from this research project were translated and printed in English. These included Gösta Bagge, Erik Lundberg, and Ingvar Svennilson's *Wages in Sweden, 1860–1930*, Gunnar Myrdal's *The Cost of Living in Sweden 1830–1930*, Karin Koch's *A Study of Interest Rates*, Erik Lindahl's *National Income of Sweden, 1861–1930*, and Gunnar Myrdal's "Industrialization and Population." Later studies included Karl Edin and Edward Mutchinson's *Differential Fertility in Sweden* and Dorothy Thomas's *Social and Economic Aspects of Swedish Population Movements, 1750–1933* and *Population Movements and Industrialization, Swedish Counties, 1895–1930*.

Myrdal's essay on industrialization and population represented the only result of his earlier demographic research published under his own name.[61] In this essay, he described population as "an interdependent mechanism" that "must be supposed to undergo changes under the influence (or, better, in some relation to) social and economic changes of greatly different kinds." He offered here his first published attention to the dramatic recent decline in Sweden's birthrate. Myrdal concluded "that birth control of some sort in the beginning of the period and up to the War was more relied upon in agricultural than in industrial districts, but that the neo-Malthusian movement, once having started, proceeded far more rapidly in the latter districts."[62]

It was also during this period at the university that Myrdal succeeded Gustav Cassel as Lars Hierta Professor in Political Economy and Financial Science. In 1929–30, both Myrdal and Bertil Ohlin were considered equal candidates for the coveted position. Ohlin takes credit for stepping aside, leaving a clear field for Myrdal, to whom Cassel then gave the nod. By mid-1932 Myrdal's probably succession was virtual public knowledge, although it was not announced officially until November 1933.[63]

In a small nation like Sweden, specialists like the economists formed rather tiny, often intimate, groups. An informal *Nationalekonomisk klubb* met a half dozen times every year, often in the homes of its members. This "purely intellectual" group included in its membership the "older" economists, David Davidson, Knut Wicksell, and Cassel; the "middle aged" group, Eli Heckscher, Sven Brisman, and Gösta Bagge; the "younger" ones, including Myrdal, Erik Lindahl, Ohlin, Ingvar Svennilson, and Dag Hammerskjöld; and selected students. In more stable economic times, discussions covered a wide variety of topics, including the "optimum population" question.[64]

The worldwide economic depression did not reach Sweden until early 1931, when business and bank failures, unemployment, and a deflated currency became the leading issues of the day. The economists' attention quickly shifted to a new analysis of the business cycle and the crafting of a response.

The historiographic debate on the emergence of the Social Democratic economic program and its neo-Wicksellian justification is extensive.[65] Gunnar Myrdal played a role in developing the economic theories of the so-called "Stockholm school" of economists, which justified active government intervention into the economy to reduce unemployment. Among his contributions to the heated economic crisis debate,[66] the most important in terms of Myrdal's later social policy work was his appendix to the 1933 budget proposal of the Social Democratic government. Even more than his formal 1934 report to the Unemployment Investigation Committee on financial policies social-economic effects, this work served as a foundation document for the development of future Swedish policy.[67]

In advocating the adoption of an extensive public works program during the depression, Myrdal argued that there always existed a backlog of needed projects that could be pursued. From a purely financial standpoint, it would be cheaper and more economical to implement public works projects in the period of stress than to wait for the future. Governments usually underestimated needs and resources. To restrict or delay public works would not only sharpen the economic distress, but also increase the long-term costs for projects that would someday be built and so raise unnecessarily the long-term tax burden. Recession-driven restrictions on public works thus represented a misdirected form of saving.

Myrdal stated that the national budget ought to give consideration to the relationship between total production, income formation, and consumption and the degree to which the existing means of production were being utilized. Public expenditures that brought about an economic expansion should go hand in hand with an increase in tax income as the tax base grew. Given idle production factors, however, one could begin with an increase in public expenditures—that is, unbalance the budget—and the growing tax revenues should come as a consequence. Hence any increase in the nation's product and real capital formation where unused means of production were brought back into operation would imply a general strengthening of the state's long-term financial base.

In the current situation, Myrdal continued, where an important percentage of labor power and capital resources was unused, the "real extra costs" for public works that placed unused means of production back into service represented only a small fraction of the income generated by increased consumption. In short, "public works possess a stimulating effect on private economic life."[68] The "real extra costs" of such projects also fell when one took into account the positive social effects on workers and their families of having work again.

Myrdal acknowledged that certain "negative" effects could derive from such a program. He mentioned the possible development of a negative balance of trade, which in turn would influence balance of payments and rate of exchange. Nevertheless, he argued that the variety of monetary and trade policy tools already available to the government and the national bank could meet problems that might arise.

Myrdal admitted that no precise formula existed to determine what policies were needed at any given time. Fortunately, though, those would be a lag between the time when state public works projects began and when their effects on the balance of payments appeared. This meant that one could confidently set in motion the projects deemed necessary and later adopt suitable financial, trade, and monetary measures to meet consequences as they arose.

In sum, Myrdal used the level of employment volume, rather than fiscal equilibrium, as the central variable in economic theory and policy development. Money became the vehicle to effect changes in employment and production. Myrdal's motivation here was social-political, rooted in concern for "the human waste" that accompanied economic depression. His tools—budgetary deficits and surpluses, state borrowing, tariffs, and monetary policies involving credit and discount rates—would be utilized in a flexible manner to restore production and consumption during periods of economic stress and to rebuild the state's financial base in periods of prosperity.[69]

Through Myrdal's economic work, certain perspectives on social policy were affirmed. The commitment to creating employment, rather than welfare, for the unemployed represented a "preventive" social policy act. Attention to public works emphasized the interrelated character of social and economic policy: to create employment could also mean to build new hospitals and schools. Effective economic policy also implied comprehensive social planning. By early 1934, Myrdal was widely regarded as this concept's most effective proponent in Sweden.[70]

Sweden's ongoing agrarian crisis, marked by the decay of the family community, also drew Myrdal's attention in the early 1930s and influenced his later work on population.[71] He gave a number of addresses and wrote numerous articles in this period stressing the need to raise the living standard of the rural population. By 1932, he had concluded that only a comprehensive, centrally organized planning mechanism could succeed.[72] Rejecting production restrictions and "dumping," he argued that increased consumption of farm products would be the best solution to low levels of farm income and investment.[73] Government interventions could include subsidy of production costs, price setting, price rebates to large families, and nutrition programs designed to raise the quantity and quality of the Swedish diet.[74]

The most direct link between Gunnar Myrdal's early policy work and later population ideas derived from his activity on the housing question. Concurrent with industrialization, the pressure on housing within Sweden's major cities grew considerably after 1900. A boom in housing construction started in the 1920s. However, by the economic depression in the 1931–33 period, overcrowding remained a serious problem. A study by a group of radical graduate students at the University of Lund in 1928 showed that over half of all urban Swedish families lived in a dwelling of only one room and a kitchen or less. While an investigation of rural housing conditions had been conducted by the Riksdag in the late 1920s, formal government involvement in the urban housing question was nonexistent.

Myrdal's work on family housing grew out of his contacts with the circle of designers, architects, and urban planners cited earlier and, in particular, from his friendship with Alf Johansson. The role of the latter deserves greater attention.

Alf Johansson, a small, intense man, studied social history and economics at the University of Stockholm in the mid-1920s and later served there as docent. Through early contacts with the politicized architects, he developed a strong interest in housing problems. A powerful and influential expression of this appeared in a February 1930 *Tiden* article titled "Housing Needs and Housing Production" ("Bostadsbehov och bostadsproduktion").[75]

The article called for government action to alleviate the crippling overcrowding of families. Johansson rejected endless attention to comparative wages and rents between various countries: "Our high wage standard implies essentially the privilege for workers to pay a greater rent for a small house. . . . That one room and a kitchen is utterly insufficient as the normal family dwelling does not need to be even discussed."[76] He subsequently turned to a consideration of "the housing question and population movements." While only three pages in length, this segment deserves close attention, for it presented for the first time a pronatalist argument for a socialized Swedish housing program.

Johansson noted that R. R. Kuczynski's 1926 work presenting comparative "net reproduction rates" had revealed the sharply declining birthrate in Sweden. The Swedish people—discovering that they were "dying out"—grew alarmed, he reflected, and turned to moralizing about irreligion and urban vice. Johansson cautioned, with tongue in cheek, that a certain decline in numbers was nothing to become excited about: the "Mongolian invasion" would not occur before Sweden dealt with its own unemployment problem. But he added that it was "unavoidably necessary" to either raise nativity or reduce mortality in the long run to prevent a fairly rapid depopulation of Sweden.

Referring to Sven Wicksell's work, Johansson suggested that a further sinking of the birthrate was likely as "birth rationalization" spread to new social groups, particularly to the rural population, which had hitherto been somewhat isolated from this process. He also doubted whether future declines in the mortality rate would be large enough to make a fertility increase unnecessary. While predictions of future developments in fertility and mortality rates had to be necessarily uncertain, Johansson stated that certain facts did stand out clearly: cities, particularly the large ones, were consuming the very body of society, and evidence suggested, from a race-biological viewpoint, that current demographic relationships between rural and urban areas resulted in an antieugenic process.

Johansson regretted that "population movements" in the past had usually been seen as mystical events. While not delineating the cause of the nativity decline, he stated that an intimate connection existed between this demographic change and the social revolution over the previous hundred years that had brought the emergence of the modern urban culture. While accepting birth control as a component of progress, Johansson pointed to the resulting social dilemma: "Relationships, particularly urban relationships, have developed to such an extent that . . . people's ordinary, reasonable, and conscientious adaptation to the social reality in which they are set does not harmonize with the best interests of society."[77] Stated more simply, the individual's rational self-interest and society's general interest were at odds over the birth question. Johansson criticized the moralists, particularly priests, who "in older, more spiritualized times" preached from the Scriptures "to be fruitful and fill the earth and in particular the church graveyard." He argued that attempts to reverse the nativity decline through "reactionary measures," such as keeping people on the farm, represented a battle against natural developments and were, in any case, bound to be ineffective.

He concluded that there was only one way to turn around a "birth strike" caused by "unacceptable social conditions": the adoption of measures that would lead to better living conditions. The availability of housing opportunities would be of the greatest importance. "Good ample housing is certainly no guarantee for an adequate birth rate," he stated, "but certainly at present and more so under future conditions [it represents] a necessary prerequisite." Johansson found it incredible that a people and a culture proved so incapable of solving their housing problem and even more incredible that people worried about Swedish "vigor" (*livskraft*) while ignoring the necessary social changes that would allow young couples to place children in the world responsibly. He called for a socialized housing policy that would allow parents to raise an average of three children per family.[78]

The central themes found in this short discourse on housing and population were identical to those adapted by the Myrdals on a more general basis four years later. That rarest of political creations—a new policy idea—had been born.

Gunnar Myrdal's first important article on the housing question appeared in a 1932 volume titled *Arkitektur och samhälle*. In his section, Myrdal applied his work in economic policy to housing needs. He argued for public programs as measures that would put the unemployed back to work, help democratize society, and improve low housing standards. He felt that an excessive concentration on the actual "cost" of such a project gave little credence to its potential social good and stimulative effect on production. Private builders, he continued, could not construct sufficient housing on rational principles. Only a policy of public subsidies and government direction could ensure an adequate housing supply.[79]

Gunnar Myrdal developed his closest association among the architects with Uno Åhrén. In late 1932, Myrdal and Åhrén met with the new Social Democratic social minister, Gustav Möller. The pair declared to Möller that it was time for the government to recognize the housing question as a serious social problem, possibly involving a remedy for economic depression, and a component of a planned economy. They proposed to Möller that they conduct social research of housing needs in Göteborg, where Åhrén was currently chief city planner, and use this data base to draw up guidelines for a general state housing program.

Möller listened to them, Myrdal later recalled, with indifference. The social minister stated that he had his hands full with the battle against unemployment, which was "the labor movement's highest priority." Myrdal also suspected that Möller viewed Åhrén and him as two examples of the "species" that trade unionists and party politicians trusted the least: "young idealists from the intellectual upperclass without practical experience."[80] Myrdal feared that their offer to perform the research without the normal remuneration paid for such work only confirmed Möller's suspicions.

While disappointed over their initial rejection, Myrdal and Åhrén turned to the Department of Finance, where responsibility for housing statistics lay. Finance minister Ernst Wigforss immediately accepted their idea and ordered the necessary paraphernalia that went with an investigative commission, including the letter of commission from the king. Åhrén and Myrdal engaged friends to assist them in the project, including Sven Bouvin on the statistical work and Rolf Bergman on matters dealing with health. The whole project, particularly the housing policy recommendations that were "smuggled in," was broadly discussed with Alf Johansson and other friends. "It became to a high degree an expression of the group's collective values and opinions."[81]

The resulting study emphasized the relationship of overcrowding to low income and a large number of children. The authors argued that the cause of overcrowding (defined for families as a dwelling smaller than two rooms and a kitchen) lay not in poverty or in low incomes, but rather in basic attitudinal and structural problems of society: "Only somewhat over a fifth of the overcrowded housing in Göteborg could, . . . according to these basic research principles, be attributed to economic incapacity on the basis of low income, while four fifths must be attributed to other causes."[82] These were identified as unsatisfactory habits and arrangements in home and family life. Large numbers of families, they found, had diverted a significant portion of their income from better housing, which they could theoretically afford, to amusements, clothing, and other items.

This result of their study—that many families were poorly housed by choice and despite relatively high incomes—made a sharp impression on Myrdal.[83] Surprised to learn that people did not have the sense to choose "what was good for them," Myrdal resolved to implement policies on the basis of a rational allocation of resources. His commitment to the provision of "in kind," as opposed to "in cash," social services as more direct and efficient correspondingly emerged.

Turning to recommendations, Myrdal and Åhrén proposed an intensive nationwide investigation of housing standards with an emphasis on the relationship between overcrowding and income. They stressed the need for an immediate investigation in order to tie the production of new housing into the general counterdepression program. The results of such an inquiry should be widely distributed among the Swedish people. A general "housing enlightenment" was necessary, they remarked, to show the psychological, moral, and physiological effects of overcrowding. The fact that a majority of families in overcrowded housing had adequate income to pay for better homes meant that improved "dwelling habits," not government subsidies, were generally needed.

With some self-contradiction, Åhrén and Myrdal also urged the utilization of state funding to stimulate housing production in Sweden. While direct support for the well situated could not be justified, Myrdal and Åhrén did advocate a policy of housing subsidy for the poorest families. On the basis of their Göteborg research, they identified the need for the immediate construction of sixteen thousand new apartments, each having at least two rooms and a kitchen. This pilot housing program would cost something over 1 million kronor annually.[84]

While the study was published as an official report, Myrdal and Åhrén approached a sympathetic socialist editor, who agreed to a special private printing of the document. Myrdal and Åhrén sent thousands of copies, at their own expense, to women's clubs, youth groups, and study circles throughout Sweden, with the recommendation that they pressure Social Minister Möller to make a government commitment on the housing question.[85] Expanding their campaign, Myrdal argued in a series of 1933 speeches that "a complete socialization of housing is in my mind the only solution to urban-industrial society's dwelling problem."[86] He added that the state alone could provide housing built on both qualitative and quantitative bases. The Stockholm architects added their voices to the call for a broadly based housing investigatory commission.[87]

Acceding to pressure from many fronts, Möller established the Social Housing Investigation on 6 October 1933. It was chaired by Bertil Nystrom, chief of the Social Bureau, and other members included Gunnar Myrdal, Uno Åhrén, and architect Sven Markelius. Statistician Richard Sterner (henceforward Myrdal's able and indispensable number cruncher) would give assistance in data collection and analysis, while Alf Johansson became the panel's secretary. Myrdal and Johansson dominated the investigation's work.[88]

The investigation's first report was released in January 1935, with others to follow in September 1935 and November 1937. While their content will be discussed thoroughly in a later context,[89] a significant philosophical change in the committee's work that occurred in mid-1934 should be mentioned here. Pronatalism was an implicit theme in Myrdal and Åhrén's original report, but its primary emphasis was on overcrowding as an explicit social problem and on the link between housing and economic policy. The Social Housing Investigation took form around these same basic thrusts. In mid-1934, however, pronatalism became the determining argument in the committee's work. Two of the three reports prepared by the investigation, for instance, dealt exclusively with the needs of large families.

While the crucial correspondence is not intact, it appears that a series of memoranda prepared by Alf Johansson and Gunnar Myrdal in the first half of 1934 resulted in this shift of emphasis. Both commitment and tactical considerations were involved. As Johansson wrote to an unidentified correspondent in June 1934: "To turn now to families with children is both proper and tactically opportune. . . . The generation of excessive babies problem is touched only sporadically [in cases of] an additional child."[90] The timing factor also correlated with the Myrdals' renewed generic interest in the population question.

The first committee report used pronatalist arguments as a justification for the reorientation of Sweden's housing policy. After reviewing statistics on Swedish fertility decline and noting that better housing was needed to reduce the infant mortality rate, the report added that "a positive population policy" that would prevent depopulation should not only be concerned with reducing the mortality rate, but also "must . . . above all seek to increase marriage formation and to stimulate fertility."[91] The report warned that unless Sweden implemented a far-reaching population policy over the next decade while the age structure was still favorable, depopulation would occur, with serious economic effects. While noting that psychological and social psychological factors played a role in the birth decline, the report emphasized the economic motive: "At a given level of income, the standard of consumption is primarily affected by number of children. [Only] by diminishing the number of children can the individual family maintain a higher standard of living for the parents and those children already born."[92] The report affirmed that the construction of healthy and adequately sized family housing was a necessary prerequisite for raising marital fertility. Over the long run, it continued, every married couple must bear an average of three children if the population stock was to be maintained.[93]

In the autumn of 1934, Gunnar Myrdal gave a series of lectures that stressed the link between the crowding of large families and the decline in the birthrate.[94] In a short popular work coauthored by Myrdal, Alf Johansson, and others and published in October, Sweden's falling birthrate became the imperative behind the push for better housing. Johansson's contribution, in particular, emphasized the relationship between the housing and population questions. Pointing to the new research of Karl Arvid Edin, which showed for Stockholm that fertility rose in direct relationship to income among the highest classes, he concluded that an increase in family living standard would result in more births. Social reformers, he concluded, should not shy away from using the population issue as a powerful argument for a radical solution to the housing problem.[95]

By mid-November 1934, an editorial in the leading Social Democratic newspaper linked the sinking birthrate to the housing question. It noted that Sweden's fertility was the lowest in the world and that at current rates the Swedish people would die out in about three hundred years. Social relationships were such, it added, that people had made children secondary to their effort to hold up their living standard. The conservative argument to keep the poor in "sexual slavery" was rejected. Rather, "[t]he Social Democrats' reasonable and therefore opposite recommendation is: reduce rents and build houses worthy of human beings."[96]

In short, there was a direct continuity between the housing question and the population question, with the socialist pronatalism of Alf Johansson as the connecting link. Following the establishment of the Population Commission in April 1935, the Social Housing Investigation served as junior partner in the commission's development of family-oriented social policy.[97]

Returning from Geneva in 1931, Alva Myrdal developed her newly found interest in social policy along lines parallel to, yet distinct from, her husband's. As one indication of her recent "politicization," she officially joined the Social Democratic party.

In November, Alva Myrdal organized Sweden's first "study circle" for parents on the proper methods of child rearing. Significantly, the course of study she developed included a section on the social factors in children's lives—"family; play comrades; the school; the social milieu; the modern era's need for collective activity."[98] As she noted in a later lecture, parenthood represented one of society's most important roles, yet it required no competency test, no personal qualifications, and no education. Since society could not increase its control over relationships between parent and child, it must improve its method of parent education as part of "the evolution towards a rationalization of human life." This should include improved communications between home and school and, more important, study circles for lectures and discussions.[99]

Alva Myrdal's first step into public controversy grew out of the housing question. Her contact with the Stockholm architects blossomed through close association with Sven Markelius in their joint development of an experimental "collective house." Based on a "rational" understanding of the changing family structure, a belief in women's right to work outside the home, and an ideological commitment to the socialization of children, Myrdal and Markelius planned and actually saw through to construction a collectivized housing form.

As developed in 1932–34, the "collective house" consisted of a high-rise placed within a park area providing fresh air, sunshine, and a play area. The main building had large central corridors linking various family units. The latter included closet, bathroom, dumbwaiter, cupboard space, and bedrooms for the adults and older children. There was a central kitchen where all food was prepared, using "rational" restaurant procedures. It could be delivered to the family units either through the dumbwaiter or in the central dining hall. Central lounges were available for discussions, family matters, meetings and games. Collective reading rooms "encouraged study." There were also collective sun rooms, gyms, storage rooms, and telephone centers. Most important was the collective nursery. Here could be found an infants' section, where children under two years of age would be cared for twenty-four hours a day by competent attendants and in "the most hygenic conditions." The nursery section was for children under school age and provided a well-lited playroom with safe, "pedagogically correct" playthings, staffed by "highly trained personnel." Children received under this arrangement "needed peer-group contact," outdoor play, nutritional meals, and psychological attention, all designed to produce socially adaptable youth.[100]

Alva Myrdal's ideological defense of this project came in a December 1932 article for *Tiden*. She noted that the institution of the family was subject to social frictions and pressures and that it changed over time. The family, she insisted in an echo of her American mentors Ogborn and Burgess, had now passed to a new form. Cries by reactionary politicians for a return to the traditional family and statements that "a woman's place is in the home" rang hollow. Such a family structure had already lost its content and had a sterile character, as evidenced by the modern one- or two-child families, crammed into overcrowded urban dwellings, with little light and unserviceable furniture. The real problems of families, she insisted, were organizational or institutional in nature.

She traced changes in the family's organization to the disappearance of the handicraft and peasant economy. Accordingly, the family had ceased to be an economic entity. The productive function in the home had generally disappeared, and "even married women" had been drawn into the industrial labor force: " . . . work, productive work, is a woman's demand, and as such a social fact, which lies completely in line with general tendencies of development."[101] Another reality marking existing family structure was that families had become smaller: "Birth control is [a] social fact, which we must consider in all attempts to reorganize the family."[102] Because of these changes, moreover, the home could no longer serve as a suitable place for raising children, and alternatives needed to be devised. Young working couples simply refused to bear a child into "gloomy solitude," where the baby would be left during the day with an expensive but unqualified "sitter."

The solution Alva Myrdal offered was the rational cooperation found in a "collective house." This great experiment in new family organization would serve as an example and propaganda center for socialized child upbringing and meal preparation, the last traditional functions to which families clung. The author emphasized the need for proper day care within the collective house. The Swedish *barnkrubborna*, which had grown to meet the needs of working mothers, did not usually reach minimum pedagogical standards. She proposed instead the model of the American nursery school. Children needed a social education, she argued, and certainly from age three on had a psychological need for peer group contacts. Existing family structures—particularly "the little modern family"—failed to provide this interaction. Only a collectivized preschool education was socially and psychologically adequate for all children. Behind the collective house ideal, she concluded, was a vision of a new and better world: "There lies behind this talk of 'social education' and 'common organization' a new ideal vision. There lies a certain belief that the new age shall build more on constructive cooperation. There lies a certain protest against the unbridled individualism which characterizes the [dying] bourgeois century."[103]

In a subsequent article in *Hertha*, a women's magazine, Alva Myrdal specified that the most important function of the collective house was the care and raising of children. It assisted the mother and provided psychologically needed companionship for the young. "The modern miniature family," she declared, "is . . . an abnormal situation for a child."[104] In a later article, she stated: ". . . 4 to 6 hours daily of being together with children of the same age is a pedagogical and psychological necessity so that children shall be raised to be effective members of society, not overexcited homebodies."[105]

Alva Myrdal's feminism found additional expression through active participation in the Business Women's Club of Stockholm, of which she was elected vice chairwoman in mid-1932. Her vision involved the total integration of women into the labor market outside the home, a lessening of the burden associated with child rearing, and an alteration of traditional sex roles. She argued that women were handicapped from birth by the "only a girl" mentality, which retarded their intellectual development, confined them to the home, and often resulted in emotional problems.[106]

In a July 1933 article for the Social Democratic women's magazine, *Morgonbris*, Myrdal discussed the political imperatives implicit within recent changes in the family. The old saying "the family is the cell of society" incorrectly implied that the institution of the family was stable. Rather, she said, the patriarchal family had a direct connection with the preindustrial milieu of farmers and handworkers. This old family had economic, old-age security, and educational, as well as biological, functions. However, the transformation from self-sufficient households to a "wage economy" had largely eliminated the economic links that bound together the members of the old family. Welfare, security, and educational functions had now passed to the state. She concluded that "we no longer have the justification to talk about the 'family' and mean the same thing in the present [as we did] one hundred years ago."[107] Families had also become smaller, she remarked. Few of them now contained relatives beyond parents and children. The number of children had also declined as the one- and two-child system increasingly became the norm.

In short, society had entered a period of vast social revolution. Material changes had gone before, while social change trailed behind. Yet the latter could already be seen in laws against child labor and for obligatory school attendance. Family relationships within the city, Alva Myrdal stated, must be understood as wholly different from those of a disappearing rural culture.

In her approach to the modern family, Alva Myrdal rejected a reactionary return "to society before industrialization," an approach that handicapped the fascist governments' approach to family problems. She also denied the communist effort to revolutionize the family through striving for "absolute freedom" from emotional bonds. She advocated instead an alternative that would save the best of the "old family" system while providing a new form of family support. From the old family form she hoped to save marriage as a relationship of love, devotion, and sharing, parenthood with its joy of bearing children and its fulfillment of the child's need for understanding and security, and the sense of "home" that gave children a warm environment. The basic change needed was for society to assume responsibility for a much greater share of children's support and welfare.

Simply put, "a portion of the traditional family tasks must be socialized. Modern society must free families from the anxieties which modern society itself has placed on families."[108] Such a socialist program, she added, could be seen as conservative if one looked to its desire to protect the essentially important core of family life. But it would also be radical in its demand for reform of essential family functions.

Alva Myrdal sharpened this vision in a series of articles that appeared in another women's magazine, *Tidevaret*, in August–September 1933. These were written in response to an article by Margarete Bonnevie published in early August in the same magazine. Bonnevie had proposed the creation of a family allowance scheme with the Swedish wage structure, based on the French model, to provide families with additional income determined by the number of children within each family.[109]

Alva Myrdal opened by agreeing that a father's income was no longer always sufficient to support a family; the family wage system had failed. It was illusory to expect that this situation would improve "if only women abandoned the labor market and the patriarchal paradise became realized on earth."[110] Rather, she argued that Swedes must place the child support problem within the larger framework of accepting a woman's place in the labor market, recognizing the real risks of unemployment and acknowledging the need for a qualitative increase in children's welfare and living standards. The situation demanded a basic struggle for a children's policy.

Myrdal rejected Bonnevie's suggestion of cash payments built into the wage system. First, Myrdal complained that such cash payments were often designed to bind women to the home, noting that "right wing" individuals and groups such as Eleanor Rathbone of Great Britain and the Sweden's Housewives League also advocated cash payments to families to obviate the need for women to work outside the home. The author doubted that one could justify a wage for housework when both the number of children and burden involved had declined significantly in recent decades.[111] Myrdal emphasized that what mothers really needed was the opportunity to have more time for themselves, to live their lives as they desired, and to assume jobs outside the home. Second, the author argued that society could not ensure that cash child-support payments, regardless of the form they took, would actually be used for the child's benefit. In many cases money would be placed in the general family budget, thereby diluting what actually reached the children.[112] Third, she maintained that any system based on wages offered a variety of problems. It confused the competitive market basis of the wage system and promised to violate the "equal pay for equal work" principle that women were seeking.[113] Fourth, Myrdal repeated the argument, sometimes heard in France, that cash payments—particularly through the wage system—tended to depress general wages. Nominal wage increases to large families in this case were often used by employers to avoid general wage increases and hence came at the expense of the whole workers' movement. Fifth, the "voluntary" French-Belgian system represented only horizontal redistribution of income between the "child-poor" and the "child-rich" within social classes. Under such a structure, the socialist call for redistribution between classes was not met. Finally, while Myrdal doubted that child support of any sort would have a significant influence on stimulating births, cash payments could provide such an economic motive if large enough. Such socially "purchased" children, though, would commonly be the offspring of asocial, undesirable parents. Such births would, in most cases, be unwanted for eugenic reasons. She added that a Swedish program "should not be inclined to special premiums for quite large numbers of children." She took no position on the need or desirability of stimulating or restricting births, noting only that both would be social-political possibilities.[114]

As her alternative to cash payments Myrdal argued that society should assume the largest portion of the child-support function. Her reform line would "diminish the costs and the inconveniences associated with children through social and collective arrangements and divide these costs more equally among the whole population through taxation." Such a socialized child welfare program would assist all children, regardless of degree of poverty or wealth. Measures to be included were: bachelor taxes on the childless, tax deductions for men and women with children, rent subsidies for families with children, free school lunches, free medical and dental care, free school clothing, maternity assistance, collective infant care, free kindergartens and day-care centers, and the establishment of educational institutions to train preschool teachers. She added that cost would not be a problem, since collectivized programs in medicine, nutrition, and child care would prove to be cheaper than if choices were left up to each parental pair.[115]

Binding together these varied facets of Gunnar and Alva Myrdal's political work was a common perspective on social policy, rooted in a unique vision of a radicalized social science. Gunnar gave this approach systematic expression in an important two-part 1932 article titled "Social Policy's Dilemma."[116]

During the pre-1914 period, Myrdal began, Malthus's pessimistic teachings on population pressure largely shaped classical liberalism's attachment to economic and property conservatism. This left most liberals skeptical of basic reform or any change in general property arrangements. Marxism, meanwhile, with an ideology riveted on accelerating capital concentration, class war, and proletarian revolt, left no room for a reforming social policy. Yet a social-political compromise did emerge prior to 1914, characterized by a "liberal-infused socialism" and "a socialist-infused liberalism" held in tension. This compromise rested on the understanding that future social policy would concern only productive arrangement and not the redistribution of property.

Accordingly, the "socialist-infused liberals" abandoned the pessimism of Malthusianism and embraced neo-Malthusianism instead. The rational limitation of births, through contraceptives, became an essential component of the prewar liberal faith. Meanwhile, the liberal-infused socialists of the prewar era were transformed into gradualist politicians, working within the system. Once agreeing to accept measures in the worker's short-run interest, the socialists succumbed to a democratic taming: "Evolution replaced revolution. . . . The democratic system's structural effect pointed towards a bourgeois stabilization of the workers' movement."[117] These liberalized socialists and socialized liberals worked together, and the period was marked by the "reign of experts" in fields such as employment, housing, schools, and the control of prostitution.

Nevertheless, liberal-socialist compromise had broken down after the world war. The basic conflict between a liberal commitment to provide social assistance as charity and the socialist demand that many forms of assistance be seen as a "right" reemerged. The postwar depression also shook liberal hopes that the system could provide rational solutions to production and distribution problems. As the compromise fell apart, old liberals had moved either to the right or the left; most went to the right, where new ideologies such as fascism and national socialism formed. Socialists, meanwhile, found the prewar vision of social reform no longer possible or productive.

For the workers' movement, Myrdal concluded, there was no longer any option but a reradicalization and a new push for basic alteration of the existing system. Liberalism, simply put, was dead. The workers' movement now needed "to become a true . . . popular reform party" to keep youth from turning to the communists for answers.[118] In this vein, the party should aim for implementation of a new form of preventive social policy. Prewar social policies had been symptom-oriented, giving assistance to the poor, the sick, the unemployed, and the alcoholic. Over the last decade, Myrdal countered, social policy experts armed with the research apparatus of social science had increased their call for policies that would prevent problems from emerging. When based on human-oriented value premises and a rational science, the author stated, preventive social policy led to the natural marriage of the correct technical with the politically radical solution.[119] Myrdal pointed to the existing "family crisis" as an example of the "social lag" of institutions behind social and economic realities. Here, as elsewhere, a rational sociological analysis would produce effective and radical recommendations for change.

This marriage of the technical and the radical was the result of logic founded on value premises that avoided institutional conventionalism. A scientific social policy, a centrally planned economy, and a leveling of wealth, Myrdal believed, would emerge from this new approach.[120]

The preceding survey of Alva and Gunnar Myrdal's work in the 1928–34 period indicates that their socialist, pronatalist program grew out of their independent work, without significant influence from other European sources. The impetus behind their interest in sociological and population questions and their commitment to a radical politics lay in their year spent in the United States. While a few strains of the population argument can be found in the Myrdals' early work, most of their social-political involvement prior to 1934 was motivated by concerns other than Sweden's low birthrate—be they purely scholastic, economic, political, humanistic, psychological, sociological, or feminist in inspiration. The Myrdals' new approach to the population question—which would bind their early work together—appears to have originated among their circle of close friends, particularly Alf Johansson. This theme, while stillborn in the unpublished article the Myrdals wrote in the spring of 1931, would reemerge in early 1934.

The first indication of this renewed interest came in a speech made by Gunnar Myrdal in Copenhagen on 9 February 1934. Titled "Social Housing Policy," the prepared text focused on Myrdal's analysis of the housing problem. It included a proposal for the building of collective houses to assist large families and the state subsidy of rents. During a question-and-answer session, Copenhagen's mayor, Peder Hedepol, rose with great indignation and charged that ideas like collective housing would have no effect on a woman's willingness to bear children: "Women will not have children. And why? They would rather own a car, take a summer trip, go to the movies and dance jazz. . . . There is nothing of a specific economic nature which hinders women from bearing children; that is shown by the poor part of the population, which has the most children."[121]

Myrdal rose in response. The modern young woman, he replied, would "happily have children and she wants to have more than one . . . although perhaps not more than two or three." She does not want as many children as her grandmother, Myrdal continued, for basic health reasons. The modern sexual revolution had made the birth of children more systematic: "Young people in our day will gladly have children, but now want to determine themselves when and how many."

Myrdal also referred for the first time to the recent research of Karl Edin, which showed that after a certain point the number of children per family rose in relation to income and social position. Myrdal concluded that young people would bear more children if social relationships, including housing possibilities, were rearranged to make it economically easier for them to do so.[122]

Sometime in the intervening weeks, the Myrdals shifted their primary attention to the natalist question. The direct stimulus may have been a fuller appreciation of the significance of the Edin statistics, the turn to natalist themes by the Social Housing Investigation, or perhaps the Myrdal-Hedepol discussion in Copenhagen. By mid-March, Alva

Myrdal was referring to the fact that women were bearing fewer children "as a social danger of the most serious kind."[123]

A pair of speeches delivered on 24–25 March by both Gunnar and Alva Myrdal in Åbo (Turku), Finland, to the Åbo Akademi represented a relatively complete expression of the pronatalist theme. Gunnar Myrdal's speech, "Viewpoints on the Population Question," began with a discussion of the "optimum population" theory, which he rejected for its faith in an abstract theory divorced from reality. Myrdal noted that in Stockholm alone, only one-third of the number of children needed for a stable population were being born. While longer life spans would prevent a rapid depopulation of Sweden, he offered reasons "from a worker's perspective" for efforts to reverse the decline in births, such as preventing the importation of cheap labor from outside Sweden. Myrdal concluded that only radical income redistribution through social policy could reverse the birth decline. The strong desire of people in the modern period to raise their standard of living had to be accepted as a basis of policy. Any effort to stimulate interest in children required that the largest proportion of the costs and encumbrances associated with them be transferred to society.[124]

Alva Myrdal's complementary address dealt with now familiar themes: disintegration of the patriarchal family under the impact of urbanization and industrialization, the need for efforts to rectify the problem of women's work outside the home, and the poor psychological atmosphere of the miniature family for the small child. She mentioned collective houses and day-care centers as solutions to these problems. Significantly, her vision was now, for the first time, wrapped in pronatalist garb.[125]

In early spring of 1934, Alva and Gunnar Myrdal decided to return to their 1931 Geneva manuscript on the population question and revise, update, and expand it into book form. For this purpose they rented a cabin in the Norwegian mountains for the summer, worked out their remaining theoretical differences, and produced a manuscript originally titled *The Population Question and Social Policy*.[126] Gunnar was responsible for the historical, theoretical, economic, and statistical chapters, while Alva drafted the chapters on families, children, and specific program suggestions. The major difference resolved was over their respective commitments to pronatalism. Gunnar had an authentic desire to increase the birthrate; Alva held firm to feminist and neo-Malthusian tenets. They eventually agreed on the need for a stable population, which necessitated at that point an increase in nativity of 40 percent.[1]

The Myrdals took the completed manuscript to *Kooperativa förbundets bokförlag* for possible publication. Editor Johannes Lindberg rejected it, citing KF as a "people's movement press" that had to show consideration for the opinions on birth control held by the working class. Gunnar Myrdal later recalled that he grew angry and stormed over to Tor Bonnier, head of Sweden's largest publishing house. The latter read the manuscript the same day and responded to Myrdal, "I am personally opposed to the whole concept. But this is brilliantly written and we'll take it." Bonnier did make one change. He termed the title "clumsy" and proposed instead the title *Kris i befolkningsfrågan* or *Crisis in the Population Question*, which the Myrdals found acceptable both as more interesting and as an accurate expression of their themes.[2] The book was released in mid-November 1934.

Notes

1. Quotations from Gunnar Myrdal, "A Worried America," an address given to the Tenth Annual Meeting of the Lutheran Council in the USA, Philadelphia, Pa., 11 March 1976. See also Gunnar Myrdal, *Against the Stream: Critical Essays on Economics* (New York: Pantheon, 1972); and *Current Biography* (March 1975), pp. 29–30.
2. Annette Kullenberg, "Jag vill städa samhället," in *Det gäller vårt liv* (Stockholm: Folkhuset, 1976), pp. 10–11; and "Några data i Alva Myrdals liv," *Det gäller vårt liv*, pp. 44–45. Interview, Alva and Gunnar Myrdal, Stockholm, 20 July 1976.
3. Egon Glesinger, "Gunnar Myrdal," mimeographed biography presented to Gunnar Myrdal on his fiftieth birthday, 6 December 1948, p. 1, in Gunnar Myrdal Archive, Arbetarrörelsens Arkiv, Stockholm (hereafter GMA).
4. See Ulrich Herz, "Två livs öden i vår tid," *I fredens tjänst* (Stockholm: Rabén and Sjögren, 1971), p. 28; and interview with Richard Sterner, Stockholm, 29 June 1977.
5. Uno Willers, "Alva och Gunnar Myrdal," *I fredens tjänst*, (Stockholm; Rabén and Sjögren, 1971), p. 15.
6. G. Myrdal to W. I. Thomas, 10 February 1931, Gunnar Myrdal Archive Letter Collection, Arbetarrörelsens Arkiv (hereafter GMAL).
7. Bertil Ohlin, *Memoarer: Ung man blir politiker* (Stockholm: Bonniers Förlag, 1972), pp. 10–11; and Glesinger, "Gunnar Myrdal," p. 2.
8. Alf Johansson, "Minnesbilder," *Det gäller vårt liv* (Stockholm: Folkhuset, 1976), p. 17; interview with Alva Myrdal, Stockholm, 20 July 1976; and interview with Alf Johansson and Britta Åkerman, Stock-

holm, 26 July 1976.

9. Gunnar Myrdal, *Prisbildningsproblemet och föränderligheten* (Uppsala: Almquist and Wiksell, 1927).

10. Bertil Hammer to the Rockefeller Foundation, 1 March 1929, unfiled letter in Alva Myrdal Archive Letter Collection, hereafter AMAL; and interview with Alva and Gunnar Myrdal, Stockholm, 20 July 1976.

11. Gunnar Myrdal, *Vetenskap och politik i national ekonomi* (Stockholm: P. A. Norstedt and Söner, 1930). First English edition: *The Political Element in the Development of Economic Theory* (London: Routledge and Kegan, 1953).

12. Interview with Richard Sterner, Stockholm, 29 June 1977; and "Förord till den nya svenska upplagan, 1972," in Gunnar Myrdal, *Vetenskap och politik i nationalekonomi* (Stockholm: Rabén and Sjögren, 1972).

13. Gunnar Myrdal, *The Political Element in the Development of Economic Theory*, p. 192.

14. Ibid., pp. 193–99.

15. Ibid., pp. 199–204.

16. Ibid., pp. 204–206. As reformulated in 1933, Myrdal explained: "Das Paradox liegt darin, dass die praktische Nationalökonomie nur dadurch Objektivität gewinnen kann, dass die politische Wollen umurhullt in allen seinen wichtigen Varianten beobachtet wird und dass diese dadurch direkt in die wissenschaftliche Analyses als ihre alternativen Wertprämissen eingefugt werden." From Gunnar Myrdal, "Das Zweck-Mittel-Denken in der Nationalökonomie," *Zeitschrift für nationalökonomie* (4 March 1933): 329. This understanding of the "value problem" in economics permeated all of Myrdal's later work. He came to see the use of "value premises" as necessary to make economics again a moral science. He wrote in 1972: "When thereafter in many fields of study I have tried to apply this insight, and worked under the discipline of stating my value premises and justifying their selection, I have restored the character of economics to that of moral science." From Gunnar Myrdal, *Against the Stream*, pp. vii–viii. See also the important methodological appendix to Gunnar Myrdal, *An American Dilemma—The Negro Problem and Modern Democracy* (New York and London: Harper, 1944).

17. The lesson plan book that Myrdal submitted to the university for spring of 1928 contained the following entry: "Maj 10—kritik av teorin om befolkningsoptimum." From "Dagbok för Stockholms Högskola," GMA 4.1.4 Myrdal's correspondence in early 1928 also reflected this interest in the "optimum population" question. See Gunnar Myrdal to Holger Koed, 6 February 1928, GMAL.

18. With subtitle, it read: "Sjätte kapitel: Befolkningsfrågan. Kritik föreställningarna om ett 'befolkningsoptimum." In GMA 4.1.2.

19. This first draft of *Vetenskap och politik* is found in GMA 4.1.3. The "optimum population" discussion is found on pp. 30–37, with several unnumbered handwritten pages inserted between numbered pages.

20. Gunnar Myrdal to Ernst Wigforss, 10 May 1931, GMAL. Myrdal's comments included in the published text are found in *Vetenskap och politik* [1972], pp. 70–71.
21. GMA 4.1.3, p. 32. See also a fragment from his redraft of the chapter on population: "Förarbeten till vetenskap och politik i nationalekonomi," GMA 4.1.5 (11).
22. GMA 4.1.3, pp. 34–35.
23. GMA 4.1.3, p. 37.
24. On this latter point, interview with Alva and Gunnar Myrdal, Stockholm, 20 July 1976.
25. Gunnar Myrdal, "Till Stockholms Högskola Fakultet," 4 October 1928, GMA 4.2. This same early interest in the dynamic relationship between economic and demographic developments in the agrarian and industrial sectors is reflected in Gunnar Myrdal to Johan Åkerman, 12 August 1929, GMAL.
26. See, for instance, Gunnar Myrdal, "Kritisk studie av Marxism," GMA 4.2.
27. Gunnar Myrdal, "Folket och samhällsklasserna;" "Samhällsrörelser och organisationer;" and "Staten och ekonomiska livet," in Nils Herlitz, *Svensk samhällslära* (Stockholm, Svenska bokförlaget, 1929, 1948), pp. 11–13, 13–23, and 98–100.
28. Gunnar Myrdal, "Lantbrukets bristande räntabilitet," *Svensk Tidskrift* 18 (1928): 463–76.
29. Interview with Gunnar Myrdal by Eric Nyhlén (1973), GMA 96.2.1, p. 23.
30. This strengthened a relationship between the Myrdals and the Rockefeller Foundation, founded in 1928, that was to last for several decades. Both Alva and Gunnar Myrdal served as advisers to the foundation in the 1930s and 1940s.
31. Alva Myrdal to Bertil Hammer, 15 September 1929, AMAL.
32. Interview with Alva Myrdal, Stockholm, 20 July 1976.
33. See Alva Myrdal, "Vi föräldrar måste fostra oss," *Idun*, 4 July 1936, p. 7.
34. Alva Myrdal, in an interview with Laura Waples McMullen, "Population Problems," *American Swedish Monthly*, August 1938. On Alva Myrdal's year in the United States see also AMA 3.000, which contains her class and reading notes from the period; AMA 4.000, which contains printed material and additional notes on her visits to American experimental schools; Gösta Bagge to John van Sickle (Rockefeller Foundation), 3 September 1932, GMAL; an important interview with Alva Myrdal, widely reprinted as "Duktiga Kvinnor," *Foket* (Eskilstuna), 2 May 1936; inteveiw with Alva Myrdal, 20 July 1976; and letter from Gunnar Myrdal to Gustav Cassel, 29 October 1929, GMAL.
35. Gösta Bagge to John van Sickle, 3 September 1932 ("Rockefeller Foundation Correspondence"), GMAL; and interview with Gunnar Myrdal, Stockholm, 20 July 1976.

36. Gunnar Myrdal to Gustav Cassel, 29 October 1929, GMAL.
37. Ibid. Cassel's reply to this letter is of some interest. He agreed with Myrdal that demographic investigations were of great importance, particularly as they might explain the "most recent changes" that had occurred in Europe. This was especially true for Germany, he noted, where the economy in recent years had been influenced by changes in the German population's composition. He saw the same general effect emerging in Sweden and felt it important "that all of our economy [*folkhushållning*] and especially our social policies be adjusted in accordance with the demographic outlook for the coming decades." Gustav Cassel to Gunnar Myrdal, 9 December 1929, GMAL.
38. Gunnar Myrdal to Gustav Cassel, 18 January 1930, GMAL.
39. Gunnar Myrdal to Gösta Bagge, 3 February 1930, GMAL. On Myrdal's growing interest in demographic questions see also Gunnar Myrdal to Gösta Bagge, 6 February 1930, GMAL.
40. See Dorothy S. Thomas to Gunnar Myrdal, 15 September 1930, GMAL. This was the first letter of a long and voluminous correspondence. See also Gösta Bagge to John van Sickle, 3 September 1932, GMAL.
41. Interviews: Alva and Gunnar Myrdal, Stockholm, 20 July 1976; Gunnar Myrdal, Stockholm, 26 July 1976; Alva Myrdal in "Duktiga Kvinnor, *Folket*, 2 May 1936; and Gunnar Myrdal, "Socialism eller kapitalism i framtidens Amerika?," *Tiden* 23 (1931): 205–30. See also Ulrich Herz, "Intervju med Alva och Gunnar Myrdal [Geneva, July 1970], "*I fredens tjänst fredens tjänst* (Stockholm: Rábén and Sjögren, 1971), pp. 109–110; and Herz, "Två livs öden i vår tid," p. 25.
42. Summary from Gunnar Myrdal, fragment of "Short Notes on an Investigation of the Swedish Population at Present Being Carried on at the University of Stockholm," in AMA 12.103–1. Myrdal's proposed methodology is summarized in a letter to Gösta Bagge, 23 July 1930, GMAL. His immediate project involved analyzing statistical materials for the 1895–1930 period, with the hope of later extending his methodology back to 1860. This would include a detailed review of the data from the 1904, 1914, 1924, and 1930 censuses. He established categories that differentiated agricultural from forested communes and distinguished "progressive, stationary and regressive" industrial, wooded, and agricultural communes. He then proposed calculating the percentages of population increase between these categories and comparing the differences in emigration, age group structure, and sex ratios between the old, dying rural communes and the growing, modern industrial communes.
43. See Gunnar Myrdal to W. I. Thomas, 1 December 1931, GMAL; and Gunnar Myrdal to Johan Åkerman, 8 September 1930, GMAL. On Myrdal's publication proposal and planned collaboration with the Thomases see Gunnar Myrdal to Gustav Cassel, 7 February 1931, GMAL; and Gunnar Myrdal to Dorothy Thomas, 10 February 1931.

On Myrdal's invitation to the Rome population conference see Corrado Gini to Gunnar Myrdal, 17 March 1931, GMAL.

44. Gunnar Myrdal to Dorothy Thomas, 10 February 1931; Glesinger, "Gunnar Myrdal," p. 1; Ohlin, *Memauarer*, p. 142; interviews with Alva Myrdal, Stockholm, 20 July 1976 and 7 July 1977; note from Alva Myrdal to the author, 23 July 1977; and Herz, "Intervju med Alva och Gunnar Myrdal," pp. 110–11.

45. Alva Myrdal, "Duktiga Kvinnor," *Folket*, 2 May 1936; and interview with Alva and Gunnar Myrdal, Stockholm, 20 July 1976.

46. Gunnar Myrdal to Ernst Wigforss, 10 May 1931, GMAL; and Ernst Wigforss to Gunnar Myrdal, 19 May 1931, GMAL.

47. Glesinger, "Gunnar Myrdal," p. 3; interview with Alva and Gunnar Myrdal, Stockholm, 20 July 1976; and interview with Alf Johansson, Stockholm, 26 July 1976.

48. Bengt Nystrom, "Sekelskrifte, brytningstid," *FORM* 66, No. 6–7 (1970): 268–72.

49. Ingela Lind, "Hemutställningen 1917," *FORM* 66 No. 6–7 (1970): 273–80.

50. Olle Svedberg, "Funktionalismen-fokus på 1920-talet," *Att bo*, June 1973, pp. 14–17; Sven Wallander, *Minnen, Del I: HSB's öden från 1920-talet till 1957* (Stockholm: HSB's Riksförbund, 1965), pp. 68 and 70; Brita Åkerman, "Goda grännar på 1920-talet—och på 70-talet, "*Att Bo*, June 1973, pp. 18–23; and Dag Widman, "20-talet—på gränsen till en ny tid," *FORM* 66, no. 6–7 (1970): 281–85.

51. Svedberg, "Funktionalismen—fokus på 1920-talet," p. 15; and Kajsa Pehrsson, "Samtal med Alf Johansson," *Att bo*, June 1973, pp. 8–9.

52. See Per-Göran Råberg, "Stockholmsutställningen 1930," *FORM* 66, no. 6–7 (1970): 286–93.

53. Gunnar Asplund et al., *Acceptera* (Stockholm: Tidens Förlag, 1931), p. 9.

54. Ibid., pp. 16–25.

55. Ibid., p. 119. Also pp. 45, 56, and 117–22.

56. Ibid., pp. 123, 140, and 171.

57. Ibid., pp. 186–88 and 198. In a 1932 work, Gregor Paulsson expanded on architecture's political imperative. He described the role of architects in creating the "classless city," where the human and urban scars of industrialization would be removed. Housing would no longer reflect class structures. Rather, architects were pursuing the goal of "a total democratization" of the bourgeois city. See Gregor Paulsson, "Arkitektur och politik," in Gregor Paulsson et al., *Arkitektur och samhälle* (Stockholm: Bröderna Lagerström, 1932), p. 15.

58. On the politicization of Sweden's architects see also "Våra arkitekter har väknat till radikal inställning," *Stockholms Tidningen—Stockholms Dagblad*, 24 January 1933. For a discussion of the relationship between functionalism and Swedish socialism see "Bostadsnöd och samhällsproblem," *Social-Demokraten* (Stockholm), 18 November 1934. This

editorial argues, for instance, that "[o]nly in a socialist system, where society's interest dominates, could functionalism's beautiful principles be realized."

59. Excerpts from minutes of the meeting of the University of Stockholm's humanities faculty, 12 May 1931, GMAL (under "Bagge"). Myrdal remained involved with the research council through the 1930s and in frequent communication with the Rockefeller Foundation. See Gunnar Myrdal to Tracy B. Kittredge, 28 March 1935, and attached appendices, GMAL. Also, Gunnar Myrdal to W. I. Thomas, 10 February 1931, GMAL (in English), where Myrdal wrote of Bagge: "He has an ambition. He is more of an organisator [sic] and scientific promoter than of a scholar, and he loves power too." See also "Gösta Bagge," *Nya Dagligt Allehanda* (Stockholm), 8 November 1931.

60. On this point see Gunnar Myrdal to Miss Walker, n.d., GMA 13.2.7.

61. Dorothy Thomas's *Social and Economic Aspects of Swedish Population Movements, 1750–1933* (New York: Macmillan, 1941) also adopted much of Myrdal's earlier work. On her relationship to the project see W. I. Thomas to Gunnar Myrdal, 23 January 1931; W. I. Thomas to Gösta Bagge, and Gunnar Myrdal, 25 November 1931; Gunnar Myrdal to Gösta Bagge, 28 November 1938; and Dorothy Thomas to Gunnar Myrdal, n.d. (circa August 1939), GMAL.

Myrdal was disappointed by his poor output in the migration study. After accepting the Carnegie Foundation's offer to study the American Negro problem in 1938, he wrote: "I shall work on the Negro—I will do nothing else: I shall think and dream of the Negro 24 hours a day, for I will do a really good job not like the Migration [study], which I always defrauded for other things." Gunnar Myrdal to Dorothy Thomas, 1 March 1938, GMAL.

62. Gunnar Myrdal, "Industrialization and Population," *Economic Essays in Honour of Gustav Cassel* (London: George Allan & Unwin Ltd., 1933), pp. 437–57, particularly pp. 449–57.

63. Ohlin, *Memoarer*, p. 112. Myrdal had not applied for the chair in economics that Ohlin was appointed to at the Business School in Stockholm. Also: Gunnar Myrdal to Dorothy Thomas, 24 June 1932, GMAL; Rockefeller Foundation to Gösta Bagge, 24 June 1932, GMAL; and *Svenska Dagbladet* (Stockholm), 6 November 1933.

Myrdal's appointment marked the first time that one of the university's own students had assumed a professorial chair. See Ivar Öhman, "Gunnar Myrdal: Charmorprofessorn," *Folket i bild*, May 1935, pp. 30–32.

64. See "Utilitaristisk inslag i modern ekonomisk teori," GMA 4.1.5(8).

65. For general surveys of the Swedish response to the economic crisis see Ralph E. Holben, *Swedish Economic Policy and Economic Stability* (Ann Arbor: University Microfilms, 1951); Harrison Clark, *Swedish Unemployment Policy, 1914–1940* (Washington, D.C.: Public Affairs, 1941); Leif Lewin, *Planhushållningsdebatten* (Uppsala: Political Sci-

ence Association, 1967); and Arthur Montgomery, *How Sweden Overcame the Depression* (Stockholm: Albert Bonniers Förlag, 1938).
On the political background to the emergence of the Social Democratic government in 1932–33 see Olle Nyman, *Krisuppgörelsen mellan socialdemokraterna och bondeförbundet, 1933* (Uppsala: Political Science Association, 1944); and Olle Nyman, *Svensk Parlamentarism, 1932–36: Från minoritetsparlamentarism till majoritetskoalition* (Uppsala: Almqvist and Wiksell, 1947).

66. See Gunnar Myrdal, *Sveriges väg genom penningkrisen* (Stockholm: Natur och Kultur, 1931); Gunnar Myrdal, "Om penningteoretisk jämnvikt. En studie over den 'normala räntan' i Wicksells penninglära," *Economisk tidskrift* 33 (1931): 191–302; in English translation: Gunnar Myrdal *Monetary equilibrium* (London: Hodge, 1939); Gunnar Myrdal, "Sverige och Krisen," lecture before National okonomisk förening in Copenhagen, 19 January 1932 (Copenhagen: Nielsen and Lydiche, 1932).

67. Reprinted as Gunnar Myrdal, *Konjunktur och offentlig hushållning: En utredning* (Stockholm: Kooperativa Förbundets Bokförlag, 1933). His formal report to the Arbetslöshetsutredningenkommittee was printed as: SOU 1934: 2, *Finanspolitikens ekonomiska verkningar* (Stockholm, 1934).

68. Gunnar Myrdal, *Konjunktur och offentlig hushållning*, p. 72.

69. For a general summary, ibid., pp. 71–76. See also *Social-Demokraten* (Stockholm), 12 January 1933. For an example of the critical bourgeois response to the "Myrdal budget" see "Halsbrytande budgetsexperiment," *Nya Dagbladet Allehande* (Stockholm), 11 January 1933.

70. See, for instance: *Lunds Dagbladet*, 27 February 1934; *Dagens Nyheter* (Stockholm), 14 January 1934; *Stockholms Tidningen—Stockholms Dagblad*, 21 November 1934; *Dagens Nyheter* (Stockholm) 21 November 1934; and the report on Gunnar Myrdal's inaugural address as Lars J. Hierta Professor of Economics, 1 March 1934, in *Dagens Nyheter* (Stockholm), 2 March 1934.

71. For a contemporary discussion see Mauritz Bonow, *Staten och jordbrukskrisen* (Stockholm: Kooperativa Förbundets Bokförlag, 1935).

72. From Gunnar Myrdal, *Det svenska jordbrukets läge i världs-krisen, föredrag vid lantbruksveckans allmänna sammanträde*, 14 March 1932 (Stockholm: Norrtelje, 1932); and Gunnar Myrdal, "Lantbrukets kris," *Svenskt Land* 16 (1932): 30–31.

73. See *Arbetet*, 12 June 1935; *Uppsala*, 12 June 1935.

74. In response to complaints about the interest rates for agrarian credit offered by mortgage institutions, the Swedish minister of agriculture on 24 June 1933 appointed a royal committee of experts to investigate the situation and make recommendations to the Riksdag. Nils R. Wohlin, Agrarian party politician and subsequent chairman of the 1935 Population Commission, was appointed chairman. The committee also included two bankers, a representative of the National Debt Office, an

agrarian Ministry official, and Gunnar Myrdal. The report issued by the committee in 1935 noted that while rent levels had generally declined over the past four years in line with the decline in agrarian income, the interest payments on loans agreed to prior to 1931 remained at a high level relative to conditions prevailing in a depressed economy. This placed an abnormal financial pressure on already troubled farmers and resulted in a significant number of foreclosures. In response, the report called for the national government to subsidize the losses experienced by credit institutions, which would accompany a reduction of the interest rates on agrarian loans agreed to prior to the outbreak of the depression. See "Ett magert betänkande beträffande stadsfästighets-krediten," *Sveriges Fastighetsägare Tidning* (official organ for Sveriges "Fastighetsägareförbund), 24 August 1935; Gunnar Myrdal, "Jordbrukspolitik—planmässig och på längre sikt," *Konsumentbladet* 22 (1935): 3f; Gunnar Myrdal, "Jordbrukspolitikens svårigheter," *Nationalekonomiska föreningens förhandlingar* (1938): 57–98; and Gunnar Hellstrom, *Jordbrukspolitik i industrisamhället med tyngdpunkt på 1920- och 1930-talen* (Stockholm: LTs Förlag, 1976).

75. Gunnar Myrdal emphasizes the importance of this article in "Bostadssociala preludier," reprint from *Bostadspolitik och samhällsplanering: Hyllningsskrift till Alf Johansson* (Stockholm: n.p., 1968), p. 10. In their population book, this article also receives revealing attention. Alva and Gunnar Myrdal, *Kris i befolkningsfrågan* (Stockholm: Albert Bonniers Förlag, 1934), pp. 150–51.

76. Alf Johansson, "Bostadsbehov och bostadsproduktion," *Tiden* 22 (February 1930): 74.

77. Ibid., p. 76.

78. Ibid., pp. 76–79.

79. Gunnar Myrdal, "Kosta sociala reformer pengar?," *Arkitektur och samhälle* (Stockholm: Bröderna Lagerström, 1932), pp. 42–44.

80. Gunnar Myrdal, "Bostadssociala preludier," pp. 10–11. Also interview with Richard Sterner, Stockholm, 29 June 1977.

81. Ibid., p. 11.

82. Gunnar Myrdal and Uno Åhrén, *Bostadsfrågan såsom socialt planläggningsproblem: Under kris och på längre sikt. En undersökning rörande behövet av en utvidgning av bostadsstatistik: jämte därmed förbunda bostadspolitiska frågor* (Stockholm: Koopertiva Förbundets Bokförlag, 1933), p. 45. For their statistical definition of overcrowding see p. 13. The general section on overcrowding is found on pp. 44–48. The government version of the report, with the same title, was published as SOU 1933:14, Finansdepartmentet (Stockholm, 1933).

83. Interview with Richard Sterner, Stockholm, 29 June 1977.

84. Myrdal and Åhrén, *Bostadsfrågan såsom socialt planläggningsproblem*, particularly pp. 62, 65–69, 82–86, and 108–111.

85. Gunnar Myrdal, "Bostadssociala preludier," pp. 11–12.

86. Social-Demokraten (Stockholm), 30 March 1933.
87. Social-Demokraten (Stockholm), 13 March 1933.
88. Wallander, *Minnen*, p. 95; Kajsa Pehrsson, "Samtal med Alf Johansson," *Att bo*, June 1973, p. 9.
89. See chapter 5.
90. Alf Johansson to an unidentified member of the Social Housing Investigation (with a copy to Gunnar Myrdal), 4 June 1934, GMAL.
91. SOU 1935:2, Socialdepartementet, *Betänkande med förslag rörande lån och årliga bidrag av statsmedel för främjande av bostadsförsörjning för mindre bemedlade barnrika familjer*, (Stockholm, 1935), p. 50.
92. Ibid., p. 51.
93. Ibid., pp. 51–52.
94. See *Vår bostad*, October 1934, pp. 8–9; *Svenska Dagbladet* (Stockholm), 15 November 1934; and *Eskilstuna Kuriren*, 15 November 1934.
95. Gunnar Lange et al., *Bostaden och vår ekonomi* (Stockholm: Hyresgästernas Förlag, 1934), specifically Alf Johansson, "Vad betala vi för bostaden?," pp. 35–40.
96. *Social-Demokraten* (Stockholm), 18 November 1934.
97. Interview with Gunnar Myrdal, Stockholm, 20 July 1976. On the continuity between the Myrdal/Åhrén study on housing and *Kris i befolkningsfrågan* see also Johan Vogt, "Sverige—den gyline middelvei," *Arbeiderbladet*, 17 September 1936; and Gunnar Myrdal, "Bostadssociala preludier," pp. 11–14.
98. See course syllabus and notes in AMA 5.200 and 5.500. The announcement on the formation of the study circle is found in *Social-Demokraten* (Stockholm), 4 November 1931.
99. From a lecture to the Göteborg kvinnliga diskussionsklubb, 1 November 1933. Draft of the complete lecture found in AMA 6.202–201. See also *Morgontidningen* (Göteborg), 2 November 1933; and *Göteborgs Posten*, 2 November 1933.
100. A copy of Markelius's *kollektivhus* plan is found in AMA 6.201. See also Sven Markelius, "Kollektivhuset," in Gregor Paulsson et al., *Arkitektur och samhälle* (Stockholm: Bröderna Lagerström, 1932). Contemporary feminist interest in the Myrdal-Markelius house remains strong. See Delores Hayden, *Redesigning the American Dream* (New York: W. W. Norton, 1984), pp. 226–31.
101. Alva Myrdal, "Kollektiv bostadsform," *Tiden* 24 (December 1932): 602.
102. Ibid.
103. Ibid., p. 607.
104. Alva Myrdal, "Kollektivhus," *Hertha*, January 1933, pp. 9–16.
105. Alva Myrdal, "Yrkeskvinnans barn," *Yrkeskvinnor klubbnytt*, February 1933, p. 63.

The proposed collective house set off a widespread public debate. Critics of the proposal blasted the separation of the mother from the child, charged Alva Myrdal with a poor grasp of child psychology (e.g., when one baby cries in a common nursery, all cry), argued that such an arrangement would depress fertility, questioned whether disease and infection might not spread quickly among "communalized" infants, and generally saw the program as overly idealistic.

For critical reviews see *Social-Demokraten* (Stockholm), 7 December 1932; and *Dagens Nyheter* (Stockholm), 12 December 1932. For additional treatments see also Eva Wigforss, "Ett forenklat liv," *Morgonbris*, 11 January 1933; Margit Palmar, "Barnens karlek och kvinnans verk: Blir kollektivhuset moderskärlekens renassans?" *Dagens Nyheter* (Stockholm), 5 February 1933; and interview with Alva Myrdal, *Morgontidningen* (Gothenburg), 24 January 1933.

This housing experiment attracted Scandinavian-wide attention. See Sigrid Tang, "Kollektivhuset: Ett nytt svensk eksperiment," *Nynorsk Vikeblad*, 15 September 1934.

The Markelius-Myrdal Kollektivhus in Stockholm was completed, on a somewhat reduced scale, in Feburary 1936. See "Markelius och hans utställningsplaner," *Vecko-Journalen*, 28 August 1938; and Brita Åkerman, "Goda grännar på 1920-talet och på 70-talet," *Att bo*, June 1973, p. 21.

106. See Alva Myrdal, "Uppfostran till 'Äkta Quinnlighet,'" *Idun*, 25 February 1934, pp. 190, 202; *Eskilstuna-Kuriren*, 10 February 1934; and *Stockholms Tidningen—Stockholms Dagblad*, 5 February 1934. On the background to the women's movement in Sweden see Ellen Key, *The Woman Movement*, trans. M. B. Borthwick (New York: Putnam, 1912); and Lydia Wahlstrom, *Den svenska kvinnorörelsen* (Stockholm: P. A. Norstedt och Söner, 1933).

107. Alva Myrdal, "Familjen göres om," *Morgonbris*, July 1933, p. 13.

108. Ibid., p. 15.

109. This series of articles included Margarete Bonnevie, "Barnförsäkring," *Tidevarvet* no. 28 (July 1933); Alva Myrdal, "Vem skall försörja barnen?," *Tidevarvet* no. 31 (Aug. 1933); Margarete Bonnevie, "Familjelön eller 'barnetrygd,'" *Tidevarvet* no. 32 (Aug. 1933); Alva Myrdal, "Barnförsörjningen I," *Tidevarvet* no. 34 (Aug. 1933); Alva Myrdal, "Barnförsörjningen II," *Tidevarvet* no. 35 (Sept. 1933).

110. Alva Myrdal, "Vem skall försörja barnen?"

111. Alva Myrdal, "Barnförsörjningen II" and "Vem skall försörja barnen?"

112. Alva Myrdal, "Vem skall försörja barnen?"

113. Alva Myrdal, "Barnförsörjningen I."

114. Ibid.

115. Alva Myrdal, "Vem skall försörja barnen?"

116. In two parts: Gunnar Myrdal, "Socialpolitikens dilemma," *Spektrum* 2, no. 3 (1932): 1–13 and 2, no. 4 (1932): 13–31.

117. Gunnar Myrdal, "Socialpolitikens dilemma I," p. 10.

118. Gunnar Myrdal, "Socialpolitikens dilemma II," pp. 16–23.

119. Ibid., pp. 26–27.
120. Ibid., pp. 28–31. Myrdal expanded this latter point in a May 1933 interview. Responding to the question, "What is your basic goal?" he stated, "I should naturally desire to have a socially directed, methodically planned and organized economic community, which makes a secure and human-worthy existence possible for the great mass of people." Interview with Gunnar Myrdal in *Morgonbris*, May 1933, p. 17.
121. *Politiken* (Copenhagen), 10 February 1934.
122. Quotations from *Stockholms Tidningen—Stockholms Dagblad*, 14 February 1934; and *Västerbottens Folkblad* (Umeå), 20 February 1934.
123. *Göteborgs Morgonpost*, 17 March 1934.
124. Reported in *Hufvudsstadsbladet*, 26 March 1934.
125. *Åbo Underrättelse*, 26 March 1934.
126. Early title found in letter, Bonniers boktryckeri to Gunnar Myrdal, 10 September 1934, GMAL.
127. Interview with Alva and Gunnar Myrdal, Stockholm, 20 July 1976; interview with Gunnar Myrdal, Stockholm, 26 July 1976; interview with Alva Myrdal in "Duktiga kvinnor"; Gunnar Myrdal to Jacob Viner, 1 October 1934, GMAL.
128. Quotations from Gunnar Myrdal to archivist Stellan Andersson, notation concerning GMA 10.1.4 ("The rejection of 'Kris i befolkningsfrågan' by KF; acceptance by Bonniers") in n.a., *Preliminär förteckning över Gunnar Myrdals arkiv* (Stockholm: Arbetarrörelsens Arkiv, 1976), p. 9. Also interview with Alva and Gunnar Myrdal, Stockholm, 20 July 1976; and interview with Gunnar Myrdal, Philadelphia, Pa., 10 March 1976.

3

A Socialist Pronatalism

As the new title of the Myrdals' book, *Crisis in the Population Question*, implied, the crisis facing Sweden was more than one of the declining numbers. It also represented an ideological crisis over how to think about the population issue and social policy. The Myrdals argued that only a totally fresh, multidisciplinary vision could identify the causes lying behind the birth decline and offer plausible solutions.

The opening sentence set the tone: "The population question, more than any other social problem, rouses agitated emotions."[1] Swedish conservatives, the Myrdals noted, saw a reduction in population size as degeneracy or "race suicide" and a geopolitical threat to national boundaries. Conservatives also opposed birth control as an "unnatural interference in the order of creation," as something "against the Christian religion." While this kind of thinking had dominated the early years of the twentieth century, a radical neo-Malthusianism advocating birth control had since spread widely among the population. Indeed, by the 1930s this ideology had met such success that it had become excessive: "The birth rate has fallen catastrophically. And it continues to fall: a bottom can still not be discerned."[2] While the economic crisis had certainly aggravated the nativity decline, the Myrdals argued that fluctuations in the business cycle should not be considered the source of the long-term problem. Rather, its roots lay far deeper and any prognosis for the future suggested only a growing crisis: "We even believe that [the population question] will come in the next generation to dominate the whole socio-political debate."[3]

The Myrdals turned to a historical survey of Malthusian and neo-Malthusian doctrine. Since 1911, radical neo-Malthusianism had become closely identified with the labor movement. While unsuccessful in repealing the 1911 anti–birth control laws or in liberalizing abortion, the neo-Malthusians had succeeded in reaching most elements of Swedish society. The use of birth control had become nearly universal among the upper, middle, and urban working classes. Recent research by the Royal Medical Board also suggested that nearly twenty thousand illegal abortions occurred annually in Sweden.

The Myrdals insisted, however, that Malthus was wrong and Malthusianism misguided. The English parson's original mistake, they said, came from viewing biological development as a constant. Modern birth control practices showed that human reproduction could now be considered a socioeconomic variable. The Myrdals also rejected the "optimum population" theory advanced by Mill and the later neo-Malthusians. Referring to the American experience, and specifically to the work of Ogburn, they blasted Mill's assumption that the tempo of technical development would eventually slow down so that society could settle into a nondynamic utopia. Accordingly, it was impossible for any country to find a quantitative "population optimum." Living standards actually proved to be independent of population size.[4]

In crafting another base on which to build a population policy, the Myrdals listed their assumptions. Technological developments, they said, would proceed in the future, which doomed any effort to arrive at some proper population size. They emphasized the moral responsibility of their generation biologically to renew the Swedish nation. This meant that the Swedish family could not be allowed to grow sterile through birth control carried to its extreme. In contrast to other theorists, they also rejected all class or racial distinctions in determining hereditary worth.[5] They affirmed that all healthy Swedes, regardless of social class, were of equal biological value and their children of equal desirability.[6]

Citing the "bankruptcy" of all existing population theories, the Myrdals presented a radically different, hybird perspective. The spread of birth control practices, they maintained, must be seen as an integral part of modernity. Motives for the use of birth control were closely tied to the breakthrough in the West of secularized rationality and of industrialization. The new problem was psychological, not biological: "People simply do not want to have as many children as before." Hence the population question demanded study as a social-cultural and a social-psychological problem.[7]

Looking to the future, the Myrdals projected a further drop in the birthrate. While fertility rates were still relatively high in rural areas, the growth of industry would pull ever more rural people into the cities and so accelerate the birthrate decline. Even among the remaining rural population, better communication would eventually eliminate the "rural-urban" fertility differential and bring still another decline in the nation's fertility. Moreover, the number of illegitimate children born in Sweden was bound to fall further as birth control methods became more widely known. The continued high fertility of very poor families could also be explained by a lag in the rationalization process. As birth control information spread to these groups, another depression in births could be expected. Finally, even the Swedish middle class seemed to rely heavily on coitus interruptus, a relatively unpredictable contraceptive technique that would over time give way to more reliable methods.

For these reasons, the Myrdals concluded that a third to a half of all births in Sweden were still unwanted. This posed a disastrous future for a nation whose birthrate was already the world's lowest and well below the replacement level. Rather than moving toward some mythical "optimum level," Sweden's birthrate showed every sign of accelerating decline: "This means depopulation."[8] Such threat demanded an immediate response from the state. As their primary recommendation the Myrdals called for a massive governmental investigation into the causes of the "depopulation of our land."[9]

Beyond the prospect of the disappearance of the Swedish people, the Myrdals pointed to the negative consequences of a declining birthrate and the aging of the nation. As the number of the young shrank relative to older age groups, an ever greater share of the national income would go to the latter's support. Given current trends, there would be in a generation's time twice as many retired people demanding social support, per working person, as there were in 1934. The opportunities available to younger people for advancement would also shrink as the percentage of the old holding seniority grew. As the power of old men spread, a depressing, psychologically debilitating form of socialism could develop, marked by a bureaucratic, senile character and presiding over the slow liquidation of a people. The whole expansionist psychology of the past few generations would be lost as the aged inherited the earth.[10]

The Myrdals also argued that a shrinking population would produce serious economic disturbances. While the per capita amount of capital would increase for a while among a diminishing people, it would decline over the long run through a crimping of the whole economy. As the age structure stabilized, extra disturbances in the demand function would disappear. With the population no longer able to absorb the wasteful mistakes of individual entrepreneurs, the latter's risks would grow and their propensity for investment decrease. This development would eventually retard increases in living standards and choke off economic progress.[11]

The Myrdals also pointed to population pressures from outside. The risk was high that a depopulating country like Sweden, with rich natural resources and a strong pension system, would attract foreign peoples. While migration from Scandinavian neighbors would be acceptable and even desirable as a positive step toward Nordic integration, the Myrdals thought it more likely that prospective immigrants would come from elsewhere: Southern and Eastern Europe or Africa and Asia. Such groups were difficult to assimilate and posed a threat to Sweden's own cultural heritage. The Myrdals also emphasized the problems for the labor movement that this influx of immigrants, willing to work for a cheaper wage, would cause.[12]

The Myrdals' "mild nationalism" and ethnocentrism represented a dramatic break with the internationalism that had marked Democratic Socialism. While their later work and reputations are largely based on "internationalism," their population work was distinctly oriented toward Sweden. This could be seen as but another example of the abandonment by many interwar European intellectuals of historic doctrine, as they dug in to weather the economic and political crises swirling about Europe.[13] Indeed, this unilateral focus on Swedish self-sufficiency could be seen in Gunnar Myrdal's general work. For example, in a 1935 speech on the farming crisis he stated that "Agrarian policies must first and foremost involve a monopolization of the whole home market, and within this monopolized home market must be built price and market policies that raise profitability."[14] Adversion to immigration, moreover, could be dismissed as merely another example of organized labor's aversion to "cheap labor" as producing "cheap men."[15]

Yet such explanations are less than adequate explanations for the Myrdals' reluctant, apologetic confession of a "mild Swedish nationalism." The world war, the Bolshevik Revolution, and the Great Depression wreaked havoc with socialist internationalism. The new alternative, national socialism, took more than one form in the 1930s.

While the Myrdals never abandoned their commitment to democracy, they did cast their lot with ethnocentric nationalism. For Alva, the conversion may have been largely tactical, a way of selling her feminist socialism at an emotional level. For Gunnar, though, an almost tribal devotion to the Swedish "folk" drove him in a new direction. As his speeches over the next four years would make clear, he held a true passion for "Sweden's children."

Everywhere they looked the Myrdals saw an economy and a culture out of kilter with the human drive to reproduce. Wages in an industrial economy, they emphasized, took no account of family economics. The bachelor and the man supporting a family of six may receive the same industrial wage, yet they bore obligations of support that were vastly different. For a couple to bear an extra child now meant a rise in family expenses without any increase in current or potential income. In addition, state old age pensions stripped children of economic value; in fact, the incentives were precisely reversed, and it became a rational act to avoid the voluntary expense of children, meanwhile hoping that others would be foolish enough to bear the children later to be taxed to pay for everyone's retirement.[16]

Family housing standards proved appalling. Indeed, as the number of children in a family rose, the size and quality of available housing declined. Accordingly, large families needing the most space and the healthiest structures were actually driven into the smallest, dingiest, and cheapest dwellings. Capitalism, the Myrdals concluded, was again the culprit: "One might suspect that this was an upside-down world. But such is the way of life in a capitalistic system built on 'individual self-sufficiency.'"[17]

The Myrdals turned to recent statistical studies that showed a high correlation between large families and poor nutrition among both mothers and children. Here too, they said, capitalism had failed in reconciling family needs with free competition.[18]

Unemployment also disproportionately affected those who were asked to found and rear families. The recent Unemployment Investigative Committee, they noted, had reported that 34 percent of the unemployed in November 1933 were workers under twenty-five years of age. Job uncertainty had severe psychic, physical, moral, and social consequences, affecting future willingness to marry and bring children into the world. Among older workers with families, sharp drops in income led to lower-quality housing and food and the further damaging of human potential. The farm crisis undermined the living standards of rural families in a similar way.[19]

The Myrdals charged that there was something basically "sick" about a society where married women could be driven by economic pressures to abortion, where the best housing was held by those who needed it least, where upper- and middle-class politicians and priests used contraceptives themselves while denying it to the poor through law, and where a young couple choosing to have children were driven to a lower standard of living because of that decision. Individualistic capitalism had failed utterly, they said, in delivering justice to families.[20]

Nor could the existing system set matters right through incremental change. The problem lay at the very heart of liberal ideology. The basic assumption of classical liberalism, which equated the individual's private interest with society's general interest, had broken down over the birth question. It did not hold that if each individual sought what was socially and economically best for him or her the net result would be best for society. While individuals might desire a growing population for social or economic reasons, their own self-interest dictated an extreme limitation in number of children. In short, the harmony between the individual and the collective interest had been lost in the population question. The restoration of harmony, the Myrdals insisted, would not reemerge out of the play of natural forces and free economic incentives.[21]

They emphasized that the central cause of the decline in births was economic, not moral. The dilemma to be faced was that in industrialized society children were the chief cause of poverty. Given current social organization, the refusal of young people to bear children was natural, rational, and blameless. The very persons who contributed the most to the nation's existence were dragged down into poverty, shoddy housing, poor nutrition, and limited cultural and recreational opportunities. A voluntary choice between poverty with children or a substantially better living standard without them was what young couples now faced. Young people were required to support both the retired and the needy through the social welfare system and the children to whom they gave life. Under this multiple burden, they had consciously reduced the number of children as the only factor over which they had some control. The tragedy for Sweden was that "[we] uphold at present our relative standard of living only thanks to a decline of fertility well below the replacement level."[22]

Out of this disharmony, the Myrdals charged, harmony must be created by political action. Their program involved linking the radical neo-Malthusian concepts of voluntary parenthood, sex education, and birth control and the feminist theme of women's full engagement in the labor market to the conservative, nationalist desire to raise Sweden's fertility level to a level ensuring a stable population. Trying to distance themselves from the pronatalist programs of Italy and Germany, the Myrdals termed any population increase as "out of the question," "entirely out of reach," a matter not even to be discussed.[23]

This synthesis of neo-Malthusian, feminist, and pronatalist thrusts mandated the restructuring of society to allow every fertile marriage to bear voluntarily a "normal" family of three children, and for some to bear more than three. "This average fertility is nearly forty percent greater than that now prevailing." The Myrdals built their program on the assertion that married couples would bear three or four children by choice once the state had removed the "living standard penalty" imposed by offspring.[24]

In this light, sexual reforms were urgently needed. The Myrdals rejected efforts to raise the birthrate by hindering the spread of birth control information and methods. They cited the hypocrisy of a democratic society that predicated its biological survival on keeping only the very poorest ignorant of contraceptive techniques. A "positive" population policy demanded the repeal of the anti–birth control laws and the universal spread of contraceptive information, so that each child born would be a wanted child. Sex education for children, as well as adults, was urgently necessary. Abortion, the Myrdals affirmed, was a great human tragedy and an indictment of society's failure to craft an environment suitable to family living. While supporting the procedure on strictly defined medical, eugenic, and ethical (rape and incest) grounds, the Myrdals guardedly rejected abortion when justified on a social or economic basis. Instead, they argued that universal sex education, readily available contraceptives, and a radical reform of social and economic conditions would eliminate the need for abortion.[25]

These democratic sexual reforms had to be coupled to sweeping measures that would relieve family insecurity and the extra cost that children brought to parents. A positive population policy so became:

> . . . a question concerning the quite radical redistribution of income be-
> tween families with an unequally great burden of child-support and [those
> with] an unequally great income. It concerns a preventive social policy,
> closely guided by the goal of raising the quality of human material, and at
> the same time carrying into effect radical redistribution policies making a
> significant portion of the child-support burden the concern of all society.[26]

New services must be provided free for all mothers, children, and
families, without means test, and financed through a tax structure
based on both "horizontal" and "vertical" redistributions of income.

The Myrdals' proposed program can be viewed from several perspectives. Authentically pronatalist, the Myrdals insisted that Sweden's birthrate be raised by 40 percent.[27] They called for a meaningful
transfer of wealth from the unmarried and the childless to the "child
rich." New family tax deductions and the imposition of a special bachelor tax would be used to help finance a series of family support programs and so diminish the extra costs that accrued to families with
children. This "horizontal" redistribution of wealth on the basis of
family size would represent a nationalization of differential child
costs, where the state would assume the economic burden associated
with bearing and raising the next generation.[28]

As a new form of social policy the Myrdals rejected the prevailing
"symptom-oriented" approach: "Almost the whole of our social policies have been focused on curing symptoms—helping the poor, the
unemployed and the sick, placing criminals in prisons, the mentally ill
in hospitals, alcoholics and vagrants in custodial institutions, and so
on—instead of being preventive and focusing on the cause of the social
anomalies."[29] They argued that the "poor relief" syndrome had to be
driven out of social policy and the focus turned instead to children.
Money spent here would represent an investment in the health and
efficiency of the young, an investment in the future.[30] The Myrdals
also rejected the use of cash grants or near-cash aid such as family
allowances. They cited the close connection between substandard
wages and these practices and the danger that cash supplements would
not necessarily accrue to the benefit of children. In addition, parents
oftentimes were ignorant of elementary hygiene and child development and would waste the aid in privately chosen consumptions. The
provision of public services rather than cash also meant that certain

consumption items could be socially organized and so realize economies of scale.

Ideologically socialist, the Myrdal's family support program would be universal in application, without the use of means tests. Income would be redistributed not only horizontally between the "child poor" and "child rich," but also vertically between socioeconomic classes on the basis of ability to pay. Accordingly, population policy would represent "a fundamental [new] phase of income redistribution between the various income classes."[31] These reforms formed part of what would later be termed *the socialization of consumption.* They were tied to a "full employment" policy that would virtually eliminate the threat of unemployment through tight government control of the labor market and a state planning mechanism that would ensure stabilized production levels for socialized consumption.[32] As the Myrdals phrased it:

> . . . the population question is here transformed into the most effective argument for a thorough and radical socialist remodeling of society. The population question powerfully raises the political demand that social relations in our land be altered in such a way that citizens will voluntarily bring a sufficient number of children in the world so that our nation shall not become extinct.[33]

As feminist policy the Myrdals' program stressed the acceptance of women's place in business and industry. It recognized the "right" of working women to bear children while retaining jobs and incomes. Using a favorite phrase, employed mothers were declared to be a "social fact," beyond challenge or debate. While some worked out of economic necessity and others for personal fulfillment, their presence in the labor market was a rational trend that could not and should not be opposed. Acknowledging that working women married less frequently and bore fewer childrnen, the Myrdals insisted that reforms allowing women to combine, without penalty, work and family were the only real option. While careful to endorse the value and utility of marriage, they also insisted that births out of wedlock be treated as equal to those within marriage, particularly in regard to benefits. In effect, the state should fill the provider role for women raising children without men.

The Myrdals' program also represented applied social science. In offering an economic explanation for the birthrate decline and in arguing for a transfer of income from the childless and wealthy to the "child rich" and poor, the Myrdals stood in opposition to conventional wisdom, which tied a rise in income to a decline in family size. To support their argument that raising the living standard of the bulk of the Swedish population would result in more, not fewer children, the Myrdals took refuge in the recent statistical work of Karl Arvid Edin.[34]

In his study of differential fertility in Stockholm, Edin utilized a new statistical technique that measured fertility by the average number of live births per thousand years of married life and correlated the results with the duration of marriage, age of parents, and employment of wives. He discovered an absence of significant fertility differences between occupational groups. However, in an important break with past work, he reported that observed fertility rates actually increased with income at the highest socioeconomic levels, with the significant exception of industrial workers. His evidence suggested that such results were not produced by a more favorable age distribution, nor by the less frequent employment of wives in the more educated group, nor because of the better economic position of the more educated. Moreover, they were not the product of temporary changes in fertility in the postwar years, nor an artifact of class differences resulting from the larger number of children born to lower-income wives before marriage. Edin's conclusion was simply that a higher net income resulted in more children, "a reversal of the traditional relation of fertility to social status."[35]

The Myrdals' program also had a race-hygienic cast. While denying a class- or race-oriented eugenics program, the authors affirmed the need to improve the physical, emotional, and moral position of the population through better care of children and youth. The pressures of modern life, the Myrdals argued, demanded persons of higher quality. Industrial procedures and intensified urban life made greater demands on men and women drawn off the farm. Unemployment, for example, directly assaulted human quality: "Here exists . . . the deep, tragic connection, that a long period of unemployment itself results in future low quality work and so raises not only the risk for continuing unemployment but also the possibility of deeply asocial development." In consequence, they insisted that "the primary task of a preventive social policy is to shape a better human material."[36]

Detailing the necessary qualitative reforms, the Myrdals pointed to the immediate need to strengthen the depressed economy. They advocated a series of economic and distributive reforms that would guarantee to all workers, including farmers, a basic annual income, put the unemployed back to work, and strengthen home and foreign markets for Swedish products. These included selective increases in tariffs, government management of exports, the creation of food reserves to stabilize prices, state subsidies for housing and related construction projects, and a commitment to central economic planning.[37]

Under the rubric of "quality-oriented" policy, the Myrdals described forced sterilization as a necessary option. While affirming, from a "race-biological viewpoint," the equality of genetic material among all Swedish population groups, they added that a genetically inferior (*mindervärdighet*) substrata existed within the population: the insane, the mentally ill, the genetically defective, and persons of bad or criminal character. With the German nazi program again as foil, the Myrdals stressed that their category of targeted individuals was drawn from all population and social groups. The reproduction of this inferior stock was undesirable, since offspring ran a strong risk of hereditary damage to health and intelligence. Because the government would be called upon to support genetically damaged children, the Myrdals concluded that the state had the right in limited cases to force sterilization on individuals. The guiding assumption should be to resort to the process only in recognized serious cases of illness and defect and only among those incapable of "rational decisions." Where indivduals were capable of reason, voluntary sterilization should be actively urged. Failing this, free contraceptives and eugenic abortion should be made available.[38]

In a bold move, the Myrdals also used the "quality" angle to justify social programs in the fields of nutrition, housing, health, and education. It was here, they argued, that the goals of quantity and quality converged: public programs designed to reduce the child-support burden on families for pronatalist reasons could be further justified on eugenic grounds.

Concerning nutrition, the authors affirmed the elementary "social-hygiene" desire that children should, irrespective of their parent's income, be assured a sufficient and healthy diet. Existing poor nutrition derived from both parental ignorance and low income. The former problem could be tackled through adult education, government information services, and applied social work. The latter could be countered by free school lunches and price rebates on food for families with preschoolers. They proposed that the state purchase surplus Swedish agricultural goods and distribute them through the free school meal program. This had the dual benefit of providing price supports to the hard pressed and high-fertility agrarian sector while assuring all children of a nutritional diet.[39]

The Myrdals also affirmed the joint qualitative/quantitative importance of housing policy. A connection existed between overcrowding and psychic illness and asocial tendencies. Overcrowding had been shown to affect the performance of schoolchildren and to increase disruptive behavior among youth. The authors also suggested a relationship between overcrowding and alcoholism and prostitution. With conservative sentiments obviously in mind, they added: "Even homosexual actions are encouraged by overcrowding." As a minimum, the Myrdals proposed a program that would provide every Swedish family a kitchen and separate bedrooms for parents, boys, and girls. This meant that a family dwelling with children of different sexes should have at least four rooms. Given the "evident inability" of the private sector to provide the risk capital to build such housing at affordable rates, state action was needed. Government assistance, they declared, "ought to be directed wholly towards families with children." Those who were childless could wait; large families could not.[40]

Turning to health care, the Myrdals praised Sweden's medical system for already embodying certain principles of social responsibility. From a population policy perspective, cost-free child health care was the most urgently needed reform. The costs of maintaining children's health, the Myrdals asserted, must be freed from every competing aspect of a family budget. Furthermore, public health service doctors should concentrate primarily on children, particularly preschool children, "which is completely natural, since preventive health care essentially is child care." In light of these needs, the complete reform of the medical profession became urgent. There was "little likelihood" that the private efforts of individual doctors would produce any significant change. Abuses and problems among doctors would be solved only through a "great social political program" that brought them all under state regulation.[41]

Quality- and quantity-oriented population goals required a similarly sweeping reform of the nation's educational system. The basic goal of the Swedish schools, the Mrydals argued, should be the socialization of children to make them instruments of social evolution: "Schools must be the living power through which every new generation is molded to take its place in a social order in continuous change."[42] They described the new human type (*nutidsmänniskorna*) that proved most adaptable to twentieth-century life: "people with aptitudes for personal independence—in contrast to subservient medieval men—and for collective cooperation—in contrast to private, capitalistic, competitive men."[43] They despaired that the Swedish system was still based on nineteenth-century liberalism and that curricula gave excessive commitment to an individualism relevant only to the already disappearing and historically short "private capitalist epoch." Even so-called new or free schools based on "open" educational experiences had their ideological base in bourgeois philosophy. "This tradition," they declared, "must be broken."[44]

Instead of individualism, schools should develop socialist cooperation: "The primary demand is . . . that group work, the distribution of tasks, leadership and deferring to leaders, planning, readiness to help, and the consideration of others within the group be developed within the schools."[45] All projects should be based on group, class, or schoolwide efforts, not on the striving of individuals. The exam system should be altered so that it did not place students "against each other" or "against the teacher," but instead served the goals of social equality and solidarity.[46]

The Myrdals also affirmed the growing importance of adult education as a vehicle for social change. The nation's extensive Peoples Education Movement (Folkliga bildningsrörelsen) embodied positive social and democratic ideals and should be used to elevate population policy goals in the popular consciousness.

More broadly, education should be the principal tool in shaping a new society. While the early industrial revolution had opened up many channels for social-economic advancement, a new social hardening had developed. Class origins and educational structures increasingly locked individuals into professional or income categories. The new pedagogical goal must be a regime of pure equality, where "the whole of social circulation is exclusively a pure circulation of work." Over time, this implied a continuous reduction in the real wages of upperclass professionals and a relative increase in wages among lower-paid workers. But in the interim, the authors felt that the educational system must serve as the primary means of occupational and social mobility. Young adults must be helped in choosing careers suited to their interests and abilities, without regard to class, birth, or gender. This democratization of education required removal of the financial pressures that limited educational advance, and the Myrdals advocated study stipends for students, from all social classes, with special aptitudes and interests.[47]

In their closing pages the Myrdals turned to the family. In the last analysis, they said, population policy was really family policy. They acknowledged that their proposals to remove hindrances preventing ordinary persons from marrying and bearing a "normal" number of children involved a profound alteration of the family institution.

Responding to the popular charge that the birthrate had fallen due to "moral disintegration" within the family, the Myrdals replied as good materialists, arguing that "[m]orals are essentially a function of institutions and not the opposite. And institutions are in turn to a large degree a function of total social development, which in the last analysis is propelled by technology." Rather than some conservative moral resurgence, the situation demanded an adaptation of the family institution to bring it into harmony with twentieth-century socioeconomic developments. Only then could "morality" be regained.[48]

Drawing on their American mentors, Ogburn and Burgess, the Myrdals stressed that the family had lost its productive, educational, and security functions. While in some ways the family remained the social unit of consumption, it was illusory to believe that members of a family still held common economic interests. Women's emancipation and new forms of marriages also tore at the fabric of the old family. Indeed, the Myrdals argued that "the little modern family is almost . . . pathological."[49] They concluded that "[t]he old ideals must die out with the generations which supported them. New generations with their somewhat more flexible life-values can orient themselves in a more skillful manner to changed human circumstances."[50]

Concerning the care of small children, the Myrdals charged that the "false individualistic desire" by parents for the "freedom" to raise their own children had an unhealthy origin: " . . . much of the tiresome pathos which defends 'individual freedom' and 'responsibility for one's own family,' is based on a sadistic disposition to extend this 'freedom' to an unbound and uncontrolled right to dominate others."[51] In order to raise children to greater self-reliance and as citizens of the modern world, "we must free children more from ourselves." Family bonds stood in the way of a better order.

The so-called traditional family was but a "poor compromise" between the stable precapitalist tradition and the modern era's changing conditions. This "compromise family" was "rootless" and "isolated" and doomed to "disintegration and sterility."[52]

The *barnkammarskolan*, or day-care center, and not the "diminutive," "pathological" old family, was in line with the socialist goals of eliminating social class and creating a society based on economic democracy. Universal state-funded collective child rearing would foster social growth and allow all children to pass from the bonds of the "old family" to the new, egalitarian family.[53]

Indeed, the very concept of "family" should be altered. The modern family, they said, should be seen as part of the "great national household" (*storfolkhushåll*), where economic incentives and children were again in harmony, where women stood by men "as comrades" in productive labor, where children had become a social responsibility, and where antique bourgeois attitudes had given way to social cooperation.[54]

In the current "dynamic, transition period" to this new social order the Myrdals saw conservatism "as our opponent. Conservatism is now individualistic. The society [conservatives] seek to defend is disintegrating. Therefore radicalism becomes society's defender and society's edifier. Conservatism has become liberal, radicalism social."[55] Yet within their program lay the possibility of forming a "unitary national ideology within population policy. . . where those, who once zealously supported social policies, come from the radical direction, and those who with great pathos zealously supported the maintenance of population size, come from the conservative."[56] This radical-conservative consensus on the population question could then serve as the lever for the full socialization of Swedish society.

Notes

1. Alva and Gunnar Myrdal, *Kris i befolkningsfrågan*, 7th Swedish ed. (Stockholm: Albert Bonniers Förlag, 1935), p. 7.
   In the following discussion of *Kris i befolkningsfrågan* elaborative use will be made in notes of certain later works by the Myrdals, where consistent with their original presentiative. The few changes in their posture that emerged in the ensuing debate are noted in chapters 5 and 6.
2. Ibid., p. 10.
3. Ibid., p. 13.

4. Ibid., pp. 56–66.
5. On this valuation see Alva Myrdal, "Ofrånkomlig kvalitetsvärd av den nya generationen," *Tidevarvet*, 6 April 1935, pp. 1, 4.
6. Alva and Gunnar Myrdal, *Kris i befolkningsfrågan*, pp. 66–78.
7. Ibid., pp. 79 and 87. For a later expansion of this point see Gunnar Myrdal, "Allmänna och ekonomiska synpunkter på befolkningsutvecklingen," lecture at Svenska försäkringsföreningens sammanträde, 31 January 1936; a stenographic record in Paul Bergholm et al., eds., *Nordisk försäkringstidskrift, årgangen 1936*, vol. 16 (Stockholm: Paul Bergholm, 1936), pp. 201–203. See also *Debatt i befolkningsfrågan* (Stockholm: n.p., 1935), p. 11.
8. Alva and Gunnar Myrdal, *Kris i befolkningsfrågan*, pp. 87–97. For a later expansion see Alva Myrdal, *Nation and Family: The Swedish Experiment in Democratic Family and Population Policy* (New York: Harper and Brothers, 1942), pp. 62–64, 77, 83–85. The Myrdals adapted their discussion and projections from Sven Wicksell's *Ur befolkningsläran* (Stockholm; Albert Bonniers Förlag, 1931).
9. Alva and Gunnar Myrdal, *Kris i befolkningsfrågan*, pp. 100–101.
10. Ibid., pp. 102–105. For later expansions see Gunnar Myrdal, *Population: A Problem for Democracy* (Cambridge: Harvard University Press, 1940), pp. 161–66, and *Debatt i befolkningsfrågan*, pp. 11–12.
11. Alva and Gunnar Myrdal, *Kris i befolkningsfrågan*, p. 104. For later elaborations see *Debatt i befolkningsfrågan*, p. 10; Gunnar Myrdal, *Population: A Problem for Democracy*, pp. 149–60; and Gunnar Myrdal, "Population Problems and Policies," *Annals of the American Academy of Political and Social Science* 197 (May 1938): 205–206.
12. Alva and Gunnar Myrdal, *Kris i befolkningsfrågan*, pp. 105–11. See also Gunnar Myrdal, "Population Problems and Policies," p. 204.
13. Critics of the book noted the Myrdals' failure to see the Swedish experience in an internationalist context. See "Vårt folk i dödens väntrum," *Mellanfolkligt samarbete*, February 1935, p. 36.
14. An address to the Riksförbundet Landsbygdens Folk (RLF), 12 June 1935, reported in "Trygghet för rimligt jordbruksstöd är ett oeftergivligt krav," *Landsbygdens Folk* 12 (June 1935).
15. See Alvan A. Tenny, *Social Democracy and Population* (New York: Columbia University Press, 1907), p. 88.
16. Alva and Gunnar Myrdal, *Kris i befolkningsfrågan*, pp. 118–25.
17. Ibid., pp. 134, 145.
18. Ibid., pp. 151–64.
19. Ibid., pp. 164–69.
20. Ibid., p. 52.
21. Ibid., p. 98.
22. Ibid., p. 170.
23. The Myrdals' avoidance of the question of the desirability of a growing population was strained and unnatural at best. See also Alva Myrdal,

Nation and Family, p. 105; and Gunnar Myrdal, *Population*, p. 173.
24. Alva and Gunnar Myrdal, *Kris i befolkningsfrågan*, p. 173. The Myrdals later set their estimate of the necessary average family size at 3.6 and sometimes talked about a necessary minimum of four children per fertile married couple. This meant, the Myrdals stated, that not merely the "two-child" system advocated by the neo-Malthusians, but even the "three-child" system was inadequate in Sweden to maintain a stable population. This was due to several factors: (1) nearly 10 percent of all Swedish marriages were involuntarily sterile, while another 7 1/2 percent became sterile after one child and another 5 percent after two children; (2) a large number of Swedish marriages, for reasons of late marriage, illness, poverty, or design, were voluntarily sterile; (3) Sweden had an unusually large number of bachelors and "spinsters." Hence, even with efforts to raise the number of marriages, "the four-child family... will have to be the practical minimum aimed at in all nonsterile families." Alva Myrdal, *Nation and Family*, p. 106. See also Alva Myrdal, "A Programme for Family Security in Sweden," *International Labour Review* 36 (June 1939): 729–32.
25. Alva and Gunnar Myrdal, *Kris i befolkningsfrågan*, pp. 112 and 42–55. On the abortion question see also Ann Katrin Hatje, *Befolkningsfrågan och välfärden: Debatten om familjepolitik och nativitetsoning söknig under 1930- och 1940-talen* (Stockholm: Almänna Förlaget, 1974), pp. 121–25, who severely criticizes the Myrdals for compromising on this question; and Halvor Gille, *Svensk befolkningspolitik* (Copenhagen: Socialt Tidsskrift, 1949), pp. 31–37.
26. Alva and Gunnar Myrdal, *Kris i befolkningsfrågan*, p. 11.
27. This number was actually higher than the level needed to achieve stability, reflecting the misleading nature of the net reproduction rate. See Michael Teitelbaum and Jay Winter, *The Fear of Population Decline* (New York: Academic Press, 1985).
28. Alva and Gunnar Myrdal, *Kris i befolkningsfrågan*, pp. 114–15.
29. Ibid., pp. 203–204.
30. Ibid., p. 204. See also Gunnar Myrdal, "Kontant eller in natura i socialpolitiken," *Nationalökonomisk tidskrift* 76 (1938): 69–70; and Åke Elmér, *Från fattigsverige till välfärdsstaten* (Stockholm: Bokförlaget Aldus/Bonniers, 1963), p. 96.
31. Alva and Gunnar Myrdal, *Kris i befolkningsfrågan*, p. 198.
32. Ibid., p. 285.
33. Ibid., p. 117. See also report of Gunnar Myrdal's speech given at Uppsala, 29 February 1935, in *Upsala Nya Tidning*, 1 March 1935; Gunnar Myrdal, "Allmänna och ekonomiska synpunkter på befolkningsutvecklingen," stenographic record in *Nordisk Försäkringstidskrift: årgången, 1936(16)* (Stockholm: Paul Bergholm, 1936), p. 212; and Gunnar Myrdal, *Population*, p. 209. Ivar Iverus discusses the socialist component of the Myrdals' program in *Versuch einer Darstellung, der Zusammenhanges zwischen Bevölkerung sentwicklung, Familienpolitik und öf-*

fenrlichen Meinung in Schweden (Helsinki Kir Japaino O.Y. Sana, 1953), pp. 35 and 90–91.

34. Presented in the following works: K. A. Edin, "Vårt moderna befolkningsproblem," *Sexual Hygiene* (Uppsala: Almquist and Wiksell, 1927), pp. 80–93; K. A. Edin, "The Birth Rate Changes," *Eugenics Review* (1929): 258–66; K. A. Edin, "Födelsekontrollens intrågande hos de breda längren," *Ekonomisk Tidskrift* 31 (1929): 123–52; K. A. Edin, "The Fertility of the Social Classes in Stockholm in the Years 1919–29," *Proceedings of the Second General Assembly of the International Union for the Scientific Investigation of Population Problems* (London, 1932), pp. 91–101; and K. A. Edin and Edward P. Hutchinson, *Studies of Differential Fertility in Sweden* (London: P. S. King and Son, 1935). As noted earlier, Edin's statistical work was funded partially by Rockfeller Foundation grants funneled through the Social Science Institute at the University of Stockholm.

35. Karl Arvid Edin and Edward P. Hutchinson, *Studies of Differential Fertility in Sweden* (London: P. S. King and Son, 1935), p. 89.

36. Alva and Gunnar Myrdal, *Kris i befolkningsfrågan*, pp. 205–14.

37. Ibid., pp. 173–88.

38. Ibid., pp. 217–26. See also Alva Myrdal, *Nation and Family*, pp. 96, 108, 115–17; Nils von Hofsten, *Steriliseringsfrågan från rasbiologisk synpunkt* (Stockholm: Svenska föreningens för psykisk hälsovård, 1933); and SOU 1929:14, *Betänkande med förslag till steriliseringslag* (Stockholm, 1929).

39. Alva and Gunnar Myrdal, *Kris i befolkningsfrågan*, pp. 226–29.

40. See: Ibid., pp. 232–53, 270–71; and Halvor Gille, *Svensk befolkningspolitik*, (Openhagen: Socialt Tidsskrift, 1949), pp. 85–91.

41. Alva and Gunnar Myrdal, *Kris i befolkningsfrågan*, pp. 240–54.

42. Ibid., p. 261.

43. Ibid., p. 262.

44. Ibid., p. 264.

45. Ibid., p. 267.

46. Ibid., p. 273.

47. Ibid., pp. 278–83.

48. Ibid., p. 288.

49. Ibid., p. 303.

50. Ibid., p. 295.

51. Ibid., p. 299.

52. Ibid., p. 301.

53. Ibid., pp. 309–17.

54. Ibid., pp. 317–25.

55. Ibid., pp. 320–21.

56. Ibid., p. 323.

4

The New Population Debate

The first Bonniers edition of *Kris i befolkningsfrågan* appeared in scholarly format and quickly sold out. A second was released in early 1935. Reader demand led to the publication of an edited paperback "popular" edition in March 1935, which went through four printings in 1937.

In addition to this unusually large sales volume for an academic-oriented work, the book immediately sparked a memorable public debate in Sweden. The early reaction to *Kris i befolkningsfrågan* took the form of major review articles. Appearing on the front pages of Stockholm's leading dailies, they were written by Sweden's best known economists and social scientists. These reviews both set the parameters of the bourgeois political reaction and proved instrumental in garnering Social Democratic support for the population issue.

Gustav Cassel, Gunnar Myrdal's mentor, published an unusual series of four articles in the Conservative daily *Svenska Dagbladet* beginning November 25. Cassel agreed with the Myrdals that the population question had reached a critical stage and acknowledged the importance of the Myrdals' work: "We see here the whole problem in its various aspects illuminated in the sharpest light and with notable competence . . . . In comparison to the problem we now have placed before us, all of the era's other problems become insignificant."[1]

Nevertheless, he continued, the Myrdals' whole approach to the question had to face strong criticism. Their arguments rested on a socialistic, "not to say a purely Communistic understanding of social economy." Cassel also criticized their reliance on "propaganda methods" in building their case. This had been done, he suspected, to show the Myrdals' "communistic planned economy as the only effective solution." Nowhere in the work, moreover, did the Myrdals attempt to estimate how much their proposed program would cost, a sum that he estimated would be prohibitive. They also offered no concrete proposals to stimulate capital formation, the critical element in any effort to provide for the children of the future.

For several thousand years, Cassel said, high material culture had risen only on the basis of a free market. The "incomparable advance" of the nineteenth century had been built on a liberal economic order. Consequently, only extraordinary reasons might justify casting it away and substituting an arbitrary experiment in collectivism.

In the second article, Cassel assaulted the Myrdals' contention that the Swedish people could prevent their disappearance only through a redistribution of property and income, a socialization of production, and a radical reorganization of the family. He expressed genuine anger over the Myrdals' characterization of liberalism as a "dangerous, asocial power" and their dismissal of bourgeois opposition to a socialized family policy as "individualistic conservatism's society-destroying class-egoism." Such statements, Cassel declared, were cheap and dishonest. He defended the existing system, where individual initiative and personal responsibility had delivered an ever rising living standard: "It is therefore deeply unjust to allege that the bourgeois virtues are wholly and completely asocial."[2]

It was necessary, Cassel continued, to do everything possible to improve the situation of families with children. Yet unless such attempts were based in a thorough appreciation of economic realities, they were doomed to failure. He noted that "radicalism" itself, now labeled the "cure" to the population crisis, had only a few decades earlier been part of the cause, when Knut Wicksell and other radicals promoted birth control to reduce Sweden's population to 3 million. Now the same group proposed to eliminate the individual initiative that had built industrial Sweden, in order to raise fertility. Cassel remained skeptical.

A third article dealt with the relationship of population size to job opportunities.[3] Here Cassel had few arguments with his protégé. While Cassel understood the desire of workers under economic stress to reduce the size of the labor force through birth restriction, he emphasized that any cut in labor power would also bring a decline in demand. Malthus was wrong, he said: every new person increased total demand and raised the level of employment. He pointed specifically to the United States, where economic growth and rapid population expansion through immigration had been closely bound together.

In the closing article, Cassel reiterated the urgency of the issue: "It is nothing less than the question of whether our lineage shall live." All other social, political, and cultural questions must be subsumed beneath it. He returned to praise the Myrdals' book for its comprehensive vision, rejection of neo-Malthusianism, and exposure of Sweden's "hypocrisy" in handling the sex question. While he predicted that the book would become the object of strong opposition, Cassel did not doubt that it would "clear the atmosphere" and let all Sweden see the population issue for what it was: "our nation's most urgent survival question."[4]

In a major ideological shift on his part, Cassel agreed with the Myrdals that Sweden's social policy had been overly dependent on curing symptoms of distress, not on eliminating their causes. While criticizing existing services for children as wasteful, he agreed that much more needed to be done for the nation's youth. He also endorsed the Myrdals' plans to help working mothers. Warming up to the Myrdal's "quality" theme, the conservative economist affirmed a strong interest in improving the quality of the growing generation: "We . . . must concentrate our interest on those who are fit to live and not through false humanitarianism make unreasonable sacrifices for the inferior element." While describing a growing population as desirable, Cassel affirmed the Myrdal compromise and the immediate need to raise the birthrate to a level assuring population stability. The Myrdals' unexpected nationalism also drew his praise. He emphasized the geopolitical threat that a declining population held, particularly the probable flow of non-Scandinavians to settle within Sweden. "Our defense," he concluded, "must above all be a defense of our own racial stock . . . . Sweden must remain essentially Swedish."[5]

Despite the exchange, Gunnar Myrdal and Cassel retained a close relationship. This would not be true following a lengthier, more bitter dialogue between the Myrdals and conservative economist Eli Heckscher and his wife, Ebba. The Heckscher-Myrdal exchange involved four front-page newspaper articles in *Dagens Nyheter* and fourteen private letters. Many of the latter were eight to twelve single-spaced, typewritten pages in length.[6]

The Heckschers' opening article noted that the use of population trends to justify radical social change had an old pedigree in Sweden, reaching back to Sweden's "first liberal," Anders Chydenius, in the eighteenth century. In this tradition, the Myrdals were using the population issue to advance their socialist notions. The Heckschers granted that the Myrdals' theories deserved a hearing; but the burden of proof in advocating such a radical break with the past clearly lay with them.

Unfortunately, the Heckschers added, none of the major premises of the book stood up. To begin with, the Myrdals failed to consider the psychological causes of the birth decline. Rather, they took refuge in a monocausal materialism. The Heckschers further charged that the connection between fertility decline and the proposed reform program was unclear. Indeed, the Myrdals conveniently ignored the fact that child limitation always began with the upper classes. While acknowledging the impressive results of the Edin work in differential fertility, the Heckschers highlighted Edin's own admission that his numbers did not mean that fertility had ceased to decline among the upper classes. The Heckschers asked how serious social scientists could justify a massive social program on such narrow and not terribly significant facts.

The Heckschers also charged the Myrdals with a poor grasp of economic history, dating, for instance, the emergence of a money economy five hundred years too late. Wearing "Karl Marx's old clothes," the socialist couple had also created a mythical preindustrial order that had absolutely no basis in fact. This had then been contrasted with "the evils" of the nineteenth century. The whole book, in fact, could be viewed as a diatribe against that century, an era, the Heckschers noted, marked by history's greatest population expansion and most rapid rise in personal living standards. The Myrdals had set this time span as the deeply despised and quite useless transition between the village collectivism of the preindustrial era and the new, egalitarian collectivism of the future.

The second article attacked the Myrdals' understanding of psychological and educational realities and offered an analysis of their "deeper motives." The Heckschers reiterated their objections to a monocausal understanding of the birth decline, citing the lower birthrate among the upper class and the "conscientious objectors" who refused to bear children into an unhappy world as examples of causation not explained by the economic argument.

But the Myrdals' motives in warping reality, the Heckschers explained, were not innocent. The young social scientists did not really seek to "save" the home. Rather, they were working to replace the home with a collectivist "melting pot." The Myrdals' largest mistake, the Heckschers asserted, was believing that such a move would raise fertility. Modern young women did not desire children in order to increase the population stock. They bore children to love, care for, and raise themselves within the family circle. The Heckschers could not understand how taking babies away from their mothers would raise fertility.

It was a thankless task, they added, to defend the traditional home (*gamla hemmet*) in an era when young sophisticates cast stones at it. They affirmed the positive psychological value of home life and noted that when both parents worked and placed their children in day care there was a sharp and damaging reduction in parent-child contact. They also asked why the Myrdals, who supported complex social and economic planning, objected to planned curricula in the schools and further asked what relation school reforms had to family size.

The Heckschers found their answer in the "deeper motives" of the Myrdals. When a reader observed the whole system found in *Kris i befolkningsfrågan* the intent of the authors became clear: "to reduce the time together in the home and so break the point of parental influence" on their children's intellectual development. The Myrdals' assault on "false individualism" left the conservative couple with little doubt as to who, in the "Myrdal regime," would determine what was best for "society's children." *Kris i befolkningsfrågan*'s program represented little more than the moral and intellectual kidnapping of the young.

Private letters carried the Heckschers' critique to a more personal level. "Your book abounds with attempts to rule out morally your opponents," Eli Heckscher wrote to Alva Myrdal. "Indeed, I cannot help but report the impression of intolerant self-righteousness which your book made on Cassel."[7]

In a separate letter, Ebba Heckscher redefined her basic criticisms of the Myrdals' program: she and her husband did not believe there would be any improvement for children and families through a strong, if not total, socialization of children, and they could not see where housing subsidy, state payments to large families, and school reforms would increase fertility. Raising the stakes, Ebba Heckscher also suggested that the Myrdals' program had the odor of nazi social policy, which also expressed concern for "family health" and "quality" but distorted the concepts in totalitarian and nationalist ways.[8]

The Myrdals' reply, both public and private, was equally harsh. Alva Myrdal's article in *Dagens Nyheter* answered the public charges leveled against the book. She argued that while the effect of their program on fertility levels could not be fully predicted, their work was based on "the most recent scientific thinking." The Heckschers' belief that a general increase in the Swedish standard of living would increase fertility was certainly false. The problem for families was not average standard of living, but rather the differential impact of children on a family's budget. The program outlined in *Kris i befolkningsfrågan* was designed to reduce that differential. Population policy, furthermore, had to be based on the sociology and psychology of the modern family and not on concepts such as "national income." While acknowledging probable causes of the birth decline other than economic, Alva Myrdal emphasized the economic argument as the one area where state intervention could have effect.

She repeated her charge of bourgeois sexual hypocrisy, pointing to Christians who condemned contraceptives and sex education as immoral and then went ahead and used birth control themselves. Critics of birth control should either have a biblically prescribed number of children or should be celibate or sterile; otherwise, they were hypocrites.

Similarly, sentimental attachment to the "traditional family" could not save it. Change occurred, and clearly family structure was changing. Social scientists were justified in studying this change, and politicians must deal with this reality.

Myrdal denied that she and her husband wanted to take infants from their mothers and turn them over to the state. Rather, they sought to correct the social and economic dysfunctions that prevented women from having children. State-financed day-care programs were needed to assist the poor who could not afford private care and women with jobs.[9]

Personal letters to the Heckschers expressed shock and bitterness. Writing to Eli, Gunnar Myrdal warned that this exchange would determine their future relationship: "I state in advance that the question for me is moral. It no longer concerns a difference in opinion; it concerns trust in your character.... The [population] question is so important to me that no false modesty shall stand in the way of full candor on my part."

With barely concealed rage he noted that while he and Cassel often held diametrically opposed opinions, they had never allowed this to affect their respect for each other. In contrast, Myrdal accused Heckscher of succumbing to the "pull of cheap dialectic." Rather than objectively discussing *Kris i befolkningsfrågan*, the Heckschers misused and even altered quotations and references from the book to fit their own perspective: "Your old friends, who know you better, say that you are impossible to work with, but they have confidence in your personal integrity. This is more decisive for me than the fact that you have many more enemies who do not share this opinion."

Myrdal claimed a personal dilemma. How could a good economic historian, such as Heckscher, practiced in historical research and the critical reading of documents, become such a "moralistically shallow dialetician" in the use of references, citations, and interpretations as soon as he stepped beyond the narrow circle of his knowledge? "Help me solve this?" Myrdal pleaded. "You stand before me as a moral-psychological riddle."[10]

In a lengthy letter sent the same day, Alva Myrdal said that it would henceforward be difficult for them to "be on speaking terms" with the Heckschers. She blasted the reactionary negativism of the Hechschers' approach. While crying for preservation of the "traditional family," bourgeois housewives did nothing to save or protect it. The question facing Sweden today was no longer a conflict between the "traditional family" and new family forms. Rather, it was a question of the direction of future social policy. Only a program similar to that in *Kris i befolkningsfrågan* could give families sufficient support in an urbanized, industrial, and secular future.[11]

In a subsequent letter, Alva Myrdal replied to the Heckschers' charge that totalitarianism lurked within the Myrdals' social theories. The rhetorical certainty displayed in *Kris i befolkningsfrågan*, she said, derived from her husband's commitment to clearly stated value premises at the outset of research into a social question. Rejecting imputations of nazi-styled intolerance, she stated that "the form of liberty embodied in freedom of thought and opinion is more dear to us than almost any other. Should the sacrifice of these principles be necessary for implementation ... of a successful population policy, we would not make the sacrifice."[12]

Gunnar Myrdal defended himself against the Heckschers' imputation that his population program was Marxist in inspiration. "If Marxism needed battling," he wrote, "I would commit myself to the battle .... But in our land, as you well know, no Marxism is found.... I am naturally no more 'Marxist' than you; approximately as much or as little, I would guess. Rather, a scientifically objective liberalism is to be found [in our work]...; it dominates the whole of our science."[13]

Other conservatives alternated between anger and frustration as they sought to come to grips with the Myrdals' ideological innovation. Colleague and economist Gösta Bagge expressed shock over the positivistic, uncompromising attitude of the book and his distress over the Myrdals' dismissal of "hypocrites" from the sexual question debate. (Bagge was childless.)[14] In a scathing review Sven Brisman emphasized the socialist component of the book, downplaying the urgency of the population crisis. Margit Cassel acknowledged the urgency of the population problem, but dismissed *Kris i befolkningsfrågan* as a guide, due to its ideologically determined content.[15]

The early socialist response was more complex. Neo-Malthusianism remained a strong ideological force among the rank and file. In the early months of the 1935 population debate, a number of Social Democratic newspapers reprinted Hinke Bergegren's speech "Love Without Children."[16] Correspondence from trade unionists and the unemployed filled the letter sections of newspapers with condemnations of the Myrdals for urging the poor to have more children.

At the leadership level, most Social Democrats could readily accept the "means" of the Myrdal program, but were decidedly uncomfortable with a pronatalist goal. In addition, the Myrdals remained relative newcomers to the party. While participating in development of counterdepression policies in the 1931–33 period, both were still viewed as "outsiders" by many in the party hierarchy.[17]

Early public support from the left came almost exclusively from personal friends: Herbert Tingsten, Alf Johansson, Axel Höjer, and Richard Sterner. Tingsten, writing in *Stockholms Tidningen—Stockholms Dagblad*, termed *Kris i befolkningsfrågan* "an original and radical book," rich in ideas, based on sharp, unsentimental, and scientific analysis, and offering concrete suggestions to solve an intractable problem. Swedish political debate, he concluded, had been considerably enriched.[18]

A more influential two-part review appeared a week later in the party daily *Social-Demokraten*, penned by Johansson, the activist who had first seen the powerful opportunities for political action lying in the birth crisis.[19] With the ideological sensibilities of party members in mind, he praised *Kris i befolkningsfrågan* for its deep commitment to historic Social Democratic ideals, as well as its "free, intelligent, and multifaceted social-scientific content." It was the first work on the population question that went beyond "hopelessly out-dated" neo-Malthusianism and the "hopelessly impossible" moralism of the conservatives.

Johansson affirmed that rapid depopulation was a real threat. Fertility had fallen catastrophically to a level that, in the span of only a few generations, would bring the extinction of the Swedes. While the use of birth control had once played its role in improving the living standard of the population, the situation had now changed. "[A] basic reorientation of the traditional way of looking at things is inescapably necessary. And the quicker it happens the better. There is actual danger in delay." Advocating increased fertility no longer meant propagandizing for an increased population. Rather, "it now means preventing national suicide."

Unemployment, he noted, confused many workers, and it was natural for the working class to distrust pleas for more births: "Why place more children into a world with an inadequate social order, abandoning them to unemployment, insecurity, and perhaps the hell of a coming war?" Johansson explained, though, that unemployment was not caused by the birth of children, but through the failures of capitalism. Under the current system, on the one hand, unemployment could not be relieved even if the birthrate fell further. On the other hand, unemployment clearly was a major cause of the birth decline. Therefore, the population question became "the most powerful intellectual argument for measures to abolish unemployment and to give, above all, greater security for material existence."[20]

In his companion article, Johansson drew heavily on pronatalist sources from other European countries. In discussing motives behind the birthrate decline, he accepted the validity of the Continental, proto-fascist interpretation of the "new human type" created in the nineteenth century: "upward striving" or "bourgeois" man, who had learned that an important component of upward mobility was a small family. Accordingly, many "social conventions" discouraged women from giving birth. However, Johansson affirmed the greater power of the economic argument: The human will to have children remained strong, restrained primarily by an inability to adequately feed, clothe, and house them. Better incomes, more security, and confidence in the future would "give release" to this natural fertility. As he put it, "a better living standard for certain categories [of people] and through certain kinds of redistribution is an indispensable prerequisite for increasing fertility." He embraced the Myrdals' reform program as a valid expression of the nation's common responsibility for children. In a curious lapse of solidarity and caution, he even pointed to the French family allowance system as a successful model and included a quotation from national socialist demographer Friederich Burgdörfer on the French pronatalist program's powerful effect in Alsace-Lorraine.[21]

Another strong affirmation of the Myrdals' program, by collaborator Richard Sterner, appeared in the trade union publication *Fackföreningsrörelsen*. With evident pleasure, he noted that the Myrdals' book had caused great consternation in bourgeois circles: "Liberal and conservative economists throw themselves on it with real frenzy," attacking the use of the population question "as a battering ram for the implementation of dangerous socialist and communist goals."[22] Sterner acknowledged that their fears were partly justified, for the book had a strong political tendency. Nevertheless, real concern was warranted: depopulation stood as an actual threat.

Neo-Malthusianism, Sterner stated, had once served a purpose. But its "prayer had been heard" and the movement now stood outdated. The "liberal notion"—suggesting that if each family balanced its size against its own economic resources then a population would result exactly suited to the area's natural resources—had also proven false. Rather, each family now sought to raise its living standard by limiting births, while the aggregate effect was ruinous depopulation.

Sterner endorsed the Myrdals' plan to reduce the individual's economic interest in limiting births. Such programs would not "take children from parents," but would free mothers from their child-care burdens for portions of the day, allowing them time for themselves and for paid employment. While such programs would be expensive, the cost already existed within the economy. The Myrdals' plan merely brought a redistribution of already existing costs.[23]

Other early favorable reviews appeared in the socialist press. Sven Wicksell, in *Arbetet*, praised the book and concluded that many of

Sweden's traditions might have to be sacrificed so that the nation would survive.[24] Halvar Khennet gave positive attention to the Myrdals' theories in *Tiden*, emphasizing the relationship between nativity and the old age security system.[25]

By January 1935, the population debate was spreading beyond the newspaper pages. Alva and Gunnar Myrdal became eagerly sought and widely publicized speakers. Reflecting his sincere interest in renewal of the Swedish folk, Gunnar's speeches tended to dwell on quantitative issues, stressing the need for Sweden to have 40 percent more births and for Swedish couples to produce a minimum of three or four children each. Alva Myrdal tended to focus her attention on the qualitative, day-care, and "women's" questions, a mirror of her preferred use of the population issue as a political tool.[26]

The Myrdals directed most of their attention to Social Democratic forums. On February 14 they presented a joint lecture on the working class and the population problem in a Stockholm hall "jammed" by an enthusiastic crowd of worker commune and Social Democratic district youth delegates. Following the singing of "The Internationale," the Myrdals declared to the crowd that the "social reform line" could be found at all levels of the population question and that socialist action was the only solution to the crisis.[27] At a major May Day rally in Norrköping, Gunnar Myrdal rose before the massed red flags and, in "the best agitator's style" and to "powerful applause," condemned the waffling of the bourgeois parties. He declared to the crowd of ten thousand that "our population question demands radical measures."[28] In another speech before a party audience in Falun, Myrdal again declared that "[t]he population question can only be solved through such vast social reforms that they mean a total transformation of society."[29]

Also in these months, the "benevolent neutrality" of the Social Democratic leadership toward the Myrdals' program gave way to growing acceptance.[30] The *Norrlandska Social Demokraten*, for example, editorialized in favor of the Myrdals' proposal, citing the need for a stable population. The editorial said that is was refreshing to see conservatives acting like socialists in response to the population crisis, even showing some compassion "for the first time."[31] In February, Riksdag member Fredrik Ström wrote that "[o]nly alteration of the capitalist system into a socialist system, which created security and the will to live among men, will bring a solution to the problem before us."[32] Evert Kuhn credited the Myrdals' book with rescuing the population question from "bourgeois demagogues." The Myrdals had shown that the choice facing Sweden was either to adopt socialist economic planning or watch the nation die out: "Socialism so passes over from theory to a program of action."[33] Tage Erlander later recalled that he and other young Social Democrats were shocked, then fully captivated by the Myrdals' population program.[34]

The inner circle of the Social Democratic party also faced the population question in early 1935, giving primary attention to the Myrdals' call for a special investigative commission on the population question. Party leaders clearly revealed their new attitudes at the 28 April 1935, meeting of the Social Democratic Steering Committee, the party's executive body.[35] Called to discuss the future course of the socialist government, the meeting revealed that the Social Democrats, after a highly successful two and a half years in office, were suffering from a surprising loss of confidence and a policy vacuum.

Prime Minister Hansson opened discussion of the government's future. He reported on the party's recent success and on the importance of maintaining a Social Democratic front in Scandinavia as a democratic bulwark against the dictators to the south. Turning to domestic policy questions, he affirmed that the immediate issues were improvement of the national pension system and working for "defense of the Swedish population stock." He pointed to the Social Housing Commission and the proposed Population Commission as the probable sources for new policy ideas. Hansson concluded that the party would be in a better position, leading into the 1936 elections, if it remained in power than if it returned to the opposition.[36]

Committee member P. E. Sköld responded sharply. He saw no danger if the party returned to the opposition; rather, the danger lay in staying in power too long. The party leadership, he felt, was growing distant from the concerns of Sweden's common people. Governmental responsibility increasingly proved to be a burden. The party had "harvested" the policies it had developed as the opposition in the six years prior to 1933. It was time, Sköld declared, to return to the party's roots and sow new directions. He doubted that the social housing and population commissions would provide any substantive policy directions. Several other committee members offered the same view.

Social minister Gustav Möller spoke in rebuttal. He agreed that the party needed new issues. The pension, economic, and defense issues all posed problems. Yet they ought to avoid negativism: "The Social

Housing Investigation gives promise for an expansion of welfare supports.... "The [proposed] committee on the population question can produce many policy recommendations, and in this question we ought to have the initiative." There were valid reasons for dissolving the government, he continued; but lack of a platform was not one of them.[37]

Hansson also responded to Sköld. If the Social Democrats could not accomplish anything while in power, he doubted that moving into opposition would make the situation better. Do we have fewer opportunities, he asked, when we have the whole state apparatus under our control? Adolf Olsson added that few grass-roots Social Democrats wanted the government to resign, most party members believing that the new Riksdag commissions on housing and population could give them a program for the 1936 elections.[38]

In the end, the committee rejected the motion to dissolve the government. Relative to the population issue, the meeting's significance lay in the surprising admission that the party, still far from implementing major social and economic reforms, had minimal policy direction in early 1935, in the leadership's opinion that the Social Democrats should take the initiative in the population debate, and in their reliance on the new Riksdag housing and population commissions—one already the center of Myrdal-inspired pronatalism and the other soon to be so—to set the direction for future party policy.

At a subsequent 29 October meeting of the Steering Committee, Hansson himself raised the question of government resignation, with the population issue again at the heart of the analysis. Controversy over national defense, he noted, raised the possibility of an Agrarian party/Liberal party coalition. Gustav Möller responded that major social issues before the 1936 Riksdag would be unemployment, improvement of the pension system, and the population question. This focus, he believed, would be helpful in diverting attention from the troublesome defense issue. Concerning finances, however, he warned that an increase in the budget could not be contemplated. Wigforss explained that balancing the 1936 budget must be accomplished through existing income, with no rise in taxes. Population-inspired reforms would have to be paid for within the existing progressive tax structure.[39]

The Myrdals' book also enflamed passions to the Social Democrats' left. The syndicalist newspaper *Arbetaren* labeled the Social Democrat's fear of non-Scandinavian immigration a symbol of the party's dying commitment to internationalism. Their "purely nationalistic" population program was "bourgeois" in inspiration, having no relevance to the needs of the working class.[40] The communist youth paper *Stormklockan* argued that capitalist barbarism lay behind the population crisis and that the Social Democrats were incapable of achieving the necessary social revolution. "The Soviets have no population crisis," the paper noted, "but then they have also provided the working masses with a situation making it possible for them to live and develop as humans."[41]

The Swedish National Socialist party blasted the new Social Democratic interest in the population question as a bluff. There was no difference between capitalism and Marxism, the newspaper charged. Only the National Socialists, who "battled for the future," could implement an economic, cultural and political program to "guarantee our people's future existence."[42]

On the spiritual front, the Church of Sweden registered a strong protest against the Myrdal line. In a widely reported January debate with Gunnar Myrdal, church social secretary Tord Ström rejected the argument that the cause of the birth decline was economic. Rather, he said, modern man's horizons were bound to a short, earthly existence, resulting in excessive rationality, pessimism, and anguish. The nativity crisis, he continued, was essentially a moral question: "Only a religion with an eternal perspective gives life value and meaning, conquers pessimism, sets the rational mind in its proper sphere, and gives so great a will to live that people also want to propagate life."[43]

The Myrdals' most persistent Lutheran critic was theology professor Arvid Runestam. He debated Gunnar Myrdal at several public forums, including a May 1935 church meeting in Stockholm, before 1,150 delegates from Sweden's congregations. Organizers of the seminar hoped it would stimulate hundreds of study circles on the population issue within the parishes. Runestam argued that because of their enthusiasm for collectivized child care and unfeltered sexual acts, the Myrdals had missed the underlying cause of the birth decline: a "rationalism" that blinded people to the promise of eternal life and the optimism of the Gospel. However, in a revealing admission, the theologian went on to give guarded praise to the book, agreeing that social reforms were necessary to remove the worst socioeconomic pressures on families. Indeed, he warned the church that the time for neutrality in social questions was over. If the church did not actively support social reforms to help resolve the population crisis, it was as good as "dead."[44]

Alva Myrdal, meanwhile, carried the population question to businesswomen's chapters, women's collectives, and Social Democratic women's clubs. A joint January address by the Myrdals before Stockholm's Working Women's Club generated extensive press coverage, being reported in over two dozen Swedish and Finnish newspapers. Economist Karin Koch gave *Kris i befolkningsfrågan* a highly favorable front-page review in the journal of the National Union of Housewives' Associations.[45] The women's monthly *Morgonbris* also ran a special issue in September 1935 on "the new family," "the new woman," and the population question.[46]

Other books on the population issue soon filled the stores, including Tord Ström's *Life Is Now at Question (Nu gäller det livet!)*, Emil Sommarin's *The Population Question and Agriculture (Befolkningsfrågan och jordbruket)*, and Folke Borg's *A Disappearing People (Ett utdöende folk)*. In March, Bonniers issued its paperback edition of *Kris i befolkningsfrågan*, to heavy sales.

Radio also proved an effective medium for promotion. On January 27, Gunnar Myrdal made his first radio address about population in which he offered a briefing on the issue for "youth study circles."[47] On 9 April, the Swedish Radio Service performed "a major technological feat" by linking participants in four cities—Lund, Uppsala, Stockholm, and Göteborg—in a debate on the population question. Chaired by Prof. Sven Tunberg, the discussants included Gunnar Myrdal, Sven Wicksell, George Andrén, Gustav Åkerman, Arvid Runestam, Nils von Hofsten, and Axel Höjer. One commentator termed the result "Sweden's greatest radio debate."[48]

Myrdal gave the opening presentation, concentrating on the moral question. It was incorrect, he charged, to separate morality from the necessity of social reform: "morals cannot be isolated from the question of social organization of the nation's families and of individual human lives."[49] Drawing heavy applause "from all four auditoriums," Myrdal urged the adoption of a new social policy that would raise the living standard of Sweden's families.

Other speakers followed, all of them affirming the need for a "positive population policy." Andrén emphasized the danger of an "invasion" of Sweden by peoples growing more quickly. Biologist Nils von

Hofsten agreed with the Myrdals that no catastrophic racial degeneracy would result from a shrinking population: "[o]ur people still have a racial-biologically solid core, of which the predominant part is of good material." However, in a numerically regressive situation, "asocial and undesirable elements" could grow in relative size. Since negative race hygiene such as sterilization could produce only limited effect, positive eugenics encouraging births among the "better elements" of society was more critical. Wicksell suggested that Sweden might choose to settle for a somewhat lower fertility than the Myrdals sought, such as sixteen births per one thousand people, which would be more attainable.[50]

With growing public interest in the population question, the Swedish Radio Service decided in the summer of 1935 to use this topic for its popular annual "study course" (October 1935 to April 1936). In September, the service issued a study handbook organized and edited by Gunnar Myrdal. Entitled *Acta och facta i befolkningsfrågan*, it included selected documents prepared by the Social Housing Investigation, relevant parliamentary documents, family-oriented statistics on housing, nutrition, unemployment, and consumption patterns, and discussions of working women, maternal assistance, abortion, and sterilization.[51] Composed of weekly "study letters" written in consultation with Gunnar Myrdal and broadcast lectures and debates, the series opened on 7 October with a talk by Myrdal. Later speakers included Sven Wicksell and Alva Myrdal.[52]

The study course was soon embroiled in political controversy. Communists and left socialists charged that the Myrdals' involvement in its preparation proved that the Radio Service was a "bourgeois dominated" monopoly.[53] Liberal and Conservative party leaders, for their part, questioned the propriety of allowing Gunnar Myrdal to plan the course, charging that he was using the opportunity to push his own "Myrdal propaganda."[54] The Swedish nazis labeled the radio service's study booklet "Professor Myrdal's Small Catechism."[55]

The subject soon obsessed the Swedish people. The large Swedish Cooperative Movement *(Kooperativa Förbundet)* issued a guide for study circles on the population question. The course's six sessions dealt with Myrdal-inspired themes and quoted extensively from *Kris i befolkningsfrågan*.[56] A multiparty youth conference on the population and sexual questions, held in December and attended by two hundred recognized "leaders," was built on the Myrdal formulation.[57] The

Myrdalproblem was even taken up by Swedish film makers. Ingrid Bergman and Lars Hansson starred in a 1935 motion picture, *Valborgsmassafton*, that dealt with a woman's unwillingness to have children.[58]

With this flood of media attention, the Myrdal name and the population issue became virtually synonymous. *Kris i befolkningsfrågan* became simply "the Myrdals' book" (*Myrdalska boken*).[59] The population question was relabeled "The Myrdal Question" (*Myrdalsfrågan*).[60] The existence of a *Myrdalsproblem* in other lands became a standard question by reporters to ask of visiting foreign officials.[61] Housing projects designed for large families were labeled "Myrdal houses," a lounging sofa as a "Myrdal sofa," and "to copulate" became "to Myrdal."[62] As the debate spread, the Myrdals received a flood of letters from parents of large families, either expressing enthusiasm for the program or asking for more direct forms of monetary assistance.[63] There were also many anonymous letters from conservatives fuming over the Myrdals' assault on the family and from labor union members and the unemployed, who criticized the Myrdals for asking poor families to have more children.[64]

Newspaper satirists had a field day. When the central statistical bureau released figures in mid-1935 showing that the birthrate had risen slightly in 1934, for the first time in fifteen years, one paper asked the "impossible" question: "[h]as the Myrdal propaganda had effect?"[65] A poem read:

> For myriads of fat spawn,
> The Myrdals plea.
> Rationalism thrives.
> To secure their upbringing
> Alva seeks a state nursery
> Filled with happy merriment.
> Many children, more children,
> Plea certain scholars,
> With firm jaws.
> This is our rejuvenation mill,
> Others conclude.
> Easy words! Too easy.[66]

In a cartoon entitled "Future Hope," Alva and Gunnar Myrdal were shown joyously reading the birth announcement section of a newspaper dated exactly nine months after his April radio debate on the population question.[67] Several months later, the same paper ran a picture of a new German statue showing a mother surrounded by many children. It was captioned "for Mrs. Myrdal."[68]

Some of the identification became more vicious. Left socialist writers continued to see a link between the Myrdals and Mussolini.[69] With only two children at that time, a figure below their own "minimum standards," the Myrdals received frequent slurs and attacks. Fully aware of the problem, the Myrdals worked at resolving it, with Alva suffering several miscarriages. The situation was only rectified with the birth of their third child, Kaj, in 1936.[70] By that year, the term *Myrdaleri* had come to signify virtually anything dealing with fertility, more children, or larger families, usually with a negative connotation.[71]

Even these scattered examples give an incomplete image of the effect that *Kris i befolkningsfrågan* had on public opinion. "A bombshell has dropped down," one newspaper said.[72] "Not for a long time has a book stirred up such a discussion in the Swedish press as the Myrdals' *Kris i befolkningsfrågan*," added another.[73] "The population question has with surprising quickness moved into the center of the ideological-political debate," commented a third. "The Myrdals' book has set the senses [of the nation] surging."[74] On the opening day of the 1935 Riksdag, Stockholms' liberal daily *Dagens nyheter* ran an unusually bold headline printed in red and black ink: "The Disappearance of Children: A Self-Evident Manifestation of Irresponsibility So Long As Youth Are Unemployed."[75] The paper termed population the most burning issue facing the new session.

Stimulated to action by the Myrdals' book, the Riksdag gave the population question early attention.[76] In January 1935, the Conservative, Liberal, Agrarian, and National Group parties introduced motions that revealed a surprising consensus.

Introduced by J. B. Johansson of Frederickslund, the Conservative party motion, or bill, urged the establishment of a Royal Commission to investigate the scope and nature of the population crisis and to make policy recommendations to the Riksdag.[77] Population, it declared, had replaced unemployment as the most pressing problem facing Sweden: "The population question is, in the literal sense, a question of the continued existence of the Swedish people." While Sweden's Christian traditions ensured that none were allowed to suffer from want, age, or disease, "the same Swedish people fail to provide for their own regeneration."

Such an intricate problem, the motion warned, had to be approached from a firm base in Christian morals, "where Sweden's true culture resides." The population question, like the earlier immigration and unemployment questions, could be used as a pretext for implementing unrelated reforms. Nevertheless, in a pregnant break with prior tax-oriented policy, the motion guardedly affirmed the need for a positive population policy: "The possibility that direct policy measures can affect developments in the population question is without doubt very limited. However, this understanding ought not hinder us from carefully testing new ideas of this kind." The motion continued: "The Conservative Party's national and social ideals oblige it to cooperate in such a policy without thereby giving up the principle that individual responsibility constitutes our greatest social asset."[78]

Reaching into the party's past, the Conservative motion did lay great stress on taxation. Referring to the party's 1931 plan to provide tax relief for families, it called for the better treatment of young married couples through income splitting in a joint return and an increased tax deduction for children. The motion emphasized that tax relief should be directed toward the middle class, where reproduction was more socially desirable. It also affirmed the need to increase maternity assistance, assist young couples financially in the early years of their marriages, provide extra assistance to young couples in the months preceding and following childbirth, and give special support to widows with children.

Turning to housing, the motion acknowledged some need for the construction of urban dwellings, but placed greater faith in the "single family house" and the "garden city" or suburb system. The measure endorsed subsidized loans and savings programs for young couples planning to build their own homes and expanded programs for single home construction in rural areas. The conservatives also called for rural colonization programs that would reverse the flight of the young to cities and also have an impact on fertility.

Above all, the motion said, the personal attitudes of Swedes toward this problem "must be changed." This required a renewal of "our nation's spiritual-religious" view of life. Artfully avoiding the question of women working outside the home, the Conservative motion affirmed the necessity of "all girls of school age receiving a basic education in housework," including the value-oriented study of personal, sexual, and social hygiene.

The Liberal party introduced a similar motion.[79] Calling the population issue "a question of life" for the nation, the Liberal motion affirmed the Myrdal argument that "the economic sacrifices associated with raising children need to be more equally distributed than is now the case. If the extra burden on a family's income which a child makes could be reduced, one of the most important factors contributing to family limitation would be eliminated." The motion endorsed a systematic investigation into the population question that would focus on the causes of the nativity decline and the development of new policies relevant to the future.

The small, nazi-tinged National Group introduced a motion that, somewhat unexpectedly, affirmed the economic cause of the population crisis, called for a new law protecting pregnant women from dismissal by their employers, and stressed the need for a reasoned investigation into the fertility crisis. More predictably, the motion stressed that this governmental investigation should give special attention to measures that could lead to "the creation of improved population stocks and better race hygiene." Drawing on the new program under way in Germany, the motion also suggested the establishment of "marriage loans" for young couples, which could be forgiven at the rate of 25 percent for each child born into the family.[80]

The parliamentary Social Democrats, for their part, remained cautious and submitted no motion. The government leadership was fully aware of growing Riksdag ferment over the population question. Prime Minister Hansson, in an early 1935 personal note on the Riksdag's priorities, wrote that the population question was "now the Riksdag's expressed 'wish.'" He listed maternity assistance, marriage loans, and the free school lunch as its components.[81] Gustav Möller cited "child-rich families" as the highest Riksdag priority for 1935.[82] Yet the government's January list of legislative priorities noted only that the population situation would need consideration in the future, devoting most space to minor issues such as health training in the schools.

The 17 January 1935 opening debate in the second chamber was the first of two major legislative debates on the population issue. Conservative leader Arvid Lindman, in a scathing attack on the "socialist direction" of the government's public works plans and its inadequate planning for national defense, concluded that both questions ran much deeper. What good were social reforms and defense expenditures if the people they sought to help and defend were dying out? He termed the population question "the Swedish people's great life question"; it's solution would determine their freedom and future.[83]

Responding for the government, Prime Minister Hansson agreed that the population problem was indeed the most serious question facing Sweden. He expressed pleasure that the Conservatives were showing so much interest in the problem and, for the first time, offering something more than moralistic preaching. The population question's solution would demand a great common undertaking. Indeed, the problem might not have become so serious if the bourgeois parties had shown some earlier interest in the heavy burdens carried by poor families. Hansson concluded: " . . . if we seek a solution to our serious population problem, so must we accept as a natural starting point that the problem's solution depends on the socio-economic relationships that we can offer to current and future generations, measures through which we can build a more secure existence."[84]

Left socialist Karl Kilbom attacked Hansson's position with arguments similar to those he later turned against the Myrdals. He noted with amusement the Conservative and Social Democratic "unity" on the population question and asked Lindman and Hansson whether their "empty phrases" on raising fertility really meant they were ready for the truly radical reforms that would allow couples again to set children in the world.[85]

In several January interviews, Gunnar Myrdal emphasized how the population debate had shifted: "It no longer is about whether something should be done, nor hardly more in principle what should be done, but rather and properly only how much—in which direction and in what form."[86] But he too questioned whether the bourgeois parties were clear about the kind of reforms that were needed. "The population question cannot be solved in a liberal-capitalist society," he stated. "The program must be in the last analysis: a new society imbued with social solidarity, where the whole nation in the broadest manner takes on general responsibility for those children who shall be the next generation. As the first step towards this new social reality, it will be necessary to destroy the narrow individualism which now poisons our nation's whole life and truly threatens its existence."[86] Nothing less than the elimination of bourgeois Sweden would do.[87]

On 8 April the Riksdag's Budget Committee, in an unusual display of interparty consensus, unanimously recommended the adoption of the bourgeois motions to establish an investigative commission on the population question. The committee's report represented a patchwork of the Conservative, National Group, Agrarian, and Liberal party motions on the population question, bonded to extensive quotes from *Kris i befolkningsfrågan*. While full of "conservative" language on moral responsibility and Christian values, the report's use of quotations made explicit the "radical" nature of social policy remedies.[88]

The Riksdag debated the Budget Committee report on April 10, with the "more lively" discussion occurring in the Second Chamber. The motion drew relatively little criticism from the political right. Carl Forssell in the first chamber expressed some concern over shifting responsibility for child support from parents to the state. Noting that those concerned with declining nativity seemed most interested in preserving the "Swedishness" of the country, he questioned whether selected immigration into Sweden from neighboring peoples might not be a better short-term solution. In the second chamber, Lindman welcomed the multiparty initiative as absolutely critical, yet worried about the costs that certain measures might necessitate. He recommended a close monitoring of state expenditures in the family policy area. Agrarian party member Carl-Axel Reuterskiöld offered a sour note, stating that little could be done to reverse the population decline. Nations in the past had tried to stimulate fertility, but had failed. The birth decline was a tragic, irreversible trend of the time.

Left socialists Ture Nerman in the First Chamber and Albin Ström in the Second were more vocal in their protest. They criticized the "bourgeois breeding or stud" viewpoint that dominated the report. Curiously citing the Myrdals' book, they called for radical social changes to shape a decent national home that "our children have a right to demand." While not advocating rejection of the population investigation, they protested any population increase dictated by military and expansionist considerations, and they criticized the report for not giving praise to the earlier work of Knut Wicksell and Hinke Bergegren in spreading birth control.

Conrad Jonsson of Eskilstuna and Ivan Pauli, Social Democratic members of the Budget Committee, replied by pointing to the unusual interest in social reforms shown by the bourgeois motions. Jonsson stated that he was less concerned with the "ideological" direction of the report than with the policy proposals that a population commission might produce: let the bourgeois parties have their rhetoric, so long as the substance remained socialist. The investigatory commission, they said, would work to build the "people's home," the working class's highest domestic priority.[89]

The Riksdag formally approved the committee report, so creating the new panel. On 17 May, Social Minister Möller issued his directive to the 1935 Royal Population Commission. In content and tone it too reflected the determining influence of *Kris i befolkningsfrågan*.

Möller opened with a brief discussion of the population question's background. He emphasized the growing preponderance of the aged that current fertility levels portended. "No people with unimpared energy and will," he stated, "can face the now demonstrated trends in our land and fail to take energetic measures to change the situation." He called for initiatives aimed at promoting more and earlier marriages and an increase in fertility. "Through a prudently planned education campaign," he continued, "we must reawaken within all circles a sense of responsibility for our nation's future and existence."[90] The central goal should be policies to reduce the differential costs that children imposed on families. Turning to specifics, Möller suggested that the commission consider tax relief keyed to marriage and family size, more choices for the care of children with employed mothers, marriage loans, better cash allowances for pregnant women, free school supplies and school meals, comprehensive health care for children, better employment opportunities for youth, cooperation with the Social Housing Commission in its study of family housing needs, and family-oriented urban planning.

Möller asked that the commission's work proceed quickly to achieve practical results. He urged that its recommendations be ready for consideration by the 1936 Riksdag. With this understood, he formally announced that the government had empowered him to appoint a population commission of no more than nine people, to select one of its members as chairman, to recommend a secretary for the commission, and to refer to the commission any matters that might arise that related to its work.[91]

The social minister's surprisingly strong embrace of the population issue throws into dramatic relief the impact of *Kris i befolkningsfrågan*. In early November 1934, "population policy" as a concept was still anathema to most Social Democratic politicians. By May 1935, even the cautious Möller could embrace pronatalism as a socially and politically acceptable goal.[92]

In this sense, *Kris i befolkningsfrågan* was the necessary cause behind the creation of the 1935 Population Commission. In a popular sense, the book "created" the Swedish population question; it set the terms for the explosive newspaper, radio, and political debate, and it sufficiently unsettled a Social Democratic party hitherto bonded to neo-Malthusianism to give the commission its birth.

Notes

1. Gustav Cassel, "Vårt folks livsfråga," *Svenska Dagbladet* (Stockholm), 25 November 1934.
2. Gustav Cassel, "Samhällsintresset i befolkningsfrågan," *Svenska Dagbladet* (Stockholm), 27 November 1934.
3. Gustav Cassel, "Arbete och välstånd," *Svendka Dagbladet* (Stockholm), 28 November 1934.
4. Gustav Cassel, "Liv eller död," *Svenska Dagbladet* (Stockholm), 30 November 1934. This series of essays was reprinted as *Liv eller död* (Stockholm: Albert Bonniers Förlag, 1935).
5. The Myrdal-Cassel exhange actually included two additional articles. Alva and Gunnar Myrdal, in "Avfölkning eller samhällsreform," *Svenska Dagbladet* (Stockholm), 6 December 1934, noted the similarities between their position and Cassel's. They remarked that Cassel had presented the same historical perspective, admitted the need for society to do more for children, and accepted the multidisciplinary nature of the population question. They were particularly pleased with Cassel's comments concerning working women. This was the first time, the Myrdals noted, that a prominent bourgeois economist had "shown clear colors" in the question and, if their book had played any part in this single conversion, "we shall consider our pains properly repaid."

   But they also issued rejoinders to Cassel, who in other areas of the population question stood "empty handed," content only to "repeat old sorceries." He had avoided in his commentary the great number of families at a low living standard. Cassel's faith that a rising national income was the key to a higher birthrate, they added, was wishful thinking; income redistribution remained necessary. They charged Cassel with using the term *kommunistiska* as a scare word. While admitting that costs would be high, the Myrdals believed that Sweden had no choice. The alternative was depopulation.

   Cassel's response to the Myrdals ("Svår till Myrdals," *Svenska Dagbladet* [Stockholm], 9 December 1934) dealt almost exclusively with their exploitation of the population issue to justify the radical reconstruction of Swedish society. He again took the Myrdals to task for avoiding the questions of economic expansion and capital generation. With the social program they had proposed, he concluded, "poverty [would] become so oppressive and so general, that no place could be found for the first class child care of which the Myrdals so prettily dream." He also could not understand their displeasure with the "communist" label. Programs of state control over production and consumption were clearly such.

6. The articles: Ebba and Eli Heckscher, "Befolkningsfrågan som murbräcka," *Dagens Nyheter* (Stockholm), 5 December 1934; Ebba and Eli F. Heckscher, "Familjen i stöpsleven," *Dagens Nyheter* (Stockholm), 7 December 1934; Alva Myrdal, "Folkets framtid och familjernas," *Dagens Nyheter* (Stockholm), 12 December 1934; and Ebba and Eli F. Heckscher, "Folkets framtid och familjens," *Dagens Nyheter* (Stockholm), 14 December 1934. The letters, all found in GMAL, include: Alva to Ebba and Eli, 11 December 1934; Ebba to Alva, 12 December 1934; Alva to Ebba and Eli, 12 December 1934; Eli to Alva, 13 December 1934; Alva to Ebba and Eli, 14 December 1934; Gunnar to Ebba and Eli, 14 December 1934; Eli to Gunnar, 18 December 1934; Ebba to Alva, 18 December 1934; Alva to Ebba, 19 December 1934; Gunnar to Eli, 19 December 1934; Eli to Gunnar, 23 December 1934; Ebba to Alva, 25 December 1934; Gunnar to Eli, 26 December 1934; and Eli to Gunnar, 27 December 1934.

7. Eli Heckscher to Alva Myrdal, 13 December 1934, GMAL.

8. Ebba Heckscher to Alva Myrdal, 18 December 1934, GMAL.

9. Alva Myrdal, "Folkets framtid och familjernas."

10. Gunnar Myrdal to Eli Heckscher, 14 December 1934, GMAL.

11. Alva Myrdal to Ebba and Eli Heckscher, 14 December 1934, GMAL.

12. Alva Myrdal to Ebba Heckscher, 18 December 1934, GMAL.

13. Gunnar Myrdal to Eli Heckscher, 18 December 1934, GMAL.

14. See Gunnar Myrdal to Gösta Bagge, 13 April 1935, GMAL.

15. Margit Cassel-Wohlin, "Skall vårt folk leva?," *Hertha*, January 1935.

16. See *Göteborg Minareten*, 9 March 1935.

17. Interview with Gunnar Myrdal, Stockholm, 26 July 1976.

18. Herbert Tingsten, "Befolkningsfrågan och vår sociala politik," *Stockholms Tidningen—Stockholms Dagblad*, 6 December 1934.

19. Gunnar Mrydal confirms the importance of the Johansson reviews, in G. Myrdal, "Bostadssociala preludier," (reprint from *Bostadspolitik och samhällsplanering: Hyllningsskrift till Alf Johansson* (Stockholm: n.p., 1968), p. 12.

20. Alf Johansson, "Kris i befolkningsfrågan—I," *Social—Demokraten* (Stockholm), 13 December 1934.

21. Alf Johansson, "Kris i befolkningsfrågan—II: Levnadsstandard och befolkningsutveckling," *Social—Demokraten* (Stockholm), 18 December 1934.

22. Richard Sterner, "Om en positiv befolkningspolitik," *Fackföreningsrörelsen*, 21 December 1934, p. 686.

124   The Swedish Experiment in Family Politics

23. See also Richard Sterner, "Trångboddheten i städerna," *Stockholms Tid-ningen—Stockholms Dagblad*, 6 February 1935.
24. Sven Wicksell, "Mycket av fäderneärvda tradition måste offras om vårt folk skall leva," *Arbetet*, 19 December 1934.
25. Halvar Khennet, "Befolkningsfrågan—ett förslag," *Tiden* 27 (April 1935): 199–202. See also Tor Jerneman, "Samhällets dilemma," *Social-Demokraten* (Stockholm), 11 March 1935.
26. For examples of the former see reports in *Svenska Morgonbladet* (Stockholm), 8 May 1935; and *Folkets Dagblad Politiken*, 20 February 1935. For examples of the latter see reports on Alva's speeches in *Yrkeskvin-norsklubbs klubbnytt*, February 1935, pp. 15–17; address in Norrköping, text found in AMA 7.104.2; newspaper reports in *Norrköping Tid-ningen*, 13 April 1935; and Östergöttlands Folkblad (Norrköping), 13 April 1935; and speech before the Nordiska Kvinnokonferensen on "Hur kunna vi ekonomiskt stödja hemman," reported in *Social-Demokraten* (Stockholm), 8 August 1935. Notes for the numerous speeches Alva Myrdal gave on the population question in the 1935–38 period are found in the AMA collection.
27. Reports in *Stockholms Tidningen—Stockholms Dagblad*, 15 February 1935, and *Social-Demokraten* (Stockholm), 15 February 1935.
28. Reports in *Östergöttlands Dagblad*, 2 May 1935 and, *Norrköpings Tid-ningen*, 2 May 1935.
29. From *Dala Demokraten* (Falun), 17 October 1935.
30. See *Dagens Nyheter* (Stockholm), 18 January 1935.
31. "Problemet på modet," *Norrländska Social Demokraten* (Boden) 29 January 1935.
32. Fredrik Ström, "Ökad allmän hjälp åt mödrar och barn," *Social—Demo-kraten* (Stockholm), 19 February 1935.
33. Evert Kuhn, "Befolkningsfrågan från socialistisk synpunkt," *Verdandis-ten*, May–June 1935, pp. 4 and 8.
34. Tage Erlander, *1940–1949* (Stockholm: Tidens Förlag, 1973), p. 182.
35. Present at the meeting were Per Albin Hansson, Gustav Moller, Rickard Sandler, Ernst Wigforss Fritiof Ekman, Z. Hoglund, Edv. Johnson, Ivar Vennerstrom, Albert Forslund, Helmer Molander, Bernhard Erikson, Elof Lindberg, Harold Åkerberg, O. W. Lovgren, Olivia Nordgren, Per Edv. Sköld, Mauritz Västberg, Erik Fast, Nils Andersson, Olav Anders-son, C. J. Johanson, Olof Olsson, Ruben Wagnsson, and Hemming Sten.
36. "Protokoll fört vid årsmöte med Socialdemokratiska partistyrelsen sön-dagen den 28 April 1935," in Per Albin Hansson Collection, Arbetar-rörelsens Arkiv (hereafter PAH), vol. 6.
37. "Protokoll fört vid årsmöte med Socialdemokratiska partistyrelsen sön-dagen den 28 April 1935."
38. Ibid.
39. From "Protokoll fört vid partistyrelsens sammanträde tisdagen den 29 October 1935 i Landsorganizations plenisal, Upplandsgatan 1, Stock-holm," Socialdemokratiska Arbetarsparti Arkiv (hereafter SAP)—Rulle

5, A:I:A: 17–19, *Partistyrelsens protokoll*, 1935.

40. From "Nationalistisk födelsepropaganda," *Arbetaren*, 21 February 1935.

41. "Kvacksalvare i befolkningsfrågan," *Stormklockan*, 9 March 1935.

42. From "Trots Myrdalarna önska socialdemokraterna fortsatt nativitetspaus!" *Den Svenska Nationalsocialisten*, 9 February 1935. On the development of naziism in Sweden see Eric Wärenstam, *Fascismen och nazismen i Sverige* (Stockholm: Almqvist and Wiksell, 1970).

43. "Vidräkning med borgerlig," *Social Demokraten* (Stockholm), 24 January 1935. On the church response see also "Diskussion om befolkningsfrågan," *Vår lösen*, March 1935, pp. 49–51; "Befolkningsfrågan ett moraliskt spörsmål," *Norrlands Landsbygd*, 1 February 1935; and "Befolkningsfrågan—samling i princip," *Nationell Tidning*, 2–8 February 1935.

44. See Arvid Runestam, "Befolkningsfrågan ur kristen synpunkt," *Svenska Dagbladet* (Stockholm), 24 February 1935. The speeches at the Stockholm church meeting were reprinted as Karl Arvid Edin, Rut Grubb, Gunnar Myrdal, and Arvid Runestam, *Vårt folks framtid* (Stockholm: C. E. Fritzes Bokförlag, 1935), pp. 3–4, 35, 54, and 60–62.

45. Karin Koch, "Kris i befolkningsfrågan," *Husmodersförbundets Medlemsblad*, February 1935.

46. See "Den nya familjen, den nya samhället," *Morgonbris*, September 1935.

47. Reprinted as Gunnar Myrdal, *Befolkningsproblemet i Sverge* (Stockholm: Arbetarnas Bildningsförbunds Centralbyrå, 1935).

48. "Sveriges största radiodebatt," *Morgontidningen* (Gothenburg), 10 April 1935.

49. From "Drivut fattigvården ur vår socialpolitik!" *Social—Demokraten* (Stockholm), 10 April 1935.

50. The text of the debate was reprinted as *Debatt i befolkningsfrågan* (Stockholm: Aktiebolaget Radiotjänst, 1935).

51. Radiotjänst, *Acta och facta i befolkningsfrågan* (Stockholm: Aktiebolaget Radiotjänst, 1935).

52. Radiotjänst, *Prospekt för radiotjänst kurs i befolkningsfrågan, 1935–36* (Stockholm: Aktiebolaget radiotjänst, 1935); and Svenska Radiotjänst, *Studiebrev Nrs. 1–11 i serien "befolkningsfrågan"* (Stockholm: Aktiebolaget Radiotjänst, 1935–1936).

53. See "Politik i radio," *Ny Tid* (Gothenburg), 4 November 1935; and Myrdals–propaganda i radio startar," *Folkets Dagblad Politiken*, 8 October 1935.

54. See "Befolkningsfrågan i radion," *Östgöta Correspondenten* (Linköping), 9 October 1935; and "Myrdalspropaganda i radio?," *Sunt Förnuft*, October 1935.

55. "Prof. Myrdals littakatekes utkommen!" *Den Svenska Nationalsocialisten*, 12 October 1935.

56. Kooperativa Förbudet, *Befolknings- och familjefrågor: handledning för*

de kooperative gruppernas och gillenas diskussioner (Stockholm: Koopertiva Förbundets Bokförlag, 1935), particularly p. 32.

57. See "Bättre villkor för familjerna om det blir fler barn," *Morgonbladet*, 13 December 1935.

58. See "Myrdalsproblem tas upp i ny svensk film," *Morgontidningen* (Gothenburg), 11 June 1935.

59. Bertil von Friesen, "Uppgörelse med Myrdals," *Frissinad Ungdom*, March 1935, pp. 9–10.

60. See "Riksdagsfrågorna," *Östgöta Correspondenten* (Linköping), 10 April 1935; and "'Myrdalfrågan' och brödet åt de studerade," *Göteborgs Posten*, 15 November 1935.

61. See, for instance, interview with Haraldur Gudmundson, Iceland's minister of foreign, ecclesiastical, and trade affairs, in "Myrdalsproblem finns ej för islänningar," *Stockholms Tidningen—Stockholms Dagblad*, 21 July 1935.

62. See D. V. Glass, "Population Policies in Scandinavia," *Eugenics Review* 30 (July 1938): 89–100.

63. Examples include Harry Gustafsson to Gunnar Myrdal, 23 March 1935, and Gustaf Karlsson to Gunnar Myrdal, 2 February 1935, GMAL.

64. See "1930-och 1940-talen Anonyma Brevsamling," GMAL.

65. See "Hr Myrdals propaganda resulterar?" *Smålands Folkblad* (Jönköping), 14 June 1935.

66. "Myrdal i namnversen," *Dagens Nyheter* (Stockholm), 13 November 1935.

67. "Framtidshoppet," *Stockholms Tidningen—Stockholms Dagblad*, 17 April 1935.

68. "För fru Myrdal," *Stockholms Tidningen—Stockholms Dagblad*, 25 June 1935. Also "Lunch prat alá Myrdal," *Svensk Damtidning*, 23 February 1935, and "Hundarna hinder för folkökningen," *Dagens Nyheter* (Stockholm), 23 February 1935.

69. See Gunnar D. Kumlien, "Mussolini som Myrdals föregångare," *Nationell Tidningen*, 15 February 1936.

70. Egon Glesinger, "Gunnar Myrdal," mimeographed biography presented to Gunnar Myrdal on his fiftieth birthday, 6 December 1948, p. 6; interview with Alva Myrdal, 7 July 1977.

71. See "Myrdaleri," *Länstidningen* (Södertälje), 19 November 1936; and "Myrdaleri i Skåne," *Aftonbladet* (Stockholm), 10 September 1936.

72. "Uppror bland nationalekonomerna," *Frihet*, 15 December 1934.

73. "Kris i befolkningsfrågan," *Krisianstads Läns Demokraten*, 7 January 1935.

74. "Befolkningsfrågan," *Folket Eskilstuna*, 18 January 1935.

75. "BARNMINSKNING: självklar yttring av ansvarskänsla så länge ungdomen är arbetslös," *Dagens Nyheter* (Stockholm), 10 January 1935.

76. In the 1930s, the Swedish Riksdag consisted of two chambers exercising equal parliamentary authority. The Second Chamber had 230 members, elected by proportional representation from electoral districts. The First

Chamber, also known as the Senate, consisted of 150 members chosen by local country councils, with the intention that experience in local government should be brought to bear on the central government. Members of the First Chamber need not be resident in the county that selected them.

Elections were normally held in September, with the new Riksdag assembling in January. In the interim, the government would prepare a budget, propose legislation, and plan for the opening debate *(Remissdebatten)*. Both government and private bills and motions would be referred to the standing committees, which in time reported back to the Riksdag for final decision. All measures required approval by both chambers.

The Riksdag had eight standing committees, jointly filled by an equal number of delegates from each chamber. Members were chosen to represent the proportional strength of the parties. The powerful Budget Committee *(Statsutskottet)* counted twenty-four members. The other committees were: Constitution, Revenue, Banking, Agriculture, Foreign Policy, and two for general legislation. Most of the Riksdag's work was done in committee, the chambers meeting in plenary session only twice a week. Government ministers had no direct access to the committees, except for foreign policy.

77. For the official text of the motion in the First Chamber see Första Kammaren, *Bihang till Riksdagens protokoll 1935*, nos. 1–3 (reprint); in the Second Chamber see Andra Kammaren, *Bihang till Riksdagens protokoll 1935*, 4 Saml., nos. 1–4 (reprint).

78. Ibid., p. 4.

79. Motion no. 230 in the First Chamber, by Elof B. Andersson; motion no. 475 in the Second Chamber, by Gustaf Andersson (from Rasjön). Reprinted in Radiotjänst, *Acta och facta i befolkningsfrågan*, p. 15.

80. Ibid., p. 15.

81. Handwritten note by Per Albin Hansson, from early 1935, in PAH, vol. 6 ("Handlingen Från tiden som Statsminister, 24.9.1932–19.6.1936.")

82. Handwritten note by Gustav Möller on *Huvudfrågorna* for the 1935 Riksdag, in Gustav Möller Archive, Arbetarrörelsens Arkiv (thereafter GMÖA), vol. 2. This observation from: Ann Katrin Hatje, *Befolkningsfrågan och välfärden: Debatten on familjepolitik och nativitet sökning under 1930-och 1940-talen* (Stockholm: Allmänna Förlaget, 1974), 22 to 23.

83. *Riksdagens protokoll: Andra kammaren* 4, no. 4 (17 January 1935), p. 7.

84. Ibid., pp. 7–8.

85. Ibid., p. 31.

86. Gunnar Myrdal, "Myrdals ha ordet."

87. *Svenska Morgonbladet* (Stockholm), 24 January 1935.

88. "Statsutskottets Utlåtande Nr. 71," in *Bihang till Riksdagens protokoll 1935*, pp. 2–4, 10. Newspapers noted the significance of the unanimous vote. In a major editorial, *Aftonbladet* commented that "the old anti-nationalistic phrase concerning cannon-fodder has lost its power, and

people have begun to realize that the population stock's decline also involves poverty and less work. . . . For the first time in many years a question has emerged where one nation can together affirm life as a good." In "Befolkningsfrågan till utredning." *Aftonbladet* (Stockholm), 8 April 1935.

89. See *Riksdagens protokoll: Första kammaren 1935* 24 (10 April 1935), pp. 74–80; and *Riksdagens protokoll: Andra kammaren 1935* 26 (10 April 1935), pp. 95–104.

90. "Befolkningskommissionens direktiv," in Radiotjänst, *Acta och facta i befolkningsfrågan*, p. 29.

91. Ibid., pp. 31–34.

92. Tage Erlander saw Möller's reaction to the population commission as grounded in both principle and political expediency. See Erlander, *1940–1949* (Stockholm: Tiden Förlag, 1973), pp. 182–83.

5

An Exercise in Ideological Control

The use of special investigative commissions was quickly becoming a tradition of Swedish democracy. The practice was to study a given issue utilizing the services of commission members, paid staff, and supplemental experts. These panels prepared formal reports, including proposed legislative changes, that were distributed widely. Unlike counterpart congressional or presidential commissions in the United States, the work and recommendations of the Swedish bodies were always taken seriously by the Riksdag. This seems, at least in the beginning, to have been a reaction by the Riksdag members to the tradition-bound bureaucracy inherited from the old kingdom.[1]

By the 1930s, the commission system also coopted and provided tangible employment for Sweden's younger academicians. This close linkage of the social sciences and the political system was probably unique to the Scandinavian countries in this period. As Alva Myrdal later noted, it also served a larger purpose: "Politics has . . . been brought under the control of logic and technical knowledge and so has been forced to become . . . constructive social engineering."[2]

On 22 May, the government announced the new members of the Royal Population Commission. Nils Wohlin, a leader of the Agrarian party in the First Chamber, received appointment as chairman. Other members included Andrea Andreen-Svedberg, a medical doctor active in the women's movement; Prof. Nils von Hofsten, a specialist in biology, genetics, and eugenics; Karl Magnusson i Skövde, a gardener by trade and Conservative party member of the Second Chamber; Johan A. L. Persson i Tidaholm, a matchstick worker and Social Democratic member of the Second Chamber; statistician Sven D. Wicksell; Disa Västberg, a homemaker and leader of the Social Democratic women's movement; journalist A. L. E. Österström, a Liberal party member in the Second Chamber; and Gunnar Myrdal.[3] Two aspects of this list—the exclusion of Alva Myrdal and the appointment of Wohlin as chairman—deserve more attention.

Concerning the former, Gunnar Myrdal later recalled that when Finance Minister Wigforss approached him concerning service on the commission, he suggested that Alva be selected instead, citing her greater interest and competence in the practical aspects of the problem. Wigforss, however, was adamant that the Social Democrats "have a male, not a female, leading representative" on the panel. It appears that the Social Democratic leadership simply distrusted the party's feminist wing.[4]

Concerning the latter, the Agrarian party served at the time as the coalition partner of the Social Democrats. Given the socialists' shaky commitment to pronatalism, and with Myrdal considered too young and inexperienced for the chairmanship, the selection of someone from the rural party to chair the new commission seemed natural. Within these parameters, Nils Wohlin proved the logical choice.

Wohlin was a generation older than Myrdal and had played a prominent role in the population debates of the early twentieth century, serving as a member of the powerful Emigration Committee and as a forceful advocate of the anti–birth control laws. During the 1920s, Wohlin focused on the eugenic health of the Swedish people and protection of the Swedish family. His political activity at this time generally reflected a growing interest in the social dimensions of politics, and he expressed unusually strong concern over unemployment in the early 1930s.[5]

Wohlin's original approach to the population question derived from his commitment to rural Swedish values. Behind the rural traditionalism, though, lurked a conservative social engineer. Wohlin repeatedly stated in the 1930s that where past social reforms had been achieved by the working class alone, future social policies would need to be built on a national and conservative political base. This "progressive conservatism," Wohlin continued, did not automatically say yes to every reform project, but it did support reform measures that would improve the living standards of the poor. On population, this meant family-oriented tax cuts, a shifting of some infant- and child-support costs to the community, better family housing, protection of the rights of working mothers, and improved treatment of unmarried mothers.[6]

He was, in short, the perfect chairman for Myrdal: a public conservative persona covering an openness to state experimentation in policy.

The commission held its organization meetings in May and June 1935. On 24 May, the commission elected Gunnar Myrdal to serve as secretary until a staff member might be hired.[7] The following day, the commission appointed its first delegation, or subcommittee, to develop a special 1935 census on families. As with the others that followed, this subcommittee of experts and party representatives, with a member of the commission as chairman, had authority to investigate a specific aspect of the population question.

After a series of important strategy meetings held 4–6 June, the commission announced the first areas of concentration: maternal assistance, family taxation, marriage loans, and child care for working mothers. Gunnar Myrdal chaired the subcommittee on family taxation, supported by district judge K. Dahlberg and tax board member C. W. U. Kuylenstierna. The commission also named Myrdal to head a special subcommittee to develop the data needed for its work, supported by statisticians S. E. H. Bouvin and Richard Sterner.[8] Additional subcommittees formed in the last half of 1935 and again in 1936 and 1937. Gunnar Myrdal chaired several of these. Alva Myrdal's sole official appointment came in February 1937, when she joined the panel investigating the status of preschool children, chaired by Magnusson i Skövde.[9]

The commission reported administratively to Möller, and most of its work occurred on the subcommittee level. The commission met in plenary sessions only on an irregular basis, as dictated by the press of business, to receive reports from the subcommittees and communications from other government departments and to amend and approve reports for submission to the Riksdag.[10]

Between June 1935 and June 1938 Gunnar Myrdal devoted the greatest portion of his time to the commission's work. His lecturing responsibilities at the University of Stockholm were light. Those talks given were often based on the practical political problems confronting him in the commission. Myrdal's election to the First Chamber of the Riksdag in January 1936 (see chapter 6), basically meant an extension of his work on the commission.[11]

Without question, Myrdal was the most active commission member. He served on more subcommittees than any other member. After the commission formed a "steering committee" in August 1936 to handle regular business (Myrdal, Wohlin, and Andreen-Svedberg were its members), most meetings were attended only by Myrdal and Wohlin. Prior to March 1938, Myrdal was present at every commission and steering committee meeting, an unequaled attendance record.[12] Wohlin, with other interests, monitored certain—often quite minor— administrative matters, but left the general operation of the commission to Myrdal. Meanwhile, the Social Democratic leadership encouraged Myrdal to become the active ideological force on the panel.[13] Where other commission members often showed little interest in their task,[14] Myrdal recognized his opportunity and pursued his work with persistence and zeal.

He purposely developed a close relationship with Wohlin. Myrdal treated the elder politician as a paternal figure, frequently telling Wohlin that his appearance, method of writing, and mannerisms all reminded Myrdal of his own father. Indeed, the young socialist had a special talent for catering to the dignity of older persons like Wohlin and Cassel and for playing the role of the gifted son. While this was a shrewd political move, Myrdal also convinced himself that it was an honest relationship.[15]

Myrdal's energy and intellectual power dominated Wohlin and the commission's work. Despite numerous compromises on language, the commission reports and recommendations closely followed the "Myrdal line" through mid-1938. The commission adopted, intact, the Myrdals' emphasis on the differential cost of children as the relevant cause of the birth decline. Every contemporary commentator on the panel's work stressed Gunnar Myrdal's dominating influence.[16] He was the "dynamic force" in every debate, with the other members accepting or resisting his ideas, but never pursuing their own agenda. Only after the Myrdals' departure for the United States in September 1938 did Wohlin and the commission's "final report" spin out of Myrdal's control.[17]

Myrdal's influence came in part largely through his ability to set the terms of the debate at the subcommittee level. While records of the meetings of most subcommittees are incomplete, the careful notes and minutes kept by Richard Sterner for the Nutrition Subcommittee of 1937 offer an instructive example of Myrdal's exercise of intellectual control.

As subcommittee chairman, Myrdal delivered a "proper orientation" to the other members of the panel. At their first meeting, he told them that better family nutrition would involve establishing a school lunch program and control over agriculture production. The delegation, he continued, would also have to consider the health aspects of nutrition, the example of other nations, Sweden's existing nutrition standards, and a thorough analysis of Sweden's farm output. It was clear, Myrdal concluded, that this aspect of the population question required the development of a comprehensive "food policy."[18]

Myrdal's political adversaries only slowly came to realize how they had been taken in. Three months after the first meeting, Magnusson i Skövde charged that the ongoing investigation into food production was unnecessary, threatening to turn the subcommittee into "a mammoth commission." He advocated a narrow focus on how to provide cheaper school lunches. Myrdal replied that the delegation must deal with both the consumption and production sides of the question.[19]

Through a series of private conversations, Myrdal brought over a majority of the subcommittee to his view that all Swedish children ought to receive free lunches, without an income test, and through full central government financing.[20] Despite heated discussion at the 17 September 1937 session, the subcommittee's draft report on the nutrition question closely followed the Myrdal line.[21]

Myrdal's influence also extended to personal relationships with other commission members. Västberg and Andreen-Svedberg held views on women's equality that were compatible with the Myrdal programs and generally supported him on other questions. Myrdal easily brought fellow socialist Persson i Tidaholm to his side. Von Hofsten concentrated solely on biological and eugenic questions, while Wicksell stayed with statistics. Only Magnusson i Skövde, sometimes supported by Österström, consistently opposed Myrdal.

His control also extended to the commission's staff. At Myrdal's urging, the panel appointed statistician Richard Sterner—Myrdal's regular collaborator—to handle its statistical work. While under the nominal control of Wohlin, Sterner later reported that he took his real orders from Myrdal.[22] Torsten Gårdlund, appointed secretary to the commission at Myrdal's recommendation, was another Myrdal protégée.[23]

The research and policy recommendations of the Population Commission between 1935 and 1938 appeared in twenty reports. Sixteen of these were major documents. Perhaps more than any other evidence, they revealed the control of Gunnar Myrdal over the panel. Prior to his departure from the commission in August 1938, Myrdal claimed primary authorship of half of these reports, including "Report on the Sex Question," considered the Commission's major ideological work.[24]

The commission's first policy action was to hold a special family census. Behind the lofty statement of goals, the primary purpose of the census was to test the Edin hypothesis with a nationwide sample: did fertility actually rise with an increase in income for at least some elements of the population? The census plan was rapidly dispatched to the Riksdag, which approved it without dissent.[25]

The special enumeration occurred in two stages. The first was a general, normal counting of the nation's population. The second, novel phase was a detailed census of one-fifth of Sweden's population, or 1,300,000 persons. For this group, census takers personally visited each household and asked thirty clarifying questions. These included the time, places, and spacing of births, their legitimacy or illegitimacy, the number of children in successive marriages, and the duration of already broken marriages. The investigation also tabulated the educational level and employment status of married couples, whether the woman had given up work when married, the incidence of unemployment within the family, and reports on income and taxes. The census further contained a housing survey to meet the needs of the Social Housing Investigation, including questions about dwelling size and the number of bedrooms and a detailed survey of other rooms.[26]

The special census quickly became embroiled in controversy. Questions of this intimacy and detail had never before appeared in a Swedish census, and bourgeois columnists soon charged that the event represented a gross intrusion by the government into the private lives of families.[27]

The results of the census, compiled in 1936, generally supported the Edin thesis. It revealed that family size did rise according to income, at the highest economic levels, and throughout the country. This finding gave Myrdal all the license he needed to push his reform plan through the commission, scientifically validated: the redistribution of income and services in favor of young, fertile couples would raise fertility.[28]

The Population Commission's Ethics Subcommittee, chaired by Magnusson i Skövde, issued a formal statement in August 1935. As the first formal commission document, it was an early indication of the degree to which the Myrdal line would permeate the panel's work.

The report emphasized the changing sociology of the family. Industrialization and technical development, the subcommittee explained, were responsible for tearing apart the unity and purpose of the traditional family. Meanwhile, the "new family" had not yet found its proper form. This passage to a new era had brought a decline in the number of children per family. Under current social relationships, children meant an increased burden, a sinking living standard, and a special set of problems for employed mothers.

Sexuality was also changing. Echoing the Myrdals, the subcommittee affirmed that the use of birth control was "in line with our era's whole spirit" and widely practiced among all social classes and geographic regions. Accordingly, Swedish population policy had to be based on the principle of voluntary parenthood. While members of the subcommittee disagreed over the appropriateness of condoning premarital sex, all agreed that sex and marriage education in schools was a "psychological necessity," since a satisfying sex life was closely associated with the love, happiness, and harmony that bound a family together.

The birth decline was not a question of morals, the report continued. Rather, young couples delayed births or had smaller completed families due to their low incomes. Unemployment hit most sharply at the young, while economic realities forced women to work outside the home and avoid the creation of a family. Tax laws, meanwhile, penalized working couples.

In crafting responses, attention to family economics was central. Some members of the subcommittee suspected that the decline in family size was related to a selfish concern by parents for their own comfort and welfare. Others pointed to the concern of potential parents over bringing children into a world of hate, unemployment, and possible war. All agreed, though, that improper economic relationships were the primary cause of the fertility crisis. Government measures must be adopted to reduce the burden of children on parents by transferring the costs to society. Myrdal's intellectual triumph, in short, seemed complete.[29]

Further confirming the point, the commission made its first substantive policy recommendation in November 1935, proposing that married women working in civil service positions be given three-month "maternal leaves" for childbearing and, while on leave, continue to receive the largest portion of their regular salary. Through this measure, the commission stressed, the government would encourage births by allowing female civil servants to combine a family and career.

In December, the commission released a commentary on the housing question and the relationship of its own work to the Social Housing Investigation. Adopting Myrdal's argument, the commission affirmed that the most important housing measures were those targeted on large families. Even from a narrow housing policy perspective, this focus was natural, for large families constituted the largest percentage of households living in overcrowded tenements.

In line with Myrdal's 1933 work in Göteborg, the work of the housing investigation had shown that large families, in order to meet other expenses, often sought out cheaper, lower-quality housing than smaller families at the same income level. The commission emphasized another aspect of the housing panel's work: the finding that while some families with small children could not afford better housing, a much greater number were voluntarily overcrowded; their incomes should have allowed the rental of better housing. For mysterious reasons, these parents made irrational choices, decisions with negative social consequences. Thus society—through its vehicle, the state— should use its authority to deliver rational housing to the people.[30]

On 20 December, the commission issued its first major independent report, dealing with maternity care, reorganization of the midwife system, and preventive health care for mothers and children.[31] Citing the need for greater central financing and control, it affirmed that planned, accessible, free pre- and postnatal care would spare many lives, both maternal and infant, and prevent illness and poor health. Medical services must be offered to all mothers and infants, without charge, as an essential part of society's care for the next generation. To meet this goal, all local districts, with central funding, should organize maternal health centers. In larger cities, special maternal and infant health clinics should be established and staffed by obstetricians, gynecologists, and pediatricians. Rural districts should be serviced by maternal and infant health stations located in the existing medical officer's center. The report also detailed a massive reorganization of Sweden's midwife system, where the state would pay their full salaries and deliver their services free of charge.

At the same time, the commission released its recommendations for tax reform.[32] In a report authored by Myrdal and directly drawn from the pages of *Kris i befolkningsfrågan*, the commission stated that "[o]ne of the most important causes of lower fertility in Sweden seems to be the low frequency of marriage. A sharpening of the tax differential according to the number of children in the family would accordingly work to increase marital fertility."

To accomplish this, the commission proposed a sharp increase in the "family deduction" and a decrease in the "standard deduction" found in both the communal and national income taxes. The large number of singles and "child poor" couples in comparison to large families made it possible for the value of the new family benefit to exceed the penalty on the childless. The panel also recommended that the value of the "family deduction" increase in proportion to family size. For the third, fourth, and later children the deduction should be double the base figure. In addition, the age limit for a child's deductible status should rise from sixteen to eighteen years.

Alongside this shift in the tax burden, which had no net revenue effect, the commission recommended creation of a new "tax for family assistance": in essence, a bachelor's tax. This tax was specifically designed to raise new revenues to finance commission-developed family support programs. This tax surcharge would be 1 percent on taxable incomes of one thousand kronor for singles and two thousand kronor for married couples and rise on a progressive scale to 4 percent. Unmarried persons would pay the full tax. Married couples without children would have this tax reduced by one-third. The tax on married couples with one child would be reduced by two-thirds, while married couples with two or more children would pay no tax at all. Significantly, this tax reduction for children would apply to parents' income even after the children were grown and had left home. Adopted or deceased children, if they had lived to at least ten years of age, would also qualify. The commission estimated that this tax would deliver an additional 15 million kronor in revenue.[33]

These tax reforms were purely "horizontal" in character, involving the redistribution of income within, not between, income categories. The commission proposed no alteration of Sweden's existing progressive tax scale. Added together, the tax burden of families with two or more children would have been substantially reduced, the burden on the single person would have significantly increased, and the tax on the childless couple or the single-child family would have remained about the same.[34]

The commission released another major report on 1 January 1936, proposing a state-funded "marriage loan" system for young couples and a program to encourage savings by youth. A subcommittee chaired by Johann Persson and including Magnusson i Skövde, Gunnar Myrdal, and Sven Wicksell prepared the report. Myrdal claimed primary authorship.[35]

In calling for a marriage loan fund, the commission argued that the cost associated with setting up a household often proved to be an impediment to marriage, which depressed fertility. The program would provide young couples with immediate resources, funded through private banks, offering low-interest loans of up to one thousand three hundred kronor, to be repaid over the following two to six years. Myrdal's ideological victory lay in the rejection of direct grants, or a provision "forgiving" a certain percentage of the loan with the birth of each child, as seen in Germany and sought by Sweden's National Group. Indeed, the panel drew direct attention to the contrast between its plan and the schemes of the nazis.

A few days later, the commission issued its report on maternity benefits. In a bow to the authority of the Myrdal line, the Maternity Assistance Subcommittee emphasized in its presentation to the full commission how its recommendations adhered to one overriding principle: " . . . the fact that a family has a certain number of children should not, in and of itself, drive that family into becoming welfare recipients."[36]

In striking departure from past practices, the commission encouraged a universal system of maternal support, nationally funded, and focused exclusively on women. It recommended that a maternity bonus of one hundred kronor be granted to every woman, without regard to income or marital status. Rather than welfare, the maternity benefit should be seen as a right and an expression of public appreciation for motherhood. Existing programs that were locally funded and controlled retained the stigma of poor relief. A national system, in contrast, would be more rational and efficient. Where existing benefits to families were commonly paid to fathers as heads of households, this new benefit should go directly to mothers, married or unmarried. This recognition of motherhood would also increase the status of women within families. Additional assistance for needy mothers, of up to three hundred kronor, should also be available, particularly as a help to new mothers under stress who might otherwise turn to illegal abortion. The estimated cost for budget year 1937/38 would be 4.4 million kronor.[37]

In the latter half of 1936 and early 1937, the commission released its second and most controversial series of reports. They dealt with aspects of the "sex question": sterilization, contraception, sex education, and abortion. These extraordinary documents mark the first time in history that a government had so candidly and completely given policy direction on these sensitive subjects. Gunnar Myrdal was the principal author for three of the four documents.

The report on sterilization was the only one not authored by Myrdal. Nonetheless, it was well within the Myrdal line. The commission embraced a race-biological program rejecting the use of sterilization as a method of birth control. The panel concluded "that our land must follow the way in which the sterilization question has been dealt with by all of our Nordic neighbors, namely to . . . regulate even the right to sterilization of the mentally capable."[38] Healthy genetic material should not be squandered recklessly. Accordingly, voluntary sterilization of the mentally competent should be allowed only after approval by a central authority, in order to avoid hasty or unnecessary operations.

The commission also called for changes in the 1934 law governing sterilization of the mentally incompetent. With initiative for the operation now deemed "too widely scattered," the panel recommended that only public medical officers be given the right of initiative, with applications to be examined by the Board of Health. It also urged that medical students receive more intensive instruction in genetic science and in eugenical medical procedures.[39]

Gunnar Myrdal served as the principal author of the report on revision of paragraph 13, chapter 18, of the Swedish criminal code, or the "anti–birth control" laws. Predictably, the report declared that they should be abolished and contraceptives made available for display and sale from druggists and at small shops and kiosks. Only a simple application by the vendor to the Medical Board would be required.[40]

The commission described these reforms as based on honor and truth. Laws that contradicted the normal behavior and beliefs of people would, in the long run, undermine the moral fabric of the nation. The commission could not support, nor would the Swedish people any longer accept, the suppression of birth control. The simple fact was that the anti–birth control laws had proven totally ineffective and their goal of holding up fertility had clearly not been met. The panel said that these laws were also a cause of the high incidence of illegal abortion, as women turned to the latter as a substitute for birth control. A positive population policy for the future must be based on the voluntary parenthood principle. The existing laws were "shackles" on Sweden's feet.

The commission's core ideological treatise, *Report on the Sex Question*, appeared next. Gunnar Myrdal claimed almost exclusive authorship.[41] He chaired the subcommittee drafting it, joined by Andreen-Svedberg, provincial doctor Gustaf Ankarswärd, Dr. Alma Sundquist, Prof. Axel Westman, and medical professor Per Wetterdal. Torsten Gårdlund served as secretary.[42]

In securing unanimous commission approval for this revolutionary analysis, Myrdal called on every form of leverage available, political and personal. In October, for example, he met with commission chairman Wohlin, who had just read Myrdal's first draft. Wohlin "solemnly informed" his younger colleague that it would be impossible for him to support the document, given its detailed treatment of birth control and sex education. Myrdal replied that he already had a majority of the commission members in support of the report, as written. He challenged Wohlin to go ahead and write a minority report, in league with the hopelessly reactionary Magnusson i Skövde. Then all the "old aunts and old colonels" could nod and affirm that "Wohlin has said the right thing." Myrdal would be left "only with the youth, the women, and all thoughtful people" behind him.[43]

Wohlin, "with the politician's instinct," responded, "God, there isn't going to be a dissenting report!" and he used all his influence to push the document through the commission. He exerted particularly strong pressure on Magnusson i Skövde to close ranks and support Myrdal's draft. A notice sent to members in late October remarked that "a majority have stated themselves clearly for the report.... Even the Commission's chairman, Mr. Wohlin, stands quite positive towards the report's principal contents."[44]

Despite Wohlin's affirmation, the records of the Population Commission show a flurry of correspondence in October over the report's contents and a series of long, often heated plenary sessions. After the sexual subcommittee had finished its work, the report was referred to the Social-Ethical subcommittee, chaired by Magnusson i Skövde, which won a few minor concessions on language. The document also received its formal title here. The unanimous formal approval of the full commission followed, and the report was released on 1 January 1937.[45]

In many respects, the "sex report" represented an abridged, updated, reorganized, and more politically sensitive version of *Kris i befolkningsfrågan*.[46] It described the decline in fertility as the result of voluntary birth control: deliberate measures taken at coitus to prevent fertilization, supplemented by abortion. Sex life had been rationalized among the Swedish people. The commission reasoned that only a program combining social reform and full sexual enlightenment could restore a birthrate ensuring the Swedish people's survival.

Walking in the Myrdal line, the report emphasized that children were the direct cause of poverty. This inverse relationship between children and income was the result of a unique transition period, during which birth control knowledge spread according to the law of social gravitation. All authorities unanimously agreed that the current trend, if unchecked, represented a threat to Sweden's future existence.[47]

Happily, a new, rational order could be created that reconciled voluntary parenthood with the psychological balance of children, the desires of adults, and the needs of society. Using data compiled and analyzed by Alva Myrdal, the commission argued that doctors and other observers viewed childless and single-child families as unhappy. Even two-child families, the commission stated, were not psychologically satisfying unless the children were near the same age. Similarly, the solo child showed signs of social maladjustment, environmental psychopathy, emotional instability, introspection, and hyperactivity, when compared to children with brothers and sisters. Hence "scientific opinion" indicated that a family with three to five children spaced at about two-year intervals represented the most favorable family size. Amazingly, this was the very family size that would also deliver to the nation a stable population.[48]

At the same time, the commission affirmed that it was in society's best interest that as large a portion as possible of the adult population be married. It recognized serious social and psychological problems that came with late marriage and concluded that it was of utmost importance that Sweden work to reduce the average marriage age by several years.

To accomplish this, Sweden needed to ensure greater economic security for its young people. The out-of-pocket costs of their education, for instance, needed to be reduced. Promotion schedules should be adjusted to give youth permanent positions and better salaries at an earlier age. Early marriage would also depend on eliminating vestigial rules that brought a woman dismissal on her marriage.

Turning directly to birth control, the report emphasized that contraception should only be used to postpone childbearing to a better or more convenient time. It should not become a "bad habit" retained after the couple's financial situation had improved. With Magnusson i Skövde undoubtedly swallowing hard, the commission accepted the "Swedish custom" of cohabitation before marriage, so long as any resulting pregnancy led to marriage.[49]

Sweden's problem now lay in the fact that birth control had gone too far. The very intensity of its use threatened Sweden with a declining population. Delicately avoiding a direct form of racial nationalism, the commission simply asserted that a net immigration into Sweden was "unlikely" to occur. Any future population trend, it concluded, would depend on fertility and mortality alone.

Repeating arguments from *Kris i befolkningsfrågan*, the commission admitted that any population increase in the future would bring temporary decline in the average living standard. However, a population decline would lead to serious national deficiencies in those qualities associated with youth: courage, self-sacrifice, initiative, and creativity. A nation with a declining population could not expect to withstand pressures from overpopulated countries seeking additional land for settlement of excess people. These parameters, the commission concluded, provided the goal for Sweden's population policy: a stationary population attained by increasing fertility to the necessary level and holding mortality as low as possible. Sidestepping again a hot ideological question, the commission endorsed the Myrdals' own compromise and rejected any discussion of a population increase as "too far outside the bounds of probability."[50]

Turning to the actual act of contraception, the commission offered a host of opinions on sexual techniques. It soundly rejected abortion as a means of birth control and also urged prohibition of the importation and sale of dangerous contraceptive devices. Ejaculation outside the vagina, the commission cautioned, often failed in its purpose unless performed with perfect care. In addition, women had little control over its use. Most authorities, the commission stated, found the pessary to be the most nearly perfect contraceptive form in marriage, because unlike coitus interruptus, it allowed for the normal completion of intercourse.

The commission acknowledged that the widespread use of reliable contraceptive methods could lead in the short run to a further birthrate decline. Yet even with the unsatisfactory methods currently used, the reproduction of the nation could not be ensured. Existing anticontraceptive laws suppressed knowledge of birth control, particularly among the low-income young. Current extreme child limitation could be seen as one protest against this apparent class discrimination. Only if the display and sale of contraceptives was open and aboveboard could "a new foundation" be created among Sweden's young people for a positive orientation on the population problem.[51]

The commission added that sex education should form part of the larger effort to instill better hygienic and moral standards in the nation and to give everyone a more positive attitude toward the family. A major task for adult education, through Sweden's extensive "study circle" system, would be educating childless and one-child couples in their responsibility for the survival of the nation.

Turning to a sex and family life curriculum, the commission recommended that from grades three to six children be taught "in a plain and honest manner" how all living things, and humans in particular, come into the world. The commission endorsed sex education in the early elementary grades, including study of the human reproductive organs, spermatozoa and fertilization, pregnancy and the development of the fetus, childbirth, the child's dependency on the mother, heredity, sexual maturity, and the importance of cleanliness of the sex organs. These young children should also be told that contraception is naturally and normally practiced in marriage for hygienic, medical, and socioeconomic reasons. The psychological and demographic reasons arguing against extreme birth limitation should be presented. As youth neared marriage age, they then needed more detailed instruction. Schools should strive to instill in individuals knowledge and emotions necessary to a pleasurable family and community life. Education for parenthood should be based on recognition of the family as the most important form of mutual human existence. In a revealing final turn of the argument, the commission concluded that a proper adjustment to modern family life was partially dependent on the degree to which husbands participated in everyday housekeeping tasks, with important implications for the training of boys in homemaking skills.[52]

Among the seventeen appendices to the report were two authored by Alva Myrdal and two by Gunnar Myrdal. Alva's first contribution analyzed the psychological importance of family size, referred to above.[53] In her second contribution she focused on the social-psychological purpose and organization of parent education. Myrdal emphasized the role this program could play in developing a positive attitude toward parenthood, sexual hygiene, and fertility among younger couples. In every case she used American models for Sweden to emulate, including the recent White House Conference on Child Health and Protection, organized by Herbert Hoover, the Bureau of Home Economics, and Cornell University's Department of Home Economics. She cited "preparental education" programs found in many American schools as another example of Americans' "unanimous demand" that sex education "fit into its wider and natural connection as an education in family reponsibility." After tracing a "typical" course plan in family and sex education used by progressive American schools and the "folk movement" character of parent education studies among Americans, she noted the rapid growth of the National Congress of Parents and Teachers in the 1920s as an expression of the model American approach.[54]

Gunnar Myrdal's contributions were devoted, respectively, to a summary of methodology in the population policy area and statistical projections on future Swedish population developments. The former report again reflected Myrdal's ability to determine the outcome of the commission's work by setting out assumptions and modes of analysis that could produce no other real result.[55]

The commission released the final "sex report" on the abortion question in early 1937. Gunnar Myrdal served as its principal author.[56] Rejecting the conclusions of the 1933 Abortion Commission, the commission followed Myrdal's lead in crafting a compromise on this explosive issue. A letter from an unidentified commission member to Per Wetterdal reported finding a solution to the panel's abortion dilemma: "We have come upon an idea that could solve even this question in a manner which should remove the unnecessary opposition between two viewpoints: on the one side that we do not want to have 'social indications' [for abortion] written into law, and on the other side that we do not want to punish a woman who stands in need. As quickly as we are able to put something on paper, we shall send you an outline."[57]

As it took form, this compromise rejected the claim that a woman should have complete freedom to decide the life or death of the fetus she carried. Stating that abortion should be kept under social controls, the commission recommended its legalization only on ethical, eugenic, and "mixed" medical-social grounds. Ethical grounds would be present where pregnancy had resulted from rape or incestuous intercourse, where the expectant woman was under fifteen years of age at the time of conception, or where she had been incapable of consent due to feeblemindedness, insanity, or gross ignorance of her own liberty of action. Eugenic indications for abortion would enter where a strong chance existed that one of the parents would transmit to the offspring hereditary bodily disease, insanity, or imbecility.

The heart of the compromise lay in the category of "mixed medical-social grounds," defined as cases of exhausted mothers, whose existing burden of children was often accompanied by poor health. The commission insisted that abortion not be allowed in purely "social" cases. While acknowledging that ten thousand illegal abortions occurred each year in Sweden for reasons such as economic hardship, the commission argued that attitudes toward unwed mothers should be changed and economic assistance be given to the mother and child. The commission also rejected abortion when justified on the grounds of "dishonor" or in cases of adultery.[58]

The commission's work in 1937 focused on two subjects: free school meals and financial support for large families. The reports on these subjects provoked the greatest controversy among the commission members. Reflecting some breakdown in Gunnar Myrdal's control over events, sustained conservative opposition emerged for the first time and several of the reports included formal minority dissents.[59]

The nutrition question report, released in early 1938, was largely the work of Gunnar Myrdal.[60] Picking up on his familiar theme, the report noted the ways in which the population question and the Swedish agrarian crisis were related: the continued migration of people from rural to urban areas, the low living standards of the rural population, the fertility differential found between rural and urban areas, and the need to provide all children with adequate, nutritious diets. Utilizing statistical data, the commission concluded that the supply of calories available to individuals in families varied inversely according to family size: children in larger families tended to have poorer diets, with underconsumption of iron and vitamins particularly noticeable. Some four thousand children under one year old died annually in Sweden, many due to low nutrition standards. Children in large families again suffered the most. Parental ignorance, more than poverty per se, was often the culprit, as many families displayed irrational choices.

Emphasizing another central Myrdal theme, the nutrition study cited the close linkage of "quantitative" and "qualitative" policy approaches. "Qualitative" measures that would improve children's economic situation, increase maternal and child health standards, and reduce infant mortality rates also had "quantitative" purposes. They worked to reduce the strong motivation for extreme child limitation. The redistribution of costs and income between families with varying amounts of children also strengthened the economic base for family formation and aided the population in developing a more positive attitude toward family life. The cost accruing to the nation, the report declared, must be seen as a common investment in Sweden's future.[61]

Commission-designed programs to help both the troubled Swedish agrarian sector and large families included the free distribution of health foods, vitamins, and medicine to pregnant and nursing women, infants, and children of preschool age. The commission also proposed that a school lunch program be set up on communal initiative, with priority given to those districts with the highest unemployment rate and the greatest number of large families. When extended to the whole population over the next decade, the program would cost 34 million kronor annually, with the central government's share being 25 million. The commission viewed planned universal coverage as an essential prop for the government's fertility goals and as a way of removing class distinctions from children's access to food.

To absorb the remainder of Sweden's agrarian surplus, the commission proposed a two-tiered pricing system. It recommended that food coupons go to families with three or more children and to all single-parent or "handicapped" families with one or two children, without income restriction, for the purchase of designated foodstuffs at reduced prices.[62]

Magnusson i Skövde, the report's principal critic, challenged the planned universal nature of the school lunch program as a dangerous socialist invention. He also termed the proposed programs unrealistic, overly costly, and even detrimental to large families, as they trans-formed recipients into dependents of the state.[63]

In its report on a children's clothing allowance, the commission tackled directly the problem of cash benefits. Using the central Myrdal formulation, it termed "in kind" social assistance superior to "in cash" for three reasons: (1) children in many large families lived in an environment where cash assistance would probably not be used to their advantage; (2) in-kind social policies built on a rational basis allowed for education in proper consumption habits; and (3) in-kind social as-sistance always proved cheaper and more efficient. Despite these ad-vantages, the commission still reluctantly recommended an "in cash" allowance for clothes. Government services were simply not far enough advanced and the existing tax base was insufficient to enable early establishment of the superior "in kind" approach.

The commission called for the creation of a yearly clothing allow-ance for children under sixteen years. For those between ages seven and sixteen and having parents at an income level below 900–1350 kronor (depending on cost-of-living region), each child would receive 65 kronor annually. For children under seven, the commission set an annual allowance of forty-five kronor. The cost for the estimated 470,000 children eligible would be 22 million kronor a year. While a means test was involved, the commission emphasized that the pro-posed allowance should not be considered welfare. The justification for the allowance was to increase the health and security of children without imposing any new financial burden on families.[64]

Magnusson again authored a dissent. Going beyond specifics, he returned to a long dormant conservative argument and charged that the proposed reforms were only of secondary importance. The basic prob-lem behind the birth crisis remained spiritual, a problem of "will," which the commission had not yet properly addressed.[65]

In a report on working women, the Population Commission built on the efforts of Alva Myrdal in the Women's Work Committee (see be-low). It recommended a law, backed by financial penalties, protecting a woman's right to her job, even though she might marry, become pregnant, or bear children. This would include the right to take leave from work, for up to twelve weeks, for childbirth. Legal protection should extend, the commission believed, to both married and unmar-ried women. Using the Myrdal understanding of social causality, the commission argued that "economic circumstances" and "existing social relationships" were such that many young married women had to work outside the home. Reform was needed to make it easier for women to combine marriage, motherhood, and employment. The commission also recommended that a woman, whether married or unmarried, who had left her job to bear a child should receive a special maternity allowance of four kronor per day for a twelve-week period. This would be financed jointly by the state and by the employees' sickness benefit societies (*sjukkassa*), with the state paying three-quarters and the society one-quarter of the total.[66]

The commission's report on preschools, day care, and summer camps, in which Alva Myrdal participated, raised the ideological stakes, affirming the value of preschool education for *all* Swedish children. Early childhood learning centers, it said, should not be seen as standing in opposition to the home as a rival form of child rearing, but rather as a complement to the home. They were said to serve a dual population policy purpose, helping qualitatively by shaping a better young generation and quantitatively by easing the child-rearing burden on mothers—particularly working mothers—and so making the possibility of more children evident.

At Myrdal's urging, the commission proposed a state subsidy for schools meeting state-established quality standards. Subsidy should cover half the expense for activities during a four-hour period, with a maximum of fifty *ore* per child and day. The commission called on the institutions and local governments to carry any additional costs on their own social budgets. Meanwhile, a state subsidy would go to expand the number and quality of the child-care centers. The commission also extended the offer of financial support to after-school and recreational centers.[67]

Magnusson i Skövde issued his sharpest dissent on the day-care report. The commission proposal, he charged, pushed Sweden closer to collective child care and so served to undermine the home and family. Day-care centers, he continued, could not serve the child as a surrogate for mother, father, brothers, and sisters. Magnusson argued that society's first interest had to be the strengthening of home and family, particularly the mother at home, and not subsidizing their planned dissolution.[68]

A report on the depopulation of rural areas, requested by the Conservative party in May 1937, finally appeared in June 1938. Gunnar Myrdal, while not a member of the delegation,[69] again played a strong indirect role. His earlier work in the area, including a 1938 book on agricultural problems, the rural policy aspects of his nutrition report, and his widely publicized 3 March address before the National Economic Union on the problems of agriculture, set the broad policy parameters within which the delegation's work fell.[70] Distinguishing the "flight from agriculture" from the "flight from the countryside," the report found the principal cause of the former to be low wages and of the latter lack of opportunities. It urged the transfer of small and handwork industry into rural areas.[71]

The Social-Ethical Subcommittee summarized its work in a final report, giving particular attention to family health. Using Myrdal-inspired language, it affirmed birth control as "a social fact." Citing the need to remove impediments to marriage, the report emphasized how unemployment hit youth particularly hard. It accepted the "social fact" of mothers working outside the home and emphasized that the birth decline resulted largely from the pressures of children on family's living standards. The report's minor, but significant, deviation from the Myrdal line came on the question of policy goal, stating that Sweden sought "at least" a stable population. This subtle departure from the Myrdals' absolute refusal even to consider a growing population would reemerge full blown in the commission's final report.[72]

Other Myrdal-dominated state panels added their weight to the Population Commission's work. The three reports issued by the Social Housing Investigation in 1935–37 forcefully reflected the Myrdal line.

The housing panel viewed children as both the cause of overcrowding and the ones who most suffered from its effects. The committee concluded that housing must be seen as a social, rather than a private, matter. In line with the Myrdal preference for planned, semicollectivized dwellings, urban low- and high-rises received the primary emphasis. The committee's recommended rent subsidization scheme was directed at families with at least three children. The state would compensate such families with 30 percent of their rent if they had three children, 40 percent if they had four, and 50 percent if they had five or more.

The committee also urged new state loans to local governments or to nonprofit corporations for the construction of special multiunit family housing. These dwellings should be "child-oriented" and designed to house adequately families with three or more children under sixteen years of age. Reflecting the growing nonrecognition of marriage, the husband and wife need not be legally married.[73]

A second report embraced expanded state inspection of housing, while a third focused on single-family dwellings.[74] While endorsing a financing package, for qualified families, combining low-interest state loans with a 10 percent share provided by the householder, the overall thrust of the panel remained oriented toward more collective units.

The Women's Work Committee, with Alva Myrdal as secretary, also labored in a parallel direction. The panel originated in 1935 at the instigation of Conservative party members who complained about the "double wage" earned by families with working wives. Their nervously articulated strategy was to plot a return to a "one paycheck" family, with the mother at home. However, Finance Minister Wigforss used his power of appointment to turn the ideological tables. Kerstin Hasselgren, a liberal feminist Riksdag member, became chairman, and she and Wigforss brought Myrdal in to head the committee staff. From this position, the latter had her most significant direct influence on the course of population policy formulation.[75]

Where the Population Commission restricted itself largely to proposals for the protection of the right of working women to marriage and childbirth, the Women's Work Committee took the broad view. It dismissed, at the outset, the possibility of restoring the traditional family, this strategy being seen as naive and impossible. Working women and working mothers were "social facts." The panel focused on such detailed questions as the need to de-gender the clergy in the Lutheran state church, the prospects for women working as prison guards or in male mental hospitals, and the existing prohibition of women teaching gymnastics to male pupils at the secondary level.

Its major report, issued in 1938, affirmed the central goal of altering social and employment arrangements to allow women to combine marriage and motherhood with their desire to work. Curtly dismissing the homemaker as an artifact, it rejected proposals to provide women with a bonus or marriage loan if they would leave work to enter marriage. Social reorganization should aim at allowing working mothers additional time with their children through more opportunities for part-time work and temporary positions. Symbolically, the committee also asserted the right of married women to retain their own surname.[76]

With the exception of her work on this committee and her appendices for the "sex report," Alva Myrdal found herself largely outside the direct policy loop. Yet her work on related projects helped craft the basis for subsequent political and social change in Sweden.

In her numerous speeches from the period, Myrdal's quiet loathing of pronatalism as a policy goal frequently surfaced through her emphasis on the "qualitative" side of the question, to the virtual exclusion of the quantitative. "The population question is not a question of breeding children," she stated in an April 1936 speech at Sundsvall. "It is to shape a healthier life." The two guiding principles in the population question, she wrote in *Morgonbris*, were interest in social reforms for the benefit of children and the principle of birth control, making no mention of Sweden's low birthrate.[77]

Alva Myrdal also emphasized the socialist imperative. Noting that babies born into poor families died more frequently than those born to the rich, she argued that economic equality was of critical importance for the nation's survival. Poverty among individual families, she added, justified basic changes in the organization of industry through creation of a new social spirit.[78] In a small book defending "in kind" over "in cash" benefits, she made short shrift of the "family wage" as a stimulant to nativity. She also dismissed income equalization through cash payments as a liberal ideological concept based on the discredited principles of private responsibility and individual freedom. "An income equalization in services forms, in contrast, a framework for a socialist development of society towards a more planned—and therefore less costly and more effective and adequate—meeting of needs."[79]

Alva Myrdal's collateral work had the most influence in the field of early childhood education. Her popular 1935 book, *City Children*, declared that "[s]mall children do not belong in the city. At least not as cities are now constituted."[80] The proper rearing of city children, she concluded, could only occur in day-care centers, giving children the social health and learning opportunities not available in small urban families. Educational programs in day-care centers should be based on a creative compromise between individualism and cooperation: "Society-oriented upbringing and attention to individual needs, fixed social habits, and free activity—the principles of good day care education can be summarized in these seeming paradoxes." Myrdal offered detailed descriptions of the facilities, program, and personnel found in "a well run" day-care center, all rich in sublimated ideological content. Toys, for example, should be freely chosen, large, durable, versatile, and interchangeable between boys and girls. She denied that day-care centers were unhealthy spreaders of disease. Properly constructed and operated centers, Myrdal said, housed relatively small groups of children and featured fresh air, regular naps, visits from doctors, and health isolation rooms.

A year later, Myrdal published a widely publicized book on "proper playthings" for children. She argued for safe and psychologically acceptable toys that downplayed violence, encouraged cooperation, and proved interchangeable between the sexes.[81]

Her major achievement in this field came in October 1936, with the opening of the new Social Pedagogical Institute (*Socialpedagogiska seminariet*) on Kungsholmen in Stockholm. With Alva Myrdal as founding director and Sven Wallander as architect, the institute was the first Swedish training center for day-care workers. Financially supported by the HSB housing cooperative, the facility included study- and classrooms and an extensive library. Students studied the use of gender-neutral, nonviolent toys and theoretical courses in psychology, pedagogy, socialization, child welfare, health, rhythm and sound, and crafts. Institute graduates quickly began to flow into the nation's day-care centers and kindergartens and reshaped the direction of Swedish preschool education.[82]

"Parent education" remained another Myrdal passion. These local study circles, she thought, were the right tools for refashioning older generations into citizens of a progressive society. While she frequently cited "American models," her core purpose was to achieve the socialist goal of "a social order in continuous change."[83]

Driving these interests, of course, was Myrdal's intense commitment to feminism. Enlightened Swedes, she said, now recognized outside employment as the means of creating in women "a secure feeling of belonging to society," giving them in turn "the courage to bear children." Despite this seeming progress, though, Sweden remained a male-dominated society: "There are in these very days utterances to be read and heard of such prejudice about the superiority of men and the super rights of men that they would match the Apostolic Fathers." Indeed, she said that women found themselves in a difficult transition period, one that began hundreds of years before and would extend hundreds of years in the future, in which they struggled "to achieve a harmony between motherhood and work."[84]

This overriding struggle, she confessed, required the dismantling of the home and the home economy. Indeed, sentimentality toward "the home" was the greatest hindrance to the rationalization of household tasks, where housework would be socialized.[85] Since inherited attitudes, children's toys, and countless other customs trained little girls for inferiority, schools should teach housework to boys.[86] Myrdal also cast "home daughters"—unmarried, nonworking, middle-aged women who remained in their parents' homes—as a special target. She termed their position in modern life indefensible. "It must be our goal," she stated, "to eliminate them."[87] In other articles, she urged that women enter the Swedish priesthood and seek election as provincial governors.[88]

Myrdal served in various leadership posts for Sweden's Working Women's Clubs and helped to plan the June 1937 meeting of the International Working Women in Stockholm. The group elected her vice chairwoman at its August 1938 meeting in Budapest. The same year, she coauthored with four other women a book dissecting the "conservative myths" holding women in the home. The volume downplayed the "physical" and "intellectual" differences between men and women and advocated a sexual revolution to establish harmony between women's two roles: motherhood and productive work. She frequently urged the adoption of employment quotas designed to equalized job distribution and wage laws that delivered equal pay for work of comparable worth.[89]

Men, too, needed reshaping in line with her vision. Commenting on the "crisis of fatherhood," Alva Myrdal argued for a transformation in the "father role." Traditional "judicial" and "economic" functions should be shared with women, while men were retrained to play a greater part in daily life and activities of children.[90] The population theme rarely intruded on this ritual call for a gender-role revolution, achieved through state intervention.

In sum, the Myrdals won an amazing influence over the political and educational institutions of Sweden during the 1930s. The scope of their population formulation left conservatives off-balance and gave a fresh, popular power to the social reform line. Gunnar Myrdal's energy and creative use of social science data brought several major state investigatory panels under his control, as he translated the message of *Kris i befolkningsfrågan* into over one dozen governmental reports charting a radically different social future for Sweden. Alva Myrdal, working primarily at the nongovernmental level, quietly shed her public commitment to pronatalism and pursued her central goal of a post-bourgeois society based on gender equality and the socialization of child rearing.

Notes

1. See Nils Herlitz, "The Civil Service in Sweden," in L. D. White, *The Civil Service in the Modern State* (Chicago: University of Chicago Press, 1930); and Bjarne Braaton, *The New Sweden: A Vindication of Democracy* (London: Thomas Nelson and Sons, 1939), pp. 154–64. For Myrdal's comments on this process see Gunnar Myrdal to W. I. Thomas, 10 February 1931, GMAL. Original in English.
2. Alva Myrdal, *Nation and Family: The Swedish Experiment in Democratic Family and Population Policy* (New York: Harper and Brothers, 1941), p. 100. See also D. V. Glass, *Population Policies and Movements in Europe* (Oxford: Clarendon Press, 1940), pp. 317–19.
3. Report on the 1935 activities of the Population Commission in RA 542, vol. 2.
4. Interview with Alva and Gunnar Myrdal, Stockholm, 20 July 1976; interview with Gunnary Myrdal, 26 July 1976; and Erik Nyhlén, interview with Gunnar Myrdal (1973), GMA 96.2.1, pp. 16–17.

   This charge of a "superficial" commitment to the feminist movement by the Social Democrats was expressed elsewhere in the period. *Tidevarvet*, for example, editorialized that the party claimed that only with and through women could the workers' movement achieve success. But in truth, the article continued, this was no more true for the Social Democrats than for any other party. It went on to warn: "Hinder us not. We shall advance as quickly as we can." "Aktivisering av kvinnornna," *Tidevarvet* 17 (April 1935).
5. From Birger Hagård, *Nils Wohlin: Konservativ centerpolitiker* (Linköping: AB Sahlströms Bokhandel, 1976), pp. 344–83. This uncritical biography represents the only comprehensive work on Wohlin's long career in government. In Hagård's discussion of the 1935 Population Commission, Wohlin's leadership is stressed. He emphasizes the limited role of the Myrdals and the foot-dragging of the Social Democratic politicians. The program developed by the Population Commission, he concludes, can be largely credited to the "enlightened progressive conservatism" of Wohlin (see pp. 384–97).
6. Hagård, *Nils Wohlin*, pp. 384–88.

   As a personal footnote with certain policy implications, at the beginning of the Population Commission's work Wohlin was still married to Margit Cassel-Wohlin, daughter of Gustav Cassel and an author on family problems in her own right. This marriage broke up over the next two years. In 1937, Wohlin undertook his third marriage, this time to

Andrea Andreen-Svedberg, a comrade member of the Population Commission.

7. RA 542 (1935 års befolkningskommissionen), vol. 1. Myrdal took the minutes of subsequent plenary meetings until 12 August 1935, when Tosten Gårdland assumed this responsibility for several months, to be replaced again by Myrdal, Sterner, and others from time to time.

8. From a report on the commission's work in 1935 in RA 542, vol. 2; "Kommunike till T. T. om befolkningskommissionen," RA 542, vol. 2; and *Protokoll* for 4, 5, and 6 June 1935, RA 542, vol. 1.

9. See Nils Wohlin to Gustav Möller, 10 February 1937, Gustav Möller to the Population Commission, 19 February 1937, and Gustav Möller to Population Commission, 30 September 1937, in RA 542, vol. 5.

10. See RA 542, vol. 1; also letters from Nils Wohlin and M. D. Höglund to Population Commission, 27 January 1936, and 29 February 1936, in RA 542, vol. 3.

11. Interviews with Gunnar Myrdal, Stockholm, 26 July and 31 July 1976.

12. "Protokoll för arbetsutskottet," in RA 542, vol. 1.

13. Interview with Richard Sterner, Stockholm, 29 June 1977.

14. Ibid.

15. Ibid.

16. Åke Elmér, *Från fattigsverige till välfärdsstaten* (Stockholm: Bokförlaget Aldus Bonniers, 1963), p. 99; Tage Erlander, *1940–49* (Stockholm: Tidens Forlag, 1973), p. 183; *Social–Demokraten* (Stockholm), 20 November 1938; and interview with Richard Sterner, 29 June 1977.

17. On the Myrdal-Wohlin relationship see also: interview with Gunnar Myrdal, Stockholm, 26 July 1976; and Hagård, *Nils Wohlin*, p. 393.

18. From "Protokoll: Befolkningskommissionens delegation för näringsfrågan," 5 March 1937, in RA 542, vol. 1.

19. Ibid., for 4 June 1937.

20. See "Anteckningar från samtal mellan herr [sic] Tjällgren, Myrdal och Sterner tisdagen den Juni 1937," and "Några frågor angående skolmåltids organisationen m.m., beröende vid samtal mellan fru Andreen-Svedberg samt herr Myrdal och Wagnsson: [and fru Västberg], den 7/6 1937; enligt referat av Sterner," both found in RA 542, vol. 1.

21. See "Protokoll: Befolkningskommissionens delegation för näringsfrågan," 17 September 1937, RA 542, vol. 1.

22. *Protokoll* for 31 July 1935, RA 542, vol. 1; and interview with Richard Sterner, Stockholm, 29 June 1977.

23. Interview with Richard Sterner, Stockholm, 29 June 1977; letter from Gunnar Myrdal to Torsten Gårdlund, 3 May 1935, and Gårdlund to Myrdal, 25 May 1935, both in GMAL.

24. From notations found on the title pages of bound commission reports, deposited in GMA. Also: interview with Gunnar Myrdal, Stockholm, 26 July 1976.

The commission's reports were formally printed for distribution to members of the Riksdag, the Social Department staff, and other government officials. The total press runs varied. Two thousand copies of the "nutrition" report were printed, compared to one thousand five hundred copies of the report on preschools and one thousand copies of the report on rural depopulation. The "sex question" report attracted a commercial publisher; over twenty thousand copies appeared in various editions.

Letters: Gustav Möller to Statskontoret, 18 February 1938, RA 542, vol. 5; and Albert Förslund to Statskontoret, 18 June 1938, RA 542, vol. 5.

25. Memorial to the government, RA 542, vol. 2.

26. A collection of the materials used in the 1936 census is found in RA 1425 (1933 års bostadssociala atredningen), vol. F:1. See also Ernst Höjer, "Inför den stora folkräkningen," radio talk, GMA; and *Aftonbladet* (Stockholm), 19 December 1935.

27. See "nu kommer husbökarna—förklädda till 'folkräknare,'" *Lordagskvällen*, 25 January 1936; and "Myrdalarna villa veta huruvida avsiktlig barnbegränsning skett," *Folkets Dagblad Politiken*, 20 December 1935.

28. See Alva Myrdal, "The Swedish Approach to Population Policies: Balancing Quantitative and Qualitative Population Philosophies in Democracy," *Journal of Heredity* 30 (March 1939):113.

29. Reprinted in: "Arbetslösheten går ut över ungdomen, äktenskap hindras," *Husmodern*, 18 August 1935.

30. Memorandum from Nils Wohlin to Gustav Möller, 10 December 1935, RA 542, vol. 2, document no. 7. This policy orientation was reaffirmed in January 1938. See Nils Wohlin to the Government, 14 January 1938, RA 542, vol. 2, document no. 107. Summaries of the reports by the Social Housing Investigation are found later in this chapter.

31. SOU 1936:12, *Betänkande angående förlossningsvården och barnmorskeväsendet samt förebyggande mödra-och barnavård*, Befolkningskommissionen (Skockholm, 1936). particularly pp. 72–104. See also Alva Myrdal, *Nation and Family*, pp. 304–309 and 316–19.

32. SOU 1936:13, *Betänkande angående familjebeskattningen*, Befolkningskommission en (Stockholm, 1936).

33. SOU 1936:13, *Betänkande angående familjebeskattningen*, particularly pp. 7–12. See also: "Belkningskommissionens förslag till skattereform," *Sunt Förnuft*, February 1936, pp. 25–28.

34. See "Väl befogad och amper kritik av befolkningskommissionens 'nativitets-skattelagar,'" *Kalmar Tidning*, 12 February 1936; and "'Ungkarlskatten' orättuis och mindre sympatisk," *Kalmartidningen Barometer*, 12 February 1936.

Gunnar Myrdal, in a November 1936 address before the National Economic Union, presented an in-depth discussion of the tax question, including the need for equitable tax rates, incentives for capital formation, and relief for large families. He noted the particular danger of excessively high tax rates, which could crimp private investment. On family taxation he argued that an increase in the family deduction was

relatively cheap reform, given the small number of big families in Sweden. See Gunnar Myrdal, "Aktuella beskattningsproblem," *Nationalekonomiska föreningens förh*, 8 (1936): 89–105.
35. SOU 1936:14, *Betänkande angående dels planmässigt sparande och dels statliga bosättningslån*, Befolkningskommissionen (Stockholm, 1936); and notation from copy found in GMA collection.
36. From "Översikt av de förslag, som delegation för moderskapshjälp m.m. ärnar framlägga till befolkningskommissionen prövning," RA 542, vol. 9, pp. 6–7.
37. From SOU 1935:15, *Betänkande angående moderskapspenning och mödrahjälp*, Befolkningskommissionen (Stockholm, 1936), particularly pp. 14–26. See also a press release on the report found in RA 542, vol. 2; H. Rahm, "Befolkningskommissionens förslag angående moderskapspenning," *Svensk Sjukkassetidning*, February 1936; and Alva Myrdal, *Nation and Family*, pp. 322–23.
38. SOU 1936:46, *Betänkande angående sterilisering*, Befolkningskommissionen (Stockholm, 1936), p. 48.
39. SOU 1936:46, *Betänkande angående sterilizering*, particularly pp. 30–40, 47–50, and 74–76. See also the news release prepared by the commission on the report: "Befolkningskommissionen föreslår reglering av frivillig sterilisering," RA 542, vol. 2. Von Hofsten prepared an unpublished statistical supplement to this report in 1937; see Nils von Hofsten, "Steriliseringar i Sverige under andra halvåret 1936 och ar 1937," RA 542, vol. 5.
40. SOU 1936:51, *Yttrande angående revision av 18 kap. 13 and strafflagen m.m.*, Befolkningskommissionen (Stockholm, 1936), p. 51.
41. Notation on title page in the collection of commission reports found in GMA; interview with Gunnar Myrdal, Stockholm, 26 July 1976; and interview with Richard Sterner, Stockholm, 29 June 1977.
    Publication of *Sexualbetänkande* was an actual violation of the still existing anticontraceptive laws. From "Swedish Population Commission Issues Report Forbidden by Birth Control Law," *Science Service* (U.S. Department of Agriculture), 4 June, 1938, in AGMC.
42. *Protokoll*, for 28 May 1936, RA 542, vol. 1.
43. Interview with Gunnar Myrdal, Stockholm, 30 July 1976.
44. In a memorandum found in RA 542, vol. 3.
45. Interview with Gunnar Mydral, Stockholm, 30 July 1976; and Memorandum by Alva Myrdal, 30 September 1938, in AMA 12.102.
    For news reports on the release of *Betänkande i sexualfrågan* see "Bärgad familj hör ha 4 barn?" *Social–Demokraten* (Stockholm), 1 January 1937; and "Det rika och det fattiga Sverige," *Dagens Nyheter* (Stockholm), 24 January 1937.
    Several radical publications praised the report as marking the final victory of neo-Malthusianism in Sweden. See Gösta Rehn, "Sexual radikalismen segrar," *Clarté*, January 1937.
46. SOU 1936:59, *Betänkande i sexualfrågan*, Befolkningskommissionen

(Stockholm, 1937). The popular edited Swedish version of the report was printed as *Familj och moral*. This report was the only commission document translated into English. See Swedish Population Commission, *Report on the Sex Question*, trans. and ed. Virginia Clay Hamilton (Baltimore: Williams and Wilkins Company, 1940).

47. SOU 1936:59, *Betänkande i sexualfrågan*, pp. 15–29.
48. Ibid., pp 50–69.
49. Ibid., pp. 70–82.
50. Ibid., pp. 83–89.
51. Ibid., pp. 90–117.
52. Ibid., pp. 118–44.
53. Alva Myrdal, "Barnantalets familjepsykologiska betedelse," appendix 5 in SOU 1936:59, *Betänkande i sexualfrågan*, pp. 183–95.
54. Alva Myrdal, "Föräldrarfostrans socialpedagogiska uppgifter och organization," appendix 17 in SOU 1936:59, *Betänkande i sexualfrågan*, p. 442–52.
55. See Gunnar Myrdal, "Några metodiska anmärkningar rörande befolkningsfrågan innebörd och vetenskapliga behandling," appendix 1, pp. 144–58; and "Utsikterna i fråga om den framtida befolkningsutvecklingen i Sverige och de ekonomiska verkningarna av olika alternativt möjliga befolkningsutvecklingar," with Sven Wicksell, appendix 8, pp. 280–89, in SOU 1936:59, *Betänkande i sexualfrågan*.
56. Notation on title page of printed report in GMA. The commission report: SOU 1937:6, *Yttrande i abortfrågan*, Befolkningskommissionen (Stockholm, 1937). The report of the earlier Abortkommittee: SOU 1935:15, *Betänkande med förslag till lagstiftning om avbrytande av havandeskap* (Stockholm, 1935). Hatje gives extensive critical attention to the whole abortion debate; see *Befolkningsfrågan och välfärden: Debatten om familjepolitik och nativitetsöknig under 1930 och 1940-talen,* (Stockholm: Allmänna Förlaget, 1974), pp. 119–63, particularly pp. 121–33.
57. Unidentified commission member to delegation member Per Wetterdal, 3 October 1936, RA 542, vol. 3.
58. SOU 1937:6, *Yttrande i abortfrågan*, particularly pp. 22–33; news release on the report in RA 542, vol. 2.
59. See: Hagård, *Nils Wohlin*, p. 389, *Protokoll* for 23 October 1936, RA 542, vol. 1, p. 43; and Richard Sterner, "Barnens mat och kläder, I. Natura eller kontant i barnavårdspolitiken?" *SAP-Information*, No. 5 (1938): 70–73.
60. Notation on title page of report found in GMA; Gunnar Myrdal to Dorothy Swaine Thomas, 1 March 1938, GMAL: and Nils Wohlin to Gustav Möller, 30 January 1937, RA 542, vol. 2, document no. 84. The report: SOU 1938:6, *Betänkande i näringsfrågan*, Befolkningskommissionen (Stockholm, 1938).
61. SOU 1938:6, *Betänkande i näringsfrågan*, particularly pp. 9, 46.
62. SOU 1938:6, *Betänkande i näringsfrågan*, pp. 65–153.

Gunnar Myrdal's contemporaneous work, *Jordbrukspolitiken under omläggning* (Stockholm: Kooperativa Forbundets Bokforlag, 1938), discussed the problems of flight from rural areas, agrarian overproduction, marketing monopolies, rationalization of production costs, prices, and the international balance of trade and its relation to the agrarian sector. Proposed solutions involved the same systhesis between family, nutrition, and agrarian policy found in the nutrition report.

63. See "Protokoll, hållet vid befolkningskommissionens delegation för näringsfrågan," 4 June 1937, "Anteckningar från samtal mellan hr. Tjallgren, Myrdal och Sterner," 9 June 1937, "Protokoll hållet vid befolkningskommissionens delegations för utredning av näringsfrågan sammanträde," 17 September 1937, and K. Magnusson i Skövde, "Reservation" to *Betänkande i näringsfrågan*, attached to *Protokoll* for 31 January 1938, all in RA 542, vol. 1.

64. See SOU 1938:7, *Betänkande angående barnbeklädnadsbidrag*, Befolkningskommissionen (Stockholm, 1938), particularly pp. 68–71, 95–98, and 105–21.

65. The various drafts of Magnusson's reservations on the nutrition and clothing allowance reports are found in *Protokoll* for 31 January 1938, RA 542, vol. 1.

In a related action, the Population Commission gave its blessing in 1936 to a means-tested child allowance program proposed by the 1934 Committee on Child Allowances. The committee proposed that fairly generous child support payments be made for orphans and illegitimate children and for children of widows and invalids. See SOU 1936:6, *Utredningen med förslag rörande bidrag åt barn till änkor och vissa invalider samt föräldralösa barn* (Stockholm, 1936); and SOU 1936:47, *Utredningen med förslag rörande förskottering av underhållsbidrag till barn utom äktenskap m.m.* (Stockholm, 1936); *Protokoll* for 1 February 1936, RA 542, vol. 1; and Nils Wohlin to Gustav Möller, *Yttrande* (on child allowances), in RA 542, vol. 2.

66. SOU 1938:13, *Betänkande angående förvärvsarbetande kvinnors rättsliga ställning vid äktenskap och barnsbörd*, Befolkningskommissionen (Stockholm, 1938), pp. 19–28. See also the news release on the report found in RA 542, vol. 2.

Commission members Magnusson i Skövde and Österström, together with delegation member K. Wistrand, issued a dissent on this report over the issue of a paid allowance.

67. SOU 1938:20, *Betänkande angående barnkrubbor och sommarkolonier m.m.*, Befolkningskommissionen (Stockholm, 1938), particularly pp. 7–8, and 12–18.

68. See the draft of Magnusson i Skövde's dissent in *Protokoll* for 15 June 1938, RA 542, vol 1; and Karl Magnusson i Skövde, "Kollektiv barnafostran i stället för hemvård," *Medborgaren*, July 1938.

69. Johan Persson served as chairman, joined by Wicksell, Österström, and three outside oppointees. See *Protokoll* for 2 June 1937, RA 542, vol. 1.

70. See Gunnar Myrdal, *Jordrukspolitiken under omläggning* (Stockholm: Kooperativa Forbundets Bokforlag, 1938), and Gunnar Myrdal, "Jordbrukspolitikens svårigheter," *Nationalekonomiska foreningens forhandlingar* (1938): 57–57.

71. SOU 1938:15, *Betänkande angående landsbygdens avfolkning*, Befolkningskommissionen (Stockholm, 1938), particularly pp. 206–208.

   Other commission reports released in 1938 included a detailed analysis of the 1936 family census published as SOU 1938:24, *Betänkande med vissa demografiska utredningar*, Befolkningskommissionen (Stockholm, 1938). Commission projections for future Swedish population developments remained quite pessimistic; see pp. 131–65.

   Other related statistical summaries from the period include Carl-Erik Quensel, "Giftermålsintensiteten i Sverige under de sista årtiondena och dess framtida storlek," *Statsvetenskaplig tidskrift* 42, no. 2 (1939): 154–82; and a dissertation based on the special 1936 census: Johannes Sjöstrand, Den äktenskapliga fruktsamheten i Sverge (Stockholm: Isaac Marcus Boktryckeri, 1940), particularly tables 1, 2, and 3 and pp. 70–87.

   See also E. P. Hutchinson, "Education and Intramarital Fertility in Stockholm," *Milbank Memorial Fund Quarterly* 14 (July 1936): 285–301; and H. J. Hyrenius, "Reproduktionen inom de nordiska ländernas befolkningar," *Statsvetenskaplig tidskrift* 41, nos. 3–4 (1940): 331–40.

72. SOU 1938:19, *Yttrande med socialetiska sympuntter på befolkningsfrågan*, Befolkningskommissionen (Stockholm, 1938), particularly pp. 7–18 and 45–52.

   The commission work also included a small number of special tasks referred to it by the social minister, including a report on problems associated with the transportation of fruits and vegetables to Norrland and a never-finished investigation into "illegitimacy," See Nils Wohlin, "Till Chefen for Kungl. Kommunikationsdepartementet," 13 November 1936, RA 542, vol. 2, document no. 55.

73. SOU 1935:2, *Betäknande med förslag rörande lån och årliga bidrag av statsmedel för främjamde av bostatsförsörjning för mindre bemedlade barnrika familjer. Jämte därtill hörande utredningar*, Bostadssociala Utredningen (Stockholm, 1935), pp. 65–75

   See also Alf Johansson and Waldemar Svensson, *Swedish Housing Policy* (Stockholm: Victor Pettersons Bokindustriaktiebolaget, 1939); Statistiska Centralbyrån, *Allmänna bostadsräkningen år 1933 och darmed sammanhängande undersökningar* (Stockholm, 1936); and Alf Johansson, "Bostadsproblemet," *Hertha*, February 1935, pp. 35–37.

   On the relationship between functionalism and Bostadssociala Utredningen see "Markelius och hans utställningsplaner," *Vecko-Journalen*, 28 August 1938; and Brita Åkerman, "For ett bättre boende," *Form* 66, no. 6–7 (1970): 296–99.

74. SOU 1935:49, *Betänkande med förslag rörande andringar i vissa delar av hälsovårdsstadgan samt anordnande av förbättrad bostadsinspektion i*

städer och stadsliknande samhällen m.m. Jämte därtill hörande utredningar, Bostadssociala Utredningen (Stockholm, 1935), particularly pp. 66–100.

The bourgeois press responded sharply to this "Myrdal-inspired" invasion of private property. See "Hemvård och heminspektion," *Aurora*, 4 March 1936.

SOU 1937:43, *Betänkande med förslag rörande lån och bidrag av statsmedel till främjamde av bostadsförsörjning för mindre bemedlade barnrika familjer i engahem m.m.*, Bostadssociala Utredningen (Stockholm, 1937), particularly pp. 75–116.

75. Note to the author from Alva Myrdal, 23 July 1977.

76. See SOU 1938:47, *Betänkande angående gift kvinnas försvärvsarbete m.m.* (Stockholm, 1938); and Ingrid Garde Widemar, "I politiken," in *Kerstin Hasselgren En Vänstdie* (Stockholm: P. A. Norstedt and Söner, 1968), pp. 142–45. See also "Nya kvinnosaksfrågor," *Hertha*, January 1939.

77. "Befolkningsfrågan skall löses genom ett rikare liv och bätttre bostäder," *Nya Samhället*, 20 April 1936; and Alva Myrdal, "Den tomma siden i befolkningspolitiken," *Morgonbris*, March 1936.

78. Alva Myrdal, "3000 barn dö årligen i onödan. Skillnaden i levnadsstandard ännu förtförande stor i landet," *Social–Demokraten,* 19 September 1936; and Alva Myrdal, "Fackföreningsfolket och befolkningspolitiken," *Fackföreningsrörelsen*, 21 February 1936, p. 299.

79. Alva Myrdal, *Familj och lön* (Stockholm: Trycherieaktiebolaget, 1937).

80. Alva Myrdal, *Stadsbarn: En bok om deras fostran i storbarnkammare* (Stockholm: Koopertiva Förbundets Bokförlag, 1935), pp. 9, 80, 123–50, and 175–79. This book was inspired by Sven Wallander, chief architect for HSB, following a research trip to Vienna. Impressed by the daycare centers there, he had asked Alva Myrdal to draw up plans for a reformed nursery school program. Her sharp critique of existing facilities led him to suggest this book. Note to the author from Alva Myrdal, 23 July 1977.

On the book's influence, see Olof Johnsson, "Stadsbarnens fostran," *Arbetet* (Malmo), 2 October 1935; "Stadens barnkammare," *Tidevarvet*, 5 October 1935; Disa Västberg, "Storbarnkammare," *Social–Demokraten* (Stockholm), 24 September 1935; and "Storbarnkammaren värdelöst hjälp i barnens fostran," *Verdandisten*, 21–31 December 1935.

81. Alva Myrdal, *Riktiga Leksaker* (Stockholm: Koopertiva Förbundets Bokförlag, 1936). See also "De riktiga leksakerna," *Morgonbris*, December 1936; and "Riktiga leksaker," *Dagens Nyheter* (Stockholm), 14 November 1936.

82. Brita Åkerman, "Goda grännar på 1920-talet och på 70-talet," *Att bo*, June 1973, p. 21; and Sven Wallander, *Minnen*, Del I: HSB:s öden från 1920-talet till 1937 (Stockholm: Bonniers Forlag, 1972), pp. 100–101. See also Alva Myrdal, *Småbarnfostran* (Stockholm: Koopertiva Förbundets Bokförlag, 1937); Alva Myrdal, "Ungar och barnavård på världsut-

ställning," *Morgonbris*, August 1937; Alva Myrdal, "Frisk radikal luft behöves i vår vardag," *Morgonbris*, February 1937; and "Alva Myrdal og hennes femti apostler," *Alle Kvinners Blad*, May 1938.

83. See Alva Myrdal, *Föräldrafostrans socialpedagogiska uppgifter och organisation* (Stockholm: Marcus Boktryckeri, 1938); Alva Myrdal, "Skall foraeldre opdrages?" *Born*, 1 September 1938; and Alva Myrdal, "Vi föräldrar måst fostra oss," *Idun*,. 4 July 1936, pp. 7 and 21.

84. Alva Myrdal, "Keeping Together and Looking Forward [in English]," *Yrkeskvinnor*, June 1937; and Alva Myrdal, "Den nyere tids revolution i kvindens stillning," in Kirsten Gloerfelt-Torp, ed., *Kvinden i samfundet* (Copenhagen: Martins Forlag, 1937).

85. See Alva Myrdal, Eva Wigforss, and Edit Sköld, "Ett ord i rättan tid!" 6 (January 1938); and *Stockholms Tidningen—Stockholms Dagblad*, 30 December 1935.

86. Alva Myrdal, "Pojkar och flickor," *Morgonbris* March 1937; and Alva Myrdal, "Medborgarkunskap efter kön," *Morgonbris*, June 1937.

87. Alva Myrdal, "Hemmadottrar," *Yrkeskvinnor*, May 1937, p. 12.

88. Alva Myrdal, "Kvinnliga präster, landshövdingar och mera sådant," *Yrkeskvinnan*, March 1938; and Alva Myrdal, "Swedish Women in Industry and at Home," *Annals of the American Academy of Political and Social Science* 197 (May 1938): 216–31.

89. Alva Myrdal, Eva Wigforss, Signe Höjer, Andrea Andreen, and Carin Boalt, *Kvinnan, familjen och samhället* (Stockholm, 1938), particularly pp. 5–41; and "Per Albin och kvinnorna," *Vecko-Journalen*, 14 November 1937.

90. Alva Myrdal, "Vart tar pappa vägen?," *Idun*, 10 September 1938.

By this time, Alva Myrdal had become a public "personality." A September 1938 readers' poll conducted by a Stockholm newspaper placed Alva Myrdal seventh on a list of Sweden's ten most popular women. She finished behind Crown Princess Louise, Princess Ingeborg, Selma Lagerhof, and Greta Garbo, yet ahead of Ingrid Bergman. See *Stockholms Tidningen—Stockholms Dagblad*, 19 September 1938.

6

Constructing the New Order

During the first eighteen months of the commission's existence, political constraints delayed implementation of significant policy changes. A breakthrough, of sorts came in wake of the 1936 election and the seating of the 1937 Riksdag for its "mothers and babies" session. While rumors of war blocked further reforms in 1938, ideas and programs already in place continued their work of social transformation, in line with the Myrdals' vision.

In this phase, the Population Commission's labors faced extensive criticism. The political press gave it considerable attention, always emphasizing the Myrdals' overriding influence. In general, the bourgeois parties grew relatively predictable on the population question. The debate shifted instead to the newspapers of the far right and left, where the attack became increasingly vitriolic, bitter, and personal.

Opinions found in the moderate and conservative press continued to reflect support for efforts to raise the fertility rate, bonded to lingering distrust over use of the population question as a "crowbar" for social reform. Concern over the cost of proposed reforms, particularly by the conservative taxpayers' journal *Sunt Förnuft*[1], attacks on the materialistic assumptions underlying the commission's work,[2] and rejection of socialist themes found in the proposals[3] were common themes.

The Swedish national socialists went to considerable lengths to discredit the Myrdals and the Population Commission's work. In various commentaries, they contrasted the Myrdals' "advocacy of abortion," latent materialism, and Soviet-styled collectivism with their ideal vision based on home and family.[4] The National Group emphasized racial themes and frequently objected to the "materialistic assumptions" found in the commission's reports.[5]

The most important socialist critic of "Myrdal propaganda" by early 1936 was Karl Kilbom, editor of *Folkets Dagblad Politiken* and leader of the splinter left socialists in the Riksdag. His "Kilbom offensive" grew out of the first series of commission reports issued in 1935–36, with the tax proposals drawing particularly heavy fire. Kilbom pointed to those population groups that would suffer under this reform and charged the Myrdals and the Social Democrats with responsibility for "fascist inspired" pronatalist proposals.[6]

The Kilbom attack spread to other periodicals on the left. *Arbetaren* warned that dictatorship could result from reforms made in the name of social democracy and referred to the looming loss of individuality and personal freedom.[7] The Myrdal propaganda for more births, the socialist *Ny Dag* warned, was not popular among the working class: "Doubtless there are many who would gladly place children into the world, but who at the same time have some sense of responsibility for the future which capitalism offers their offspring."[8] Meanwhile, the communist paper *Norrskenflamman* termed the work emerging from the Population Commission "baby propaganda" imported from Hitler's Germany and Mussolini's Italy.[9]

Under attack, the Myrdals' political use of pronatalism showed further strains. Gunnar Myrdal publicly retained his natalist focus. Responding to the Kilbom charges, he stated, "If the Swedish people want to survive, they must shape social and personal conditions so that more wanted children come into the world."[10] Alva Myrdal emphasized the socialist, reform, and feminist components of their population program and at times angrily denied that the stimulation of more births had anything to do with it.[11] In a widely printed response to Kilbom, she drove home the point that "'Myrdalspropaganda' is . . . only a propaganda for social reforms for children, mothers and for the benefit of families."[12]

Kilbom's agitation found fertile soil in the latent neo-Malthusianism of the labor movement. With elections approaching in September 1936 and with the worried encouragement of his party colleagues,[13] Gunnar Myrdal authored a pamphlet titled *What Concerns the Labor Movement in the Population Question?*[14] Using the "agitator's style" of questions and answers, Myrdal lashed out at critics on both his right and left. Conservatives, he wrote, had long used the population issue to hinder women's attainment of full citizenship, to prevent social reforms, and to block the spread of birth control information to the working class. The Social Democrats, he explained, had in contrast turned the population question into a program for economic security, job creation, legal reforms in favor of women, and social measures to assist mothers, children, and families.

Back in 1935, he noted, the Conservative, Liberal, and National Group parties had expressed strong support for the major social reforms long sought by the Social Democrats. For a year or so the population question had been "the Swedish people's life question" in every small conservative newspaper. Now it was all but forgotten. At the very same time, the communists and Kilbom socialists sought "to fish in murky water," charging that the Social Democrats wanted "population increase," "uncontrolled numbers of babies," and so on. Myrdal blasted these tactics: "the splintering, the short-sighted opportunism, the callous dishonesty."

While in other countries the population question had become a weapon in the hands of reactionaries, in Sweden it had been wrested away and had become a "crowbar for social reform." The Social Democrats had transformed the population question into a problem of family living standards, which mandated the elimination of overcrowded housing, inadequate nutritional standards, poor health care, unemployment, and economic insecurity. Repeating his standing argument, Myrdal charged that it would be "impossible" to achieve an increasing population under existing conditions. While the immigration of other peoples could solve some of Sweden's problems, the friction that would result made this an undesirable option. A mild blending of nationalism with socialism would better secure Sweden's future.

As the Myrdals parried these charges from their left, the Social-Democratic press gave them increasingly strong support. Gunnar Lundberg, editor of *Social-Demokraten*, regularly endorsed the Myrdals' work and defended the couple against Kilbom's personal attacks. In the party youth publication, *Frihet*, he supported the Myrdals' program as sound socialism, emphasizing that solutions to population problems were in every case also solutions to related social problems long advanced by socialists.[15] Mauritz Västberg, writing in *Social-Demokraten*, noted that "the Social Democratic party's estimation of and support for Professor Myrdal is most evident by the fact that the government placed him on the Population Commission." This support, Västberg added, would increase to the degree that Kilbom's vicious campaign continued.[16] Tor Jerneman, writing in *Fack-*

föreningsrörelsen, reiterated the socialist components of the population question: implementation of sociopolitical changes to better the living standards of the masses and the maintenance of the population stock at a level ensuring that productive relationships and employment would not be diminished.[17]

Most of the intellectual left also rallied behind the Myrdals. Writing in the radical journal *Clarté*, Gösta Rehn emphasized the leftist social psychology found in the Myrdals' work, measures designed to engineer Swedish attitudes and behavior in a more cooperative manner.[18] *Tiden* also ran several articles in the 1935–37 period that affirmed the Myrdals' socialist core, several authored by Myrdal's protégée, Torsten Gårdlund.[19]

The population question also brought Gunnar Myrdal into direct political activity as a Social Democratic member in the Riksdag's First Chamber. In late July 1935, the Dalarna Social Democrats, under party pressure to select a representative to the First Chamber from outside their province, chose Myrdal, a "son of Dalarna."[20] News reports cited Myrdal's role in the population question and his position as one of the Social Democrat's most influential thinkers. As the opposition *Östgöta Correspondenten* commented, Myrdal also "made . . . the impression of being a properly conventional adulator of the Hansson regime."[21]

The only direct public attention given the broad population question by the Social Democratic party (as distinct from the Social Democratic Parliamentary Group) came at the April 1936 party congress. Reflecting neo-Malthusian sentiments lurking in the grass roots, the Stocksund Workers' Commune introduced a motion arguing that there was no reason to fear a population reduction. Over time, better social relationships for workers, diminished unemployment, and peace would provide a stable population. The proper party line would be concentration on economic questions, not pronatalist initiatives. "Give us those circumstances that shape security in the greatest possible dimensions in our society, and then the children will come of themselves." On this basis, the commune moved "that the Party Congress declare itself against further party support for a policy which directly aims at increasing fertility."[22]

The party Steering Committee, however, recommended rejection of the motion. It noted that the government had already established a commission on the population question and, as it produced its reports, the party would judge each according to its content. "In the party is found absolute unity," the committee declared, "that the basis for the *folk's* preservation and strengthening must be sought in circumstances which give security and a spirit of life."[23]

In a revealing floor speech on the motion, Gustav Möller expanded on the political importance of the population issue: "I do not hesitate a moment to frighten however many Conservatives and however many Agrarian Party and Liberal [Riksdag] members with the threat that our population will die out, if with that threat I can persuade them to vote for social proposals which I offer. This is my simple perspective on the population question, and it is sufficient for me."[24]

At the invitation of the party leadership, Gunnar Myrdal then rose to make a major, somewhat disingenuous address. After repeating his regular explanations, Myrdal noted that some charged him with using "birth propaganda." However, he felt that a "conservative newspaper in Skåne" was closer to the truth when it termed his radio lectures an actual deterrent to bearing children. His constant references to children as the cause of overcrowding, low family living standards, poor nutrition, inadequate health care, and youth unemployment had actually served to aggravate the birth decline. He cautioned that the slight upturn in the Swedish birthrate seen in the 1934–35 period was only a short-term phenomenon based on the large number of marriages and first children that occurred after the worst years of the depression. The tendency toward fertility decline, he predicted, would soon return.

Concerning his work on the Population Commission, he stated that its Social Democratic members refused to deal in "private politics" with the more conservative members. "We have our directive from the Social Minister," he stated, and they intended to follow closely that political line. Concluding, Myrdal noted that anyone with a Social Democratic world view must show concern for future generations. "We plan to build a new society," he stated, "and we differ from all other parties because we desire a complete revolution in economic and social relationships. We must have a people who will live in the new society which we shall build."[25]

The party congress approved the recommendation of the Steering Committee and rejected the Stocksund motion. However, while on record as supporting the Population Commission's work, the Social Democrats avoided a direct affirmation of pronatalism.

Similar foot-dragging by the Social Democratic leadership led to parliamentary delays. Möller's directive to the commission had specified that its recommendations were to be made to the 1936 Riksdag, and the first parcel of reports on maternity assistance, mothers' and children's health care, taxation, and marriage loans appeared prior to the opening of that session. Yet action was deferred until 1937.[26] The subject was not mentioned in the ceremonial speech from the throne nor in the debate that followed.[27]

However, with the first group of commission reports just released, the newly elected Dalarna *Riksdagsman*, Gunnar Myrdal, was given the unusual opportunity—particularly for a new member—of briefing the Social Democratic parliamentary group at their regular monthly meeting on the commission's work.[28] In his hour-long address, Myrdal emphasized the commission's "so-called bachelor tax," designed to raise 15 million kronor a year to finance support programs for families and parents. Stressing the interrelated nature of the commission's recommendations, Myrdal also promoted the measures to build marriages, including maternity benefits and marriage loans.

The subsequent discussion reflected the mix of attitudes toward the commission's work shown by party members in other forums. Ottilia Nordgren criticized the commission for taking on too much and for proposing overly costly reforms. Bernhard Eriksson expressed similar reservations and suggested an alternate task for the commission: accident insurance. Gustav Möller's response, however, proved more revealing and suggested the growing political power of Myrdal's formulation. While "unable" to take an official position toward the commission recommendations at this time, he did place himself "completely on the same side" of its desire to sustain the Swedish population stock. It would be unfortunate, he continued, if the Social Democrats left this issue to "reactionary elements." While aware that social programs cost money, he stated that population-related social reforms could be used to justify a new round of income redistribution that would improve the economic position of those who had the least. The party would be foolish, he continued, if it failed to use the force of the population argument in pressing for its social goals.[29]

Under questioning by the Riksdag opposition in early April, Möller cited cost as the reason for delay in consideration of the commission recommendations. The Riksdag subsequently debated the population question on 9 May, when Möller answered three questions placed before the government by commission members Wohlin and Magnusson i Skövde.[30]

Möller replied that the government, while positive toward the commission's recommendations, would delay their consideration until the 1937 Riksdag. The reports had simply arrived too late to be considered in the government's 1936 budget proposal. Since the tax and social policy recommendations were tied together, both would be held over until the following year. Möller added that he, along with other members of the government, regarded the issue "as urgent in high degree." Concerning the establishment of a marriage loan fund, he pledged that the government's 1937 budget proposal would include the necessary capital. While generally accepting the commission's maternity assistance plan, he recommended that the program remain tied for the immediate future to voluntary sickness benefit societies (*sjukkassa*). He affirmed the recommended program of providing additional assistance for needy mothers, and special allowances for the children of widows and invalids.

On the negative side, he stated that Finance Minister Wigforss felt any solution to the extra cost generated by such programs "ought not to be sought in an isolated [family support] tax," as the Population Commission suggested.[31] Necessary family programs, Möller concluded, should be financed through normal budgetary channels. Wigforss himself added that nothing would prevent the development of a family tax deduction on the scale that the commission proposed. Yet such a deduction would have to be constructed within a unified, progressive tax structure.[32]

In response, Nils Wohlin cited the popular identification of the Social Democrats with extramarital sexuality and termed the position taken by the finance minister on family taxation a "great setback" for the Population Commission's work.[33] In his "maiden speech," Gunnar Myrdal toed the political line and endorsed Wigforss's position on taxation, even though Myrdal had been both chairman of the taxation delegation and chief author of the repudiated report. He stressed the "positive side" of Wigforss's position: recognition that taxation should be adjusted according to family burden. Myrdal reiterated that population policies must reshape personal and social relationships so that persons in all social classes could responsibly bear a "normal number of children."[34]

While failing to take substantive action on most of the Population Commission proposals, the 1936 Riksdag did express strong support for large-family housing and approved the expenditure of 11.5 million kronor for the construction of "Myrdal houses."[35]

In the summer of 1936, the Social Democratic government resigned after the bourgeois parties blocked a key provision of the new pension law that would have keyed benefit size to the regional cost of living. In the subsequent election campaign, the population question became a decisive issue.

Such emphasis was not predetermined. While official party publications in early 1936 placed the population question on an equal footing with the unemployment, pension, housing, monopoly, and defense issues[36] and Hansson himself noted with pleasure the "competent" nature of the commission's early recommendations,[37] the functional attitudes of party leaders were less clear. As seen at the 1936 party congress and in the Riksdag, Möller exhibited a less-than-full embrace of pronatalist goals. Hansson's own speeches in the first half of 1936 referred to individual components of the Population and Social Housing commissions' work, but never drew them together under a "population policy" umbrella.[38] A May Day 1936 proclamation by the SAP leadership to the nation placed strong stress on the party's welfare program, yet made no mention of population policy.[39]

However, by midsummer of 1936 a strong emphasis on the party's population goals emerged. It appears that this emphasis derived from a formal plan to attract a broader base of political support. Designed to increase party strength among the middle class and devised by members of the Social Democratic Civil Servants Group, the Marx Study Society, and the Social Democratic Student Union, this proposal was submitted to the party Steering Committee in May. It advocated new emphasis on the party's commitment to family needs, specifically maternity assistance, child allowances, and housing programs for large families. The goal should be to wrap socialism in the garb of home and family.[40]

A 1936 party propaganda film, featuring a talk by Hansson, laid great stress on the "people's home" ideal and on the party's effort to create a "good home" for everyone, based on security and human dignity. He emphasized the special needs of large Swedish families.[41]

Hansson and Möller released a preelection statement on 5 August giving family policy a prominent position. In extolling their public works projects that had met the economic crisis of 1932, they emphasized the "great building program" to house large families. The same spirit, they stated, would infuse the party's future reforms. Social policies designed to create a secure existence and increase welfare for the great majority of Swedes would not be sacrificed to the military budget, as the bourgeois parties sought. Masses of Swedish children, Hansson and Möller stated, still did not receive the food they needed. The Social Democrats would direct production to meet the needs of families and children. They affirmed that a "good home and a secure existence are prerequisites for the healthy formation of families and the maintenance of the population stock" and pledged to provide nutritious food to all children, support for fatherless and parentless children, and better maternity assistance.[42]

Hansson further bound the Myrdal population policy to his "people's home" campaign theme in his major 2 September radio address. After discussing assistance to the elderly, the prime minister turned to the younger generation. Their welfare could not be neglected, for they represented the nation's future capital: "[They] shall carry Swedish achievements further, [they] shall maintain the Swedish population stock healthy and strong." Warning that "[t]he threatened shrinkage of the Swedish population has driven into the foreground questions concerning the growing generation's welfare," he urged massive support for mothers and children. The party's theme would be a "radical program" based in "reality." Measures designed to increase personal security and family welfare would also form the basis for the nation's reproduction. Hansson emphasized that the Social Democrats did not seek to divide society into socialist and bourgeois. Rather, they sought to bind all Swedes together to lay the social basis for defense of "our peace and freedom."[43]

The Myrdals played an active role in injecting population themes into the campaign and in playing to the political middle. At a major September 1936 rally sponsored by HSB, Gunnar Myrdal joined Hansson in calling for a family-oriented housing movement in the tradition of the great popular or folk movements of Sweden's past. Its goal should be providing all families with a decent home, where children could grow and learn. "This reform work," Myrdal continued, "is in the deepest sense socially constructive and socially conservative."[44] In a special election issue of *Frihet*, Myrdal described the Social Democratic program as aiming at enhanced security for young families. The regulation of production and consumption would also end the scourge of unemployment that cut most brutally at the young.[45] In another campaign pamphlet, Alva Myrdal expanded on the imperatives behind the population question. Only the Social Democratic party, she charged, could build a society where families could find protection and security.[46]

The election itself proved to be a major victory for the Social Democratic party. The appeal of the party as defender of home, children, and family played a critical role in its electoral success[47] and set the stage for the 1937 "mothers and babies" Riksdag session.

While rebuffed on taxes, the Myrdals harvested here the other fruits of their politicized social science.[48] Gunnar Myrdal served as the primary actor in this stage of the project. Reflecting the magnitude of the party's new enthusiasm for population and family themes, Möller's personal notes on the 1937 Riksdag ranked attention to mothers and children as the highest priority. He listed pregnancy assistance, maternity care, child-support payments, marriage loans, and means-tested school lunches for children as the major party-supported proposals. Family housing, a universal school lunch, and children's clothing allowances were all placed on the "waiting list."[49] Addressing the party's Parliamentary Group, Hansson stressed that their overwhelming victory in the 1936 election using family themes had created a great responsibility.[50] In its formal legislative list, the government called for favorable action on the social proposals advanced by the Population Commission.[51]

In May 1937, the Riksdag approved the commission's programs to provide prenatal care and delivery assistance to pregnant women and to reorganize the district midwife system.[52] A government decree in July 1937 implemented recommendations on maternity care, funding four hundred new maternity beds in hospitals that agreed to limit their charge to one krona per day. The cost of delivery itself would be fully subsidized. In addition, the program offered a state grant of two kronor per day for expectant mothers residing in waiting homes.

The proposed maternity bonus to assist childbearing women generated more debate. The commission had proposed a bonus of one hundred kronor provided to all women, without income test. The government recommended a somewhat means-tested program, providing a bonus of seventy-five kronor to mothers from families with a taxable income under three thousand kronor, available to married and unmarried mothers alike. This would exclude only 10 percent of mothers from coverage.

Debate centered on the proper cutoff point. The Agrarian party recommended two thousand kronor in income, the Conservatives one thousand kronor. In the First Chamber, Myrdal defended the governmental proposal. At issue, he stated, was creation of a more equal income distribution between families with a varied number of children. Repeating his key theme, he emphasized that this differential did not diminish within the middle class. Distancing himself from the right, Myrdal argued that this bonus was not a fertility premium. There was no basis in Sweden, he stated, for a national socialist or fascist inspired family policy designed to increase population size. The proposed measure, he concluded, aimed solely at removing the hindrances on individual families that prevented them from reaching a normal fertility.[53] The Riksdag approved the government's recommendation, including the three-thousand-kronor test.

The body then turned, indirectly, to the abortion question and created the special maternity aid fund for mothers under particular financial or emotional stress. Aid of up to three hundred kronor would be available, with the sum and duration set by individual circumstances. The measure created "maternity boards" on a provincial basis, with two-thirds of their members to be appointed by the central government. The program carried an appropriation of 1 million kronor for the remainder of budget year 1937/38.[54]

Turning to the marriage loan question, commission member Persson emphasized to the Riksdag that its purpose was to lower the nation's average marriage age and so make room for more natural fertility. Most debate centered on the question of which financial institutions would handle the loans. Bourgeois party members favored the private banks, while the government endorsed the national bank. The Riksdag ultimately approved a fund totaling 2 million kronor, to be paid back over a period of five years. The maximum grant size was lowered from the proposed one thousand three hundred to one thousand kronor. Loans would be handled by the national banking system, with the assistance of local commissions.[55]

Accepting the recommendations of the Population Commission, the Riksdag also created a children's allowance system for orphans and the children of widows and invalid fathers. Orphan benefits would be set at 300–420 kronor annually for the first child. Additional, yet decreasing, sums would be available for subsequent children. The offspring of widows and invalids would also receive benefits, while children under age two derived an additional sixty kronor.

Myrdal's highly publicized speech in the Riksdag supporting these programs emphasized their contribution toward removing the "poor relief" stigma attached to child welfare. Rejecting the Conservative charge that the allowance proposal would further fragment welfare assistance, Myrdal argued that experimentation and bold action were needed immediately, with this proposal but a first step.[56]

The 1937 Riksdag also became the setting for a sharp policy clash between Myrdal and Ernst Wigforss. Myrdal's first controversy with the finance minister had come over the commission's tax proposals in early 1936, with the social scientist losing that round. Their second confrontation derived from Wigforss's proposal to include children's allowances in the pay schedules for teachers and other civil servants, an "in cash" form of assistance that violated the Myrdals' emphasis on "in kind" support. Through an unusual internal party challenge, Myrdal prevailed this time, and he gave decisive direction and shape to the developing Swedish welfare state.

In his proposal, Wigforss sought to eliminate the lingering advantage in the wages paid to male teachers, as heads of households, over women. He offered a wage plan that provided equal pay for men and women and a general raise of 120–180 kronor annually. He tied to it, however, an allowance scheme providing an extra 120 kronor per child, with a maximum allowance of 360 kronor for three or more children. He justified his plan on the Social Democratic goal of redistributing income according to need. Wigforss said that his proposal recognized both women's desire for equal wages and the reality that men were more often the principal supporters of families. Family tax deductions were insufficient to meet the need, and "in kind" social measures took too long to implement. Children's allowances—similar to those provided in France and Belgium—were the quickest way to bring equality between need and income and to retain some aspect of the "family wage" economy.[57]

Wigforss's plan stirred a whirl of controversy. Opponents included many Social Democrats and the regular bourgeois opposition. The latter cited potential chaos within the wage structure and argued that there were more effective ways to build a population policy.[58]

Gunnar Myrdal, ideologically committed to "in kind" social assistance as a means of replacing parental with social choices, led the assault within the Social Democratic ranks. He opposed the "quantative" baby-generating stress of direct child allowances to the detriment of qualitative goals, and he blasted the distortion brought to the "equal pay for equal work" doctrine central to the feminist vision. Myrdal also stressed the linkage between "in kind" social assistance and the creation of a rational, radical "consumption socialism."[59]

With the support of other party members, he filed an internal motion in the Parliamentary Group opposing Wigforss. It argued that any allowance scheme should be considered only in conjunction with a national, universal system and complained that Wigforss's plan threatened to transform family policy into a bourgeois poor relief system. On April 8, the Social Democratic Riksdag members debated the issue for four hours. While a number declared themselves behind Wigforss, Myrdal's arguments carried the day. Fellow commission member Persson backed his colleague, while Fru Nordgren announced that the Social Democratic women's caucus adhered to Myrdal's motion. While additional interparty debates were held on 18 May and 24 May, a major radio dialogue between Myrdal and Wigforss on 3 May, and a Riksdag debate on 21 May, the Wigforss's proposal was effectively "dead" by mid-April.[60]

The 1938 Riksdag considered the second series of commission reports, dealing with legal reforms and the sex question. In a symbolic, predictable move, the Riksdag repealed the 1910 anti-birth control laws governing the sale and advertising of contraceptives. New regulations placed the contraceptive trade on an equivalent footing with that of pharmaceutical supplies, allowing licensed druggists and other approved vendors to sell birth control materials. While the sale of certain harmful abortifacients was prohibited, the availability of others was made subject to a doctor's prescription. Where the Population Commission had recommended making the sale of contraceptives compulsory for all druggists, the Riksdag allowed druggists to refuse to carry them according to their convictions.[61]

The 1938 Riksdag also approved a new abortion law that followed the Population Commission's recommendations, rooted in the Myrdal compromise. In place of a fairly total ban, the new law allowed abortion on medical, humanitarian, eugenic, and "mixed" social-medical grounds. Under this measure, the operating doctor and a public medical officer would have to prepare a joint report stating the grounds for abortion, to be filed with the Board of Health. Abortion on eugenic grounds required prior approval by the board and would usually be accompanied by sterilization. Significantly, the opinion of the prospective father on the abortion would have to be obtained, although an unmarried mother could veto this. Induced abortion by nondoctors remained a criminal offense.[62]

In addition, the Riksdag gave its belated approval to the commission-proposed increase in the tax deduction granted to families with three or more children. Myrdal also pressed in the 1938 Riksdag for several minor population-related reforms, including a measure making it easier for couples to adopt babies born out of wedlock[63] and another reforming medical education to give it more "social" and "social hygienic" content.[64] The subsequent 1939 Riksdag approved Myrdal-favored measures designed to support the working mother. One new law specified that employers could not dismiss female employees or reduce salary or benefits on the basis of engagement, marriage, pregnancy, or childbearing. Women also received the right to a voluntary twelve-week leave of absence at the time of childbearing, without fear of dismissal.

Yet after early 1938, the Riksdag took no substantive action on the major, more costly commission recommendations relating to school meals, children's clothing allowances, and day-care centers. This end to the implementation of commission proposals derived from the "reform pause" declared by the government in 1938. With the growing threat of a European war, the government felt obliged to divert additional funds to the military forces and to consolidate Sweden's financial status.[65] Commenting on the Riksdag's failure to consider the commission's later work, Gunnar Myrdal wrote: "The government is in favor of all the proposals, but I am sorry to say that even in our small country the present world situation makes it necessary to mortgage most of the money at our disposal for armament purposes."[66]

These circumstances led to the Myrdals' decision to leave Sweden. The Carnegie Foundation in August 1937 had tendered an offer to Gunnar Myrdal to come to the United States to direct its pending study of the Negro in America.[67] "At first I said . . . 'no,'" Myrdal commented in a letter to a friend. "We thought of all the duties of different kind [sic] in this small corner of the world which had accumulated around our work and of our house and children and so on."[68] But in early 1938 he changed his mind. A letter sent from Myrdal to Wohlin shortly after the former's departure suggests the motivation:

> And so, yet once more, thanks for these years which we threw away in common! There has been something special about this Commission. Naturally it has been a great and very influential experience for me to get to work with you. It is perhaps good that it soon is ended . . . .
>
> Now we approach the Statue of Liberty with all our children (increased by two pug-nosed, blue-eyed, red-haired twenty-year old students of the R.S.B. type to attend to the household). The youngsters are very happy about everything new. Alva and I are as excited as in youth's springtime before new adventures and achievements. It is so wonderful to be relieved of all those thousand practical duties and obligations as worn out clothes, to be able to shut up the house and place everything in a knapsack. Now we are again free researchers and not dependent on the crowd and the human masses in the guise of political representation: To sail our own ship without help and on our own responsibility. There lies an ocean between us and all those small ambitions, intrigues and daily preoccupations, which shackled all our thoughts.[69]

While not resigning from the Population Commission, Myrdal began to lose interest in and control over its concluding work. Having attended most commission meetings since the panel's organization in May 1935, he missed four consecutive meetings in May–June 1938 (due, in part, to a Carnegie-related trip to the United States) and attended meetings in July–August only sporadically. Decisions by the Executive Committee between late April and August were left entirely to Wohlin and his new wife, Andreen.[70]

However, one last dispute swelled up over the contents of the commission's final report (or *slutbetänkande*), which offers deep insight into the degree to which Myrdal had kept the commission under rigid ideological control.

As early as May 1936, Wohlin had circulated a letter to all members of the Population Commission regarding authorship of a "final or principal" report. He designated Magnusson i Skövde and Andreen-Svedberg to begin work on a draft.[71] However, in February 1938, Richard Sterner received a commission (through Myrdal) to prepare a first draft of the final report.[72]

Myrdal gave Sterner "vague" instructions to write a synopsis of all the commission reports, stressing the main ideology behind them. Absorbed by the pending move to the United States, Myrdal then gave his protégé and the drafting process little attention. Under considerable time pressure, Sterner prepared the manuscript "in a small room" at Stockholm University.[73]

Myrdal reviewed this draft in early summer of 1938 and raised a number of reservations over its content. He cited an apparent retreat from basic principles found in the earlier reports. In a telegram to Nils Wohlin (then in Dublin), Myrdal requested an urgent meeting of the commission on 10 August. He added that Persson and Österström also had questions concerning the draft.[74] At the August meeting, Myrdal received assurances from Wohlin that his reservations were relevant and that a copy of the redraft would be sent to the United States by 1 November for his comment and approval. Myrdal formally reserved the right to author a dissenting report, insisting that this agreement be written into the minutes of the commission's plenary session.[75]

Despite Wohlin's promises, Myrdal left for the United States with considerable apprehension. He wrote to Sven Wicksell: " . . . danger exists that Wohlin, now that he is under less direct control, will write up something more twaddling which better suits his antecedents. You must now maintain a watchful eye over the work; otherwise I am afraid that it will become muddled."[76] In a letter written while on the boat to the United States, Myrdal told Wohlin: "I have often found myself unhappy and occasionally annoyed during the last half year, when I would notice that we are not as wholeheartedly on the same side." He again questioned Wohlin about the recent draft.[77]

At the 26 September meeting, with Myrdal absent, the commission voted to rework the entire Sterner draft. Wohlin, von Hofsten, Österström, and Andreen would each edit chapters or parts of chapters, and the chairman would then consolidate their work. They also voted to invite Myrdal to write a new chapter on the population question's economic importance.[78] In October, Myrdal and Wohlin exchanged telegrams. Wohlin inquired about the new chapter. Myrdal advised that no new chapter be written and recommended that Wohlin talk with Alf Johansson if he needed further guidance.[79]

Yet Wohlin was already at work to ensure that Myrdal would play no significant role in the preparation of the final report. Following an unusual conversation in early October with Gustav Möller, Wohlin received a ruling from the social minister sharply limiting Myrdal's role. Since he now lived outside the country, Myrdal still had the right to recommend changes in the report where he could find cause and could, like any other member who at the time of a report's final consideration was ill or traveling in another country, request that his name be included as having taken part in the deliberations, discussion, and approval of the report. However, as an ex patria member, Myrdal would not have the right to author and attach a dissenting report to the *slutbetänkande*.[80]

The commission discussed Möller's ruling during its 2 November plenary meeting. Noting that this changed the understanding reached with Myrdal in August, the commission instructed Wohlin to write Myrdal a "friendly appeal" asking that he remain a member of the commission and approve the final report.[81]

Wohlin delayed authoring the letter until 26 November. He then wrote that while the draft of a final statistical report had received the commission's blessing on 26 September, Sterner's draft of the *slutbetänkande* had been found unsatisfactory. The various chapters, he reported, were then distributed to commission members with writing ability for substantial rework. Wohlin himself withdrew from other responsibilities for five weeks late in October and November to coordinate preparation of the report's final draft. Its first three chapters, together with the concluding seventh chapter, had received preliminary approval from the commission plenary on 22 November; the other three chapters would be discussed on 6 December.

Wohlin then turned to an explanation of Myrdal's current position relative to the commission. After summarizing Möller's ruling, Wohlin described the social minister's praise for Myrdal's contribution to the commission and explained that Möller's decision was based "exclusively on principle."[82] Such a situation, Wohlin continued, appeared to be unique in the history of the Swedish commission system. Yet it was clear that Myrdal could not enjoy all the privileges of commission membership while residing in New York City. It was absolutely necessary, Wohlin added, that the commission conclude its work in December.

"Now I can understand naturally quite well," Wohlin told Myrdal, "that you could become angry over these developments. I beg you, however, with consideration to our friendship of many years and our delightful collaboration these past years, to avoid taking some rash step and resigning your membership from the commission." He imployed Myrdal to avoid any friction that would damage their common work. After all, he stated, there was nothing so terribly important about the final report. The "great contributions" from the commission had already been made; the final report represented little more than a "literary product." It "would gladden us all," Wohlin continued, if Myrdal would simply adhere to the final draft. Magnusson i Skövde, Wohlin stated, planned to write a dissenting report from the Conservative perspective. Certain Social Democrats were increasingly attacking the work of the commission as "poor relief." Wohlin asked Myrdal to support him as he sought to hold the middle during "an unfavorable internal situation." Any response that Myrdal would care to make should be in Wohlin's hands prior to the final commission plenary meeting on December 18.[83]

Myrdal, quite simply, found himself politically outmaneuvered. Wohlin's letter and the draft arrived in New York only a few days before the commission's last meeting. In a 15 December letter (preceded by a telegram) to his "party comrades" on the commission, Myrdal complained bitterly about Wohlin's tactics. He pointed to previous examples of Wohlin's double-dealing over reports prepared by the Social-Ethical and Rural Depopulation subcommittees, where Wohlin had reneged on promises to delay final approval. Myrdal also accused Wohlin of passing on false information to the commission concerning these procedural agreements. Now Wohlin had again broken his pledge to allow Myrdal the opportunity to read and critique the second *slutbetänkande* draft.

Myrdal pointed to the nearly two-month interval between Wohlin's conversation with Möller and his communicating the social minister's opinion to Myrdal himself. Since the commission would dissolve before he even had a chance to contact the ministry to seek a delay or withdrawal, he had virtually no recourse. Wohlin had taken away his right to object to the final report through his arrangement with Möller and his right to resign from the commission in protest through his delay in communicating with Myrdal. While tempted to "go public" in castigating Wohlin's devious methods, he recognized that this could damage the commission's earlier work and hence would be counterproductive.

Under these circumstances, Myrdal pointed to the only effective solution. The other Social Democratic members, he said, must author a socialist dissent to the *slutbetänkande*. It would be dangerous, Myrdal warned, to let the final draft stand without a strong critique. Deviations from socialist principles were found throughout the manuscript.

"It smacks of Naziism from a distance," he wrote, "and the situation in Sweden makes it dangerous not to position Social Democracy apart from these tendencies in the report."[84]

Myrdal warned Persson and Västberg to avoid letting Wohlin lead them into compromise. Even a change in emphasis would not help. The report had to be "deloused" line by line. Compromise had proven important in winning bourgeois support for many reform proposals. Yet principle alone was now involved. Myrdal feared that unless a socialist critique was strongly made, "the population question could become spoiled in Swedish politics. What we have worked for above all is to prevent the population question from sinking down to a Nazi argument."[85]

Concerning specifics, Myrdal pointed to a portion of the draft that implied that "a natural population increase" could be Sweden's policy goal. "What is a natural population increase?" Myrdal asked. "Moreover the impression is made that this would be more advantageous than a stable [population]."[86] Other statements repeated the implication, hitherto foreign to the commission reports, that a slowly increasing population was the most desirable goal.

Myrdal also pointed to various phrases, giving a negative connotation to child limitation. Myrdal reiterated that the problem was not all birth control, but only the extreme child limitation characterizing the 1920s and 1930s. Failure to qualify critical comments concerning birth control, Myrdal believed, gave an entirely different and unacceptable tone to the document.[87] Later statements in the draft also offered veiled criticisms of the neo-Malthusian movement.

Myrdal pointed to unhistorical "value judgments" found in the report, such as statements that the neo-Malthusians' conservative opponents in Sweden had been a talented group or that the population discussion in the prewar period stood on a high level. It was simply wrong, Myrdal stated, when the draft maintained that the current population debate was but a continuation of that earlier discussion. The shift that the Swedish birthrate made after 1925 represented an entirely new situation. Myrdal pointed to dangerous statements implying that the population policies of dictators produced more fruitful results. He noted, in particular, a tendency toward adulation of Nazi Germany population policies. He was not sure that the child welfare program of the nazis was more effective than that of the Weimar Republic, although it was clear that the national socialists conducted a more effective publicity campaign. The nazis, he added, gave charity rather than social policy to the German people. Efforts in the draft to use certain developments in Germany as supporting evidence for Swedish programs were incorrect. Since the Swedish and German programs were founded on different assumptions, Myrdal said, the latter had no impact on the former.[88]

The *slutbetänkande* received formal approval at the Population Commission's final plenary meeting, 18 December 1938. Persson, Västberg, and Magnusson i Skövde reserved the right to add dissenting reports.[89] The former two, responding to Myrdal's entreaties, prepared a draft of a Social Democratic dissent to the report. It stands as one of the clearest short expressions of the Myrdal line in the population question.

In their draft, Persson and Västberg explained that while standing behind positive commission recommendations for reforms to assist children and families, they objected to the ideological muddling found in the final report. Reactionary forms of thinking had colored its form of delivery; important principles had been distorted and undermined.

The Swedish population policy set out in the earlier reports, they stated, was based on the democratic "voluntary parenthood" principle and on an effort to lend public support to family formation. This positive and radical program was fundamentally different from the pronatalist policies of the fascist and national socialist states. The two strongly objected to the blurring of lines between the Swedish and the German and Italian policies found in the first chapter. They disputed the implication that the "older conservative" line in the birth question had finally been adopted by the working class. The old conservatives, they noted, had been instrumental in the passage of the 1910 anti–birth control laws. Fundamental components of Sweden's new population policy represent the repudiation of the old conservatives and the final victory of the neo-Malthusian movement. The final report had no justification for blotting out these distinctions that stood "between the modern Swedish population policy on the one side and on the other the fascist and nazi ideologies of the older conservative theories."[90]

Persson and Västberg turned to other problems. They attacked the final report's criticism of the tendency toward child limitation, which failed to distinguish between normal birth control, which the commission favored, and "extreme child limitation." Concerning the report's preference for a growing population, they stated that "even if such a goal were possible, which we doubt, we would not desire an increase of fertility above what would be necessary for a constant population."[91]

They also noted that the final report confused the basic relationship between fertility and income levels. While poorer couples had a higher average fertility, this was only a result of the current "transition period." As birth control knowledge continued to spread among those with low incomes, this differential would disappear. It was folly for the report actually to promote an argument used by the commission's critics.

The Social Democratic understanding of the relationship between income level and fertility, they affirmed, had governed all the commission's earlier work. Social policies designed to reduce the living standard differential between families with varying numbers of children could make a contribution toward raising fertility. Extra children affected the living standard of all families, the wealthy as well as the poor. An effective population policy could not be class-directed or welfare-oriented. The fertility rates of couples in all socioeconomic classes were affected by the cost of the differential child. Any useful program, they concluded, should be universal in its application.[92]

Yet at the last minute and for unstated reasons, both Persson and Västberg dropped their planned dissenting report. "Will not deliver any [dissenting] report or reservation," they cabled Wohlin on 29 December. "I adhere completly to the final report," Persson added in a telegram the next day.[93] Since the final report retained the language that had troubled Myrdal, it appears that his influence and his finely tuned policy distinctions simply proved unable to span an ocean or to influence the politics of the Social Democratic/Agrarian party coalition. The final report appeared in late December. Concerning authorship, the report noted only that all commission members took part in the preparatory work and that everyone had participated in the final process "except for Mr. Myrdal, who was prevented from being present by foreign travel."[94]

The final report was generally recognized as Wohlin's work.[95] Yet public attention by early 1939 had turned elsewhere. Myrdal consoled himself by focusing on its general unimportance. Writing to Västberg in February 1939, he stated: "I received the other day [a copy of] the Population Commission's final report. As you know, I think it is to some extent rather bad, but on the other hand it will not play so great a role; the important principles are more clear and firm in the earlier reports."[96]

Notes

1. See: "Befolkningskommissionen hissar nya signaler," *Sunt Förnuft*, April 1938; Wald. Svensson, "Myrdal och det jordbrukspolitiska problemet," *Sunt Förnuft*, April 1938; and Gösta Bagge, "En socialpolitik av Myrdalstyp blir ruinerade," *Umeåbladet*, 16 September 1938.
2. "Högerkritiken mot befolkningskommissionen," *SAP Information*, June 1938.
3. "Bosättningslånen inför riksdagen," *Sundt Förnuft*, March 1937.
4. See Åke Berglund, "Socialhygienes utveckling till rashygien," *Nationell Socialism*, 15 June 1935; "Befolkningskommissionen. II," *Den Svenska Nationalsocialisten*, 22 June 1935; Åke Berglund, "Teknisk materialism eller levande utveckling," *Nationell Socialism*, March 1936, pp. 75–79; and "Befolkningsfrågan löses genom negerimport?" *Den Svenska Nationalsocialisten*, 8 January 1936.
5. *Nationell Tidning*, 14 May 1937.
6. From "Den myrdalska befolkningspropagandan," *Folkets Dagblad Politiken*, 9 January 1936, and "Myrdalsskatten skulle hårt drabba ogift jordbrukare," *Folkets Dagblad Politiken*, 13 January 1936.
7. "Slavstaten," *Arbetaren*, 6 February 1936.
8. "Myrdahlskt myrdaleri," *Ny Dag* (Stockholm), 7 January 1936.
9. "Musses och Hitlers barnavlings premier införes av Myrdal?" *Norrskensflamman* (Luleå), 4 February 1936.
10. Inteview with Gunnar Myrdal, in "Myrdal vill ej ha många barn," *Vecko-Journalen*, 5 April 1936.
11. See "I Hinkes förspår: 'Alva propaganda' contra 'Gunnar propagandan,'" *Vest. Svenska Dagbladet*, 15 February 1936. This article viewed Alva Myrdal in the tradition of Hinke Bergegren, while Gunnar Myrdal was identified with the moderate commission line.
    The Myrdals claim that no split or change in their position occurred—that each had an understood role to play in the debate and, in this instance, were only answering charges. Note to the author from Alva Myrdal, 23 July 1977.
12. "Ett inlägg från fru Myrdal," *Folket Dagblad Politiken*, 7 February 1936.
13. Prime Minister Hansson's endorsement of the volume, and its "clearing of the air," is noted in "Ett nytt socialist monopol," *Kalmar Tidningen Barometer* 3 (August 1936).
14. Gunnar Myrdal, *Vad gäller striden i befolkningsfrågan* (Stockholm: Frihets Förlag, 1936).
15. Gunnar Lundberg, "Myrdaleriet avslöjas av popularaste källe!," *Social-Demokraten* 27 March 1936; and Gunnar Lundberg, "Befolkningsfråga

och socialpolitik," *Frihet*, no. 5 (1936).

16. Mauritz Västberg, "Kilboms kaninsvindel," *Social–Demokraten* (Stockholm), 14 January 1936.

17. Tor Jerneman, "Arbetsmarknaden och vår befolkningsfråga," *Fackföreningsrörelsen*, 20 March 1936, pp. 419–24, and 27 March 1936, pp. 443–50.

18. Gösta Rehn, "Dit befolkningsfrågan hunnit," *Clarté*, June 1936, p. 22.

19. H. G. Tonndorf, "Folkminskningens ekonomiska verkningar," *Tiden* 28 (February 1936); Torsten Gårdlund, "Befolkningsfrågan i dagens politik," *Tiden* 29 (January 1937); and T. Gårdlund, "Befolkningsfrågan i dagens politik-II," *Tiden* 29 (February 1937).

20. From "Protokoll fört vid sammanträde med Dalarnas soc.-dem. landstingsgrupp den 1 September 1935 i Falun," and "Protokoll fört vid sammantrede med representanter för Dalarnas soc.-dem. partidistrikts-styrelse, Landtingsgruppen och partistyrelsen, den 21 Juli 1935 i Falun," *Verkställande utskottets bilagor* (SAP, Rolle 22 A:II:B, 16–18, 1935); interview with Gunnar Myrdal, Stockholm, 26 July 1976; and Glesinger, "Gunnar Myrdal," Mimeographed biography, 6 December 1948), p. 4.

21. "Valet i Kopperbergs län," *Östgöta Correspondenten* (Linköping), 27 July 1935.

22. *Protokoll från sverges socialdemokratiska arbetarepartis 15:e congress (Stockholm, 3–9 April 1936)* (Stockholm: Tryckerietaktiebolaget Tiden, 1937), p. 188.

23. *Protokoll från... 15:e congress*, p. 188.
The party steering committee decided at its 29–30 October 1935 meeting to recommend rejection of the Stocksund motion, with no debate on the subject recorded. (See "Protokoll fört vid partistyrelsens sammanträde tisdagens den 29–30 October 1935," *Partistyrelsens protokoll 1931–39*, SAP Rolle 5, A:I:A: 17–19.) The working group of the party steering committee subsequently assigned its chairman—Per Albin Hansson—to author the party leadership's formal response to the motion. (See "Protokoll, hållet vid sammanträde i Stockholm med socialdemokratiska partistyrelsens verkställande utskott den 7 November 1935," *Verkställande utskottets protokoll, 1935*, SAP Rolle 9, A:II:A: 8–11.)

24. *Protokoll från... 15e congress*, p. 189.
Despite his early expressions of interest, a thorough review of Möller's speeches and notes after 1935 reveals that he never embraced the full "population perspective" on social problems advanced by the Myrdals or its pronatalist justification. From 1936 on, he makes no mention of the "population focus," citing only the individual components of the Population Commission's work: marriage loans, health care for mothers and children, dental care, maternity assistance, delivery care, abortion measures, and summer camps. (See "Familjevärdande socialpolitik" and "Riksdagen 1937," notes in GMÖA, vol. 2 [Föredrag, n.a.].) His short address to the 1936 party congress on the population question was consistent with this orientation. It may be partially ac-

counted for by Möller's continued distrust of Gunnar Myrdal as an "intellectual." Interview with Richard Sterner, Stockholm, 29 June 1977.

25. *Protokoll från . . . 15:e Congress*, pp. 189–95.
26. See: "1936," handwritten note by Gustav Möller from early 1936, in GMÖa, vol. 2. This personal planning list itemized the social policy programs to be dealt with by the 1936 Riksdag, including pension reform, health care, union rights, accident and sickness insurance, the position of agricultural workers, and unemployment. Among the "deferred questions" (*väntande frågor*) were maternity assistance, support for mothers in need, health care, child allowances (for widows and orphans), and marriage loans.
27. Ruth Stjernstedt, "Kvantitativ befolkningspolitik," *Dagens Nyheter* (Stockholm), 28 February 1936.
28. See *Socialdemokratistiska riksdagsgruppen förtroenderåds protokoll*, 24 January 1936.
29. From *Socialdemokrtaiska riksdagsgruppen protokoll*, 29 January 1936.
30. *Riksdagens protokoll: Första kammaren 1936* 2 (no. 27) (24 April 1936): 14–15; and . . . *Andra kammaren 1936* 7 (no. 27) (24 April 1936): 5–6.
31. Ibid., p. 28.
32. *Riksdagens protokoll: Andra kammaren (1936)* 7, (no. 31): (9 May 1936).
33. In an interview given later that month, Wohlin reiterated that the Finance Department's opposition to the special tax placed a shadow over the commission's past and future work. The commission, he believed, would have to seriously reconsider the directions in which it had hoped to move in the future. In *Östgöta Correspondenten* (Linköping), 30 May 1936.
34. Debate from *Riksdagens protokoll: Första kammaren 1936* 3, (no. 31) (9 May 1936): 16–18; and . . . *Andra kammaren 1936* 7, (no. 31) (9 May 1936):28.
35. *Social–Demokraten* (Stockholm), 27 November 1936.
36. See *SSU, SAP studieplan i aktuell politik* (Stockholm, 1936). One of the thirteen study sessions was devoted to the population question, with the subheadings: (1) Population growth in Sweden; (2) Is increased nativity desirable?; and (3) Population policy measures?
37. Handwritten note from early 1936, fragment no. 102, in PAH, vol. Ia, II: 4.
38. Speeches found in PAH, vol. 5, 1935–36.
39. Copies of drafts found in *Verkställande utskottets bilagor* (SAP Rulle 23, A:II:B: 18, 1936).
40. Ibid.
41. Script found in PAH, vol. 5, n.d.
42. Per Albin Hansson and Gustav Möller for *Socialdemokratiska partisyyrelsen* :Till Sveriges folk," release no. 135 (1936), in *Verkställande utskottets bilagor* (SAP Rulle 23, A:II:B: 18, 1936).
43. "Inför höstens val," in PAH, vol. 5 (1936).
44. Complete text of speech reprinted in "Vår lösen är: Hemmet, Familjen,"

Hus och härd, September 1936.

45. Gunnar Myrdal, V\u00e5ra sociala syftlinjer," *Frihet*, 1 September 1936, pp. 3–4.

46. Alva Myrdal, "Familjens framtid—folkets framtid," in a brochure, *Den 20 september* (1936), Alva and Gunnar Myrdal Clipping Collection (hereafter AGMC).

47. This was Hansson's candid assessment of the election. See "Socialdemokratiska riksdagsgruppens protokoll, 11 Jan. 1937." *Socialdemokratiska riksdagsgruppens arkiv*, Stockholm.

48. For surveys of the 1937 session see Tor Jerneman, *Handbok rörande folkpensioner, barnbidrag, bidragsförskott och mödrashjälp* (Stockholm, 1938); and Andrea Andreen-Svedberg, "En epokgärande riksdag," *Morgonbris*, March 1937.

49. From Gustav Möller, notation—"Riksdag 1937," GMÖA, vol. 2.

50. *Socialdemokratiska riksdagsgruppens protokoll*, 11 January 1937.

51. Hannson made similar points in a 4 February 1937 lecture at Uppsala, where he integrated commission recommendations into his social policy vision. "Föredrag; Uppsala," 4 February 1937, PAH, vol. 5.

52. For the Riksdag debate on reorganization of the midwife system see *Riksdags protokoll: Första kammaren 1937* 3, no. 31 (12 May 1937): 29–39.

53. *Riksdags protokoll: Första kammaren 1937* 3, no. 29 (5 May 1937): 6–28, particularly 16–17. See also *Riksdagens protokoll: Andra kammaren 1937* 7, no. 29 (5 May 1937) 7–33.

54. This figure rose to 5.8 million kronor for the 1939/40 fiscal year. See Ann Katrin Hatje, *Befolkningsfr\u00e5gan och välfärden: Debarten om familjepolitik-och nativite sökning under 1930-talen* (Stockholm: allmänea Förlaget, 1974), pp. 32–35; and Alva Myrdal, *Nation and Family: The Swedish Experiment in Democratic Family and Population Policy* (New York: Harper and Brothers), pp. 229–30.

55. For the Riksdag debate see *Riksdagens protokoll: Första kammaren 1937* 4, no. 37 (29 May 1937): 130–39; and *Riksdagens protokoll: Andra kammaren 1937* 8, no. 35 (26 May 1937): 33–41.

    On the relation of the marriage loan program to the introduction of modern furniture in Sweden and the general "socialization of taste" see "Bättre och vackare hem genom bosattningsl\u00e5n," *Frihet*, July 1938.

56. *Riksdagens protokoll: Första kammaren 1937* 4 no. 41 (June 1937) 42–61. Also: "Barnbidrag och bidragsforskott," *Sunt Förnuft*, May 1937.

57. Wigforss defended his proposal in "Provisorisk löneförbättring och familjförsörjning," *SAP Information*, March 1937, pp. 65–69; and Ernst Wigforss, "Likalön och familjelön, Radiodiscussion den 3 Maj 1937," in Ernest Wigforss Collection, Arbetarrörelsens Arkiv (hereafter EW), 62.

58. On the general debate see "Hr. Wigforss barntillägg," *Dagens Nyheter* (Stockholm), 27 March 1937; and "Hr. Wigforss framstöt," *Arbetet* (Malmö), 21 April 1937.

59. See Gunnar Myrdal, "Kontant eller in natura i socialpolitiken?" *Arbetet* (Malmö), 26 January 1938; and Gunnar Myrdal, "Socialpolitik in na-

tura," *Första Maj* (1938): 31–32.

60. For the Parliamentary Group debates see *Socialdemokratiska riksdags-gruppens protokoll*, 8 April 1937, 18 May 1937, and 24 May 1937.

On the radio debate see "Radiodebatt om lika, lön och barntil-lägg," *Svenska Dagbladet* (Stockholm), 4 May 1937; and "Social lön eller marknads lön?" *Kristianstadsläns Demokraten*, 5 May 1937.

On the Riksdag debate see "Lärarnas lönefråga inför riksdagen," *Svenska Lärartidning*, 22 May 1937.

The controversy left lasting scars. Wigforss's memoirs give the incident revealing attention *(Minnen, III. 1932–1949* [Stockholm: Tidens Förlag, 1954], pp. 362–63). The finance minister also became a promi-nent force in securing passage of a universal child allowance system in 1946.

61. Hatje, *Befolkningsfrågan och välfärden*, pp. 37–39; and Alva Myrdal, *Nation and Family*, pp. 196–99. Opposition by druggists to mandatory sale of contraceptives had prevented approval of the measure in 1937.

62. Alva Myrdal, *National Family*, pp. 211–12; and Hatje, *Befolkningsfrå-gan och välfärden*, pp. 135–38.

Hatje argues that the Population Commission, and by implication the government, supported a restrictive law on abortion and an abandon-ment of "social indicators" in order to push through other social and sexual policy reforms. When the commission's promised "future vision" of a "social political utopia" that would eliminate the need for abortion failed to materialize, its rejection of "social indicators" proved a failure. The 1938 law, she concludes, only codified existing practice.

63. See "Riksdagens diskuteranda Myrdal," *Göteborgs Tidningen*, 3 March 1938.

64. See "Läkarutbildningen kräuer mer av socialt inslag," *Dagens Nyheter* (Stockholm), 20 January 1938.

65. Möller's list of the "affected proposals" is found in "Reformpausen (1938)," GMÖA, vol. 2. It includes large-family housing, school lunches, and extension of cost-free health care.

66. Gunnar Myrdal to D. V. Glass, 4 February 1939, GMAL. See also Hatje, *Befolkningsfrågan och välfärden*, pp. 43–45.

67. On the publicity surrounding the Carnegie offer and its possible relation-ship to Myrdal's population policy work in Sweden see "Myrdal tar hand om negerna," *Nya Dagligt Allehanda* (Stockholm), 14 December 1937.

68. Gunnar Myrdal to Jacob Viner, 14 February 1938, GMAL.

69. Gunnar Myrdal to Nils Wohlin, 9 September 1938, RA 542, vol. 5.

70. See *Protokoll* for May–August 1938 and "Arbetsutskottets Protokoll," April–August 1938 in RA 542, vol. 1.

71. Wohlin to members of the Population Commission, 15 May 1936, in GMA 11.2.4.

72. See "Arbetsutskottet protokoll, 28 February 1938," in RA 542, vol. 1; Nils Wohlin to Gustav Möller, 7 October 1938, RA 542, vol. 2, no. 132; and Nils Wohlin to Gunnar Myrdal, 26 Nov. 1938, GMA 11.2.4.

73. Interview with Richard Sterner, Stockholm, 29 June 1977.
74. Telegram from Gunnar Myrdal to Nils Wohlin, sometime between 7 and 17 July 1938, RA 542, vol. 3.
75. *Protokoll* for 16 August 1938, RA 542, vol. 1; and Gunnar Myrdal to Johan Persson and Disa Västberg, 15 December 1938, GMAL.
76. Gunnar Myrdal to Sven Wicksell, 29 August 1938, GMAL.
77. Gunnar Myrdal to Nils Wohlin, 9 September 1938, GMA 11.2.3.
78. *Protokoll* for 26 Septemmber 1938, RA 542, vol. 1.
79. Telegrams, Nils Wohlin to Gunnar Myrdal, 5 October 1938, and Gunnar Myrdal to Wohlin, 10 October 1938, in RA 542, vol. 5.
80. Nils Wohlin to members of the Population Commission, 11 October 1938, RA 542, vol. 3, and minutes of the meeting of the Population Commission held 2 November 1938, in GMA 11.2.4.
81. *Protokoll* for 2 November 1938, RA 542, vol. 1.
82. Nils Wohlin to Gunnar Myrdal, 26 November 1938, GMA 11.2.4., p. 4.
83. Ibid., pp. 5–8.
84. Gunnar Myrdal to Johan Persson and Disa Västberg, 15 December 1938, GMA 11.2.4., p. 4.
85. Ibid., p. 5.
86. Ibid., "P.N. med exempel ur befolkningskommissionens slutbetänkande," p. 1.
87. Ibid., pp. 1–2.
88. Ibid., p. 2.
89. *Protokoll* for 18 December 1938, RA 542, vol. 1.
90. "Särskilt yttrande av herr Persson och fru Västberg," GMA 11.2.3, p. 4.
91. "Särskilt yttrande av herr Persson och fru Västberg," p. 5.
92. Ibid., pp. 6–9.
93. The two telegrams are found in RA 542, vol. 1.
    Magnusson also decided on "no [dissenting] report," suggesting that all three potential dissenters abided by Wohlin's call for unity.
94. SOU 1938: 57, Socialdepartementet, *Slutbetänkande* (Stockholm, 1938), p. 11. For examples of the language Myrdal disliked see pp. 26–31 and 34.
95. See Birger Hagård, *Nils Wohlin: Konservativ centerpolitiker* (Linkoping: A B Sahlströms Bokhandel, 1976), p. 389.
96. Gunnar Myrdal to Disa Västberg, 25 February 1939, GMA 11.2.4.

7

The Use and Abuse of Social Science

Departure for the United States brought an end, for several decades, to the direct involvement of the Myrdals in the crafting of Swedish domestic policy. Already, though, their work was being cloned in other countries, with similar results. For example, the Myrdal line spread successfully to Denmark and Norway. In both of these countries, translations of *Kris i befolkningsfrågan* and numerous direct appearances by the Myrdals stimulated independent debates and the creation of parallel population commissions in, respectively, 1935 and 1936. Their conclusions were strikingly similar to the work done in Sweden. The Myrdals also gave direct encouragement to democratic socialists in Great Britain, which resulted in creation of the Royal Commission on Population in 1944.[1]

Yet the deeper significance of the Myrdals' effort remains in dispute. For many decades, Swedish scholars regarded the Myrdals work on population as triggering "the breakthrough" of modern Swedish social policy, the first full expression of and scientific justification for the complete welfare state.[2] Several recent historians argue otherwise. Hatje, for instance, views their book and project as little more than a compilation of existing policy ideas, stitched together into a good—if less than original—public relations package. She dismisses the 1935 Population Commission as a place where "no comprehensive reforms" were actually achieved and casts the Myrdals' involvement in the abortion debate as reactionary in its thrust, a net setback to the work of the Swedish women's movement.[3]

In her attempt to measure the actual effects of specific policies adopted in the 1930s, Kälvemark describes a mixed bag. Looking at the marriage loan program, for example, she finds an ironic result: Among the couples in a Stockholm sample who took the loans, behavior was the exact reverse of that expected. They had fewer conceptions and births than similarly situated couples who did not take the loans. In addition, the divorce rate of this group was disturbingly high: 27.5 percent of loan-receiving marriages had resulted in divorce by 1942, compared to only 12 percent among the general population.

The maternity relief program also produced contradictory results. The aid program proved to be much more "popular" than anticipated; by 1941, more than half of all Swedish women giving birth qualified for and received the special aid, five times the predicted number. However, unanticipated side effects showed up, with Kälvemark discovering that unmarried mothers receiving the aid were less likely to marry than similarly situated women not receiving the aid. More disturbing, given the Myrdals' and the commission's arguments, was the finding that relative high numbers of children could be found only among women with low ages at marriage and high rates of premaritally born or conceived children: in short, among the premodern, "irrational" couples that the new programs theoretically dismissed as anachronistic.

Only the housing programs showed a positive effect: the divorce rate among families in special family housing was lower than the national average. However, it proved impossible to determine what effect the housing program had had on subsequent fertility. Added together, Kälvemark's work suggests either the neutral impact or overall failure of the Myrdals' project.[4]

To judge their impact on these criteria, though, is to miss the larger meaning of historical change. In this light, two themes deserve attention: A review of the Myrdals use and abuse of the social sciences and an analysis of their true long-term social goals, as opposed to the momentary utility of the pronatalist and profamily messages.

Concerning social science and policy, the Myrdals' work set a widely copied model for the use of scientific data, both in the creation of a crisis and the turning of that crisis toward the growth of the state. Prior to the 1930s, "crisis" had justified state expansion only in periods of invasion, war, or (rarely) economic difficulty. National socialists in Italy and Germany had advanced the model of crisis stimulation and control during the 1920s and early 1930s, but it fell to the Myrdals to give the use of crisis a democratic spin.

At the time, demographic science was new, with only embryonic paradigms and untested theories. The Myrdals forged ahead, undaunted. To some degree, Sweden's (like Europe's) population crisis derived from the weaknesses of social science, rather than its strength. For example, the possibility or theory of "demographic transition"—a society-wide shift from a high fertility/high mortality order to a low fertility/low mortality one—was but dimly perceived at the time. Moreover, Kuczynski's widely repeated calculations of national net reproduction rates tended to overstate the fertility decline. In addition, later work revealed that a good share of the fertility dip in the early 1930s—the development giving such air of urgency to *Kris i befolkningsfrågan* and similar books—was in fact fertility delayed rather than fertility denied. The *completed* fertility of West European female cohorts during the 1920–45 period actually showed surprising stability.[5] Nonetheless, flawed calculations and poorly interpreted data proved useful to the Myrdals in turning change into crisis and crisis into political action.

The true uncertainty of their science came masked by the utter confidence and avoidance of nuance characterizing their work. Gunnar Myrdal explained, over and again, that his certainty derived from "clearly stated value premises" that merely gave direction to neutral facts. A more accurate explanation may be that Gunnar Myrdal became the most effective practitioner of the scientific jargon that came to dominate the University of Stockholm's Social Science Institute in the late 1920s and 1930s. As the relatively clean prose of sociology's nineteenth-century founders gave way to the promiscuous use of numbers and hyphenated phrases of its twentieth-century practitioners, Myrdal's distinctions between "values" and "facts" became blurred and jargon became a convenient cover for political goals.[6]

Further, the Myrdals' linkage of cause to effect to policy response proved extremely weak. The scientific justification for the transfer of income from the relatively wealthy and "child poor" to the relatively poor and "child rich" rested on Edin's finding that, at the higher income levels and for some social classes, net completed fertility rose a significant, albeit small, amount. While an important and unexpected discovery, the Edin work was a limited special case, of uncertain and perhaps transitory meaning. Indeed, the data could be read to negate the Myrdals' conclusions. To begin with, it was objectively impossible to raise the "bottom 90 percent" of the population to the same income level of the "top 10 percent," which could be the only logical policy inference drawn from some of Edin's work. At best, the relatively poor with children could be moved some notches up the income scale, but the numbers suggested that this would in fact reduce, not increase, subsequent fertility. Progressive taxation at the highest levels, moreover, would predictably drive down the fertility of one group showing a positive relationship between income and number of births.

Nonetheless, the Myrdals dominated the interpretation of Edin's work and crafted policy accordingly. The living standard case, for example, guided the construction of the Population Commission's marriage loan program. Using the argument that economic pressures led to delayed marriage and that low marriage rates and high ages at marriage for women were contributing causes of fertility decline, the commission concluded that an economic boost would deliver more marriages and more births. Curiously, data collected by Commission member Sven Wicksell showed that, except in the northernmost parts of Sweden, fertility actually was high where marriage rates were low and vice versa. Indeed, the marriage rate was highest in urban areas, where fertility was lowest. Nonetheless, marriage loans were implemented, with policy being the slave to theory rather than to statistical fact.

The Swedish experience with population policy also showed the frailty of applied social science. Most obviously, the commission recommended and the Riksdag approved national programs that had enjoyed no test. These "scientifically justified" policies would never face the true test of science: a controlled experiment. Moreover, no measures were taken or funds provided to check the results of policy actions against stated goals in later years. This failure to test results against goals remains, perhaps, the most common of errors made in applying social science to policy formation.

In short, it is difficult to see social science in this episode as little more than a new tool for rhetorical control and political advantage. Weak and inconsistent data, confusion over cause and effect, and avoidance of experimentation proved to be no obstacles to the construction and implementation of policy.

But the image of failure disappears and the seeming contradictions fall into a pattern as we turn to the deeper goals of the Myrdals. While Gunnar Myrdal showed, at times, true sympathy for the need to generate more births, the pair's central goal was the construction of a radically different Sweden. Their consistent purpose, articulated throughout the 1930s, aimed at specific triumphs by new ideas or institutions over old ones. These included:

The triumph of feminism over the old socialism. In the scale of values brought by the Myrdals to policy formation, highest priority fell to the social liberty and equality of the individual, particularly in matters related to gender. The equality of households, the democratic socialist goal in the early twentieth century, became subordinate in their scheme to the equality of individuals within households. Women and men were to be independent actors, with no bonds beyond those of freely entered affection. A family wage for breadwinners, once the central Democratic Socialist demand, became an affront in the 1930s, a vehicle of oppression and dependence. The Myrdals program of maternity relief, for example, made a fundamental break with prior policy: it was a reform intended exclusively for women. Only women could apply, and the money was reserved for mothers and their children. At a 1938 conference on maternity aid, witnesses reported on the disruptive effects of the law: "It is not a question of hardness or ill will on behalf of the men—it is just that it is all so completely at odds with general custom and tradition. Always earlier, in matters concerning money, it has been the men's money."[7]

The triumph of reason over tradition. The new programs devised and delivered by the Myrdals skewed benefits in favor of citizens governed by modern reason, at the expense of those guided by religion and tradition. Put another way, the Enlightenment's children stood as victors over the remaining pockets of old Sweden. Turning again to the marriage loan program, its irony—that participants had fewer children and more divorces—disappears as the operation comes under scrutiny. As structured by the Population Commission, the borrowers had to be employed or cite other conditions indicating their ability to repay the loans. Regulations specified that recipients be "known as steady and economically prudent" and show "a willingness to save." In short, the loan program pointed toward the selection of people with a high sense of economic rationality, the very ones who could also be expected to control and restrict births in service to other consumption goals.[8] Persons with convictions that held procreation to be a religious obligation or contraception as immoral were the ones who would probably not qualify for the state benefit, but who would be taxed to pay for it.

The triumph of the central government over the regions. While relatively unified and centrally directed by nineteenth-century standards, Sweden still enjoyed a high degree of decentralized governance in domestic matters. Poor relief and social welfare, in particular, remained into the 1930s largely a local affair, the responsibility of municipalities and rural parishes. Using the same example, the new maternity assistance program not only disrupted prevailing male-female relationships, but also shifted new power to central authorities. The funds came directly from Stockholm, and county maternity assistance boards were controlled by the central government. In the name of family, localities and regions surrendered control over community welfare to the central Social Ministry, the first phase of a massive—and now largely completed—retreat.

The triumph of the urban, multifamily dwelling over the suburban single-family model. While Western nations have witnessed, over the last 150 years, a common migration of populations from farms to modern cities, two rival housing patterns have emerged, with significantly different consequences for the family. In the United States and New Zealand, for example, policy preference fell to single-family dwellings, a choice that built the new suburbs that now define majority life in both countries. This was a way of life consciously designed to retain a symbolic ruralism, through lawns and gardens, and which appears to have contributed to the continuation of older family patterns.[9] In Sweden, however, the Myrdals were instrumental in shaping a policy focused on semicollectivized multifamily housing, steeped in a celebration of the urban and of rationalized, efficient consumption. They admitted that children had little place in an urban setting, but they were also willing to risk the disappearance of the young in their gamble that a reordered, centrally guided social system could reconcile children to the city.

The triumph of the therapeutic over the moral. As secular materialists, the Myrdals' vision held no place for the claims of revealed truth. For them, morals were a function of institutions and social evolution. If a majority of the population behaved in a manner that violated a religious or traditional code, then the code had lost its utility and needed to be brought in line with behavior. In place of displaying moral condemnation or approval, the Myrdals raised individuals as independent social actors with duties reduced largely to service to the state (principally through paying taxes and procreation). The Myrdals also inverted blame. The refusal to procreate did not lie with the moral failings of the young, who refused to marry or have children, but with the liberal capitalist society and outdated moralisms. Accordingly, the Myrdals elevated the self as an actor free from the petty bonds and tyrannies of immediate family, kin, local community, and tradition and redefined morality to mean recognizing human needs and drives, a task of social psychology.

The triumph of the state over the family. As the central goal of their project, the Myrdals took the American sociology of Burgess and Ogburn and gave it an activist spin. Seeking to strip away the remaining functions adhering to the family, they pursued the leap to a new and presumably better social order. The primary task, in this regard, was to eliminate home production and the home economy. Incentives must shift and laws must change so that women would abandon unpaid home production activities such as child care, gardening, and cooking in favor of market employment. Laws, regulations, and taxes should remove the economic benefit adhering to marriage. New programs to support the children of never-married mothers and the children of divorce should eliminate the economic necessity and functional value of fatherhood. Dependency, a universal in any society with very young, very old, and infirm people, must also be stripped away. Women should never be dependent on husbands, nor men on wives, nor the elderly on grown children, nor young children on their parents. Rather, the Myrdals envisioned a new order, where all individuals would be equally dependent on the state. Not only child care but also consumption—the last family economic function—should be socialized. Rent rebates predicated on "proper design," marriage loans stipulating the purchase of "modern, hygienic furniture," school lunch programs, in-kind food and clothing benefits: all this and more aimed at turning even the consuming side of the family over to central direction. In the end, only the sexual and procreative functions were to be left with free individuals, who might be married. The Myrdals hoped and believed that this artful combination of socialized community and moral freedom would be sufficient to secure enough children to fund the entire apparatus in the future.

It is true that the new Sweden, envisioned by the Myrdals in the early 1930s, described in *Kris in befolkningsfrågan*, and built into the work of the Population Commission, was not a reality by 1939. The old Sweden—an amalgam of the rural Christian past and the world of the middle class—remained the normative order. Indeed, when a second Population Commission organized in 1941, nationalist and traditionalist themes predominated, and its principal recommendation—the construction of a universal children's allowance program—ran counter to the Myrdals' push for "in kind" social assistance.[10]

On the surface, the 1950s proved to be even more at odds with the Myrdals' formulation. The proportion of Sweden's population that was married rose to a record height, while the average age of first marriage declined. Over 90 percent of all marriages still took place under church auspices. In 1950, a hefty 85 percent of married Swedish women remained homemakers; as late as 1965, 75 percent of Swedish preschoolers were still cared for, full-time, in their homes. Sexual traditionalism also seemed the order of the day. For example, *The Handbook on Sex Instruction in Swedish Schools*, published in 1956, deviated far from the vision of the sexual modernists. It stated that sex life must, from the start, be associated with "its objects—home, family, and children" and that it was "extremely important that pupils should realize fully that home and family are the groundrock of society, cemented together partly by love between man and woman and parent and children, partly by law .... Legal marriage has accordingly a moral value which cannot be dispensed with."[11] Even Alva Myrdal succumbed to this spell of bourgeois domesticity and coauthored (with Viola Klein) the book *Women's Two Roles: Home and Work*. While still arguing that women should plan for careers, Myrdal gave unusual attention to the psychological need of small children for the full-time care of their mothers. She argued that mothers should stay home until their children were of school age and only work part-time until the youngest child reached age fifteen.[12] Even the number of legal abortions declined during this phase, as bourgeois familism enjoyed an apparent resurgence.

Yet beneath this surface, deeper forces of change were at work. Eating away at Sweden's family system were the ideas and institutions created and mobilized by the population debate of the 1930s. As intended, programs of maternity assistance and children's aid steadily enhanced the economic power and autonomy of women at the expense of the economic utility of men. Special aid for the children of never-married women also worked to subvert the economic logic of marriage, leaving husbands increasingly superfluous. Equal pay laws, endorsed by the Population Commission as a necessary factor in the new order, progressively dismantled the semiformal family wage that had helped sustain traditional familism. Housing programs skewed toward multifamily and high-rise dwellings encouraged a decline in family-centered autonomy and the turn by individuals (particularly the young) from family to peers as the dominant force in the shaping of values. As progressive taxation and family welfare programs grew, in tandem, the effective tax burden also shifted against traditional families. Committed to unsubsidized home production activities such as child care and elder care, such families found their income (including their imputed income) taxed to pay for the new families living state-preferred lives; in effect, they would carry the burden of both systems. But over time, state economic and cultural incentives lured ever more Swedes out of traditional networks, in favor of the new and financially supported order.

The institutions and professions influenced by the Myrdals' formulation in the 1930s also remained active centers for change. While preschool teachers and day-care providers were relatively few in the 1950s, practitioners trained at Alva Myrdal's Social Pedagogical Institute and its clones continued to flow into the system, undaunted by the bourgeois domesticity around them and still committed to the vision of the 1930s. Secure in their strategic point of control, they bided their time. So did the growing cadre of social welfare experts and social workers flowing from Swedish universities into government service. Committed to an activist state and to socialist solidarity, they also shared in the Myrdal vision and waited for its new moment.

Finally, the renewed domesticity of the 1950s rested on a frail base. While educators affirmed marital fidelity, international child development experts such as John Bowlby applauded maternal care, and sociologists affirmed the need for two to four children per couple, the rationales used were always utilitarian: fidelity would increase the security felt by children; maternal care was psychologically healthy; a stable population was economically desirable. Rival metaphysical explanations for these preferences carried ever decreasing weight. Meanwhile, the authority of the social sciences as the arbiter of truth grew. Utility, though, was a fickle defender of the old family system. If and when social priorities shifted or the scientific evidence became murky or opposite in its implications, then utilitarian science would easily become the opponent of tradition.

The family system, which had found some affirmation in the expert science of the 1950s, faced a fresh, albeit familiar, challenge in the 1960s. The core idea assault came from a renewed radical feminism, stimulated in 1961 by editor Eva Moberg's 1961 essay "The Conditional Emanicipation of Women." Rejecting the argument that women's first responsibility was homemaking, Moberg said that "both men and women have one principal role, that of being human beings." Women's status could not be improved until men's roles also changed.[13] Over the next few years, public debate on sex roles became a national passion. In a revealing description of the debate's structure, analyst Edmund Dahlstrom noted that conservative viewpoints on the issue—be they the "traditional" ideology "anchored in the Judeo/Christian religion and in talismanic concepts" of men as lord of the household or the "romantic" middle-class ideology that viewed men and women as different and complementary—were "seldom championed at the 'expert' level of debate." Instead, the experts were heavily arrayed on the "liberal radical" side, denying that women could ever balance their "two roles" without total social reconstruction, necessitating the leveling of sex roles.[14]

In the influential and symbolically titled 1969 document *Toward Equality: The Alva Myrdal Report to the Swedish Social Democratic Party*, the new Working Group on Equality headed by Myrdal drew on themes she had articulated thirty-five years before, pronouncing the equivalent of a death sentence on the family. Its autonomy and strength were no longer of interest, with the focus instead on how each individual within a family could best develop his or her independent talents. Gender and parental relations should no longer determine dependency status. Equality and independence could be won only through the programs of the beneficent, equality-minded state. Families *per se* ought to enjoy no favoritism, with adults being "treated in the same manner by the society whether they live alone or in some form of common living arrangement." Cutting to the heart of the family economy, Myrdal's group affirmed "the economic independence of marriage partners" as "the basis for future legislation."[15] In short, Alva Myrdal had triumphed and the Swedish family as a distinct, autonomous social unit was doomed.

The pace of social reconstruction was already in high gear. In the mid-1960s, for example, state school officials adopted "an emphatic policy of not only refusing to perpetuate but actively counteracting the

traditional view of sex roles." At the same time, labor and social planners grew anxious over the darkening complexions of immigrants
coming into Sweden. Rather than pronatalism, though, they concluded
that housewives were Sweden's greatest untapped labor supply, certainly one easier to assimilate than southeast Europeans, Africans, or
Turks. If government economic goals were to be met, more married
women with children would have to enter the paid labor market.[16]

Over the next ten years, Swedish labor policy focused primarily on
achieving "full employment" for women. The central government directly funded the placement and training of women in traditionally
male industrial jobs, through "equality grants." In 1969, the state directed its schools "to counteract the traditional attitudes to sex roles
and stimulate pupils to question the differences between men and
women with respect to influence, work assignments and wages . . . ."
In its instructions to the 1971 Commission on a New Marriage Law,
the Social Democratic government made explicit the state's social and
economic priorities: "There is no reason to refrain from using legislation on marriage and the family as one of the instruments in the struggle to shape a society in which every adult takes responsibility for
himself without being economically dependent on another and where
equality between the sexes is a reality."

The same year, the government's tax reform initiative eliminated
income splitting and the joint return, henceforward taxing husbands
and wives separately on salary and wage earnings. Tax tables also
become more progressive. The joint effect was to sharply raise the
after-tax income of couples where both worked, while sharply cutting
the retained income of single-wage-earner families. Symbolically, the
Social Democrats sacrificed here one of their most hallowed principles—the progressive taxation of households—in order to force a tax
on the imputed income of the homemaker and to drive mothers into the
marketplace. Feminism had triumphed over socialism. As radical
leader Annika Baude put the matter, this single change in taxation
became the critical turning point in the liberation of women and the
final dismantling of the family economy. There was now a large economic gain to be had from a wife's salary, and "married men started to
look with much more favor than before on the idea of their wives
taking jobs." With the economic benefits of marriage finally and fully
stripped away, the marriage rate also fell sharply while the divorce rate
climbed higher.[17]

State subsidies flowed increasingly in favor of "new families," involving cohabitation outside of marriage or single women deliberately raising children without male presence. Meanwhile, family legislation was altered fundamentally: where prior law had stated that spouses had the obligation to support marriage through market labor or work in the home, new law deleted the phrase "work in the home." In another richly symbolic act, the Swedish government stipulated that if no official last name for a child was reported to the local office at time of birth, the child would be given the mother's name. In 1977, the National Swedish Board of Education issued a new sex education volume, which effectively dismissed marriage as in any way relevant to sexual behavior. In its place was another guiding principle: "The most important goal of instruction concerning interpersonal relations is to promote the capacity for intimacy. . . . Sexual activities can take place without intimacy, but school instruction concerning interpersonal relations argues that sexuality on a basis of personal intimacy satisfies a profound human need."[18]

By 1980, the social revolution in Sweden was complete, legally and institutionally. On occasions, it is true, the population of Sweden still showed some retardation in adapting to the new order. For example, despite twenty years of fairly systematic indoctrination, Swedish schoolgirls still tend to favor occupations in traditionally "female" fields, and "parental leave"—equally available to new mothers and fathers—is utilized primarily by women.[19] Occasionally, pronatalist sentiment wells up again, as some Swedes focus on their national future.[20] Yet these examples of ideological lag, while perhaps offering hints of truth about human nature, are already the object of intense new rounds of human engineering and government education and may not continue for long.

The true new reality in Sweden can be seen in the social statistics: Between 1966 and 1974 alone, the Swedish marriage rate fell 40 percent, and today it is the lowest among all modern nations. Based on current trends, an estimated 36 percent of Swedish women born in 1955 will not have married by the time they reach age fifty (compared to but 9 percent of women born in 1940). Cohabitation among unmarried couples, meanwhile, is high, reaching 50 percent among men ages twenty-five to twenty-nine. While overall Swedish fertility remains about 15–20 percent below the zero-growth level (a total fertility rate ranging from 1.7 to 1.8), half of current births occur outside of marriage. When divorce rate and "the dissolution rate of cohabitation couples" are added together, Sweden probably has the highest rate of "couple dissolution" in the world. Sweden also leads the world in having both the smallest average household size (2.2 persons) and the highest percentage of single-person households. Downtown Stockholm sets the pace, with 63 percent of all households containing only single persons. Meanwhile, 85 percent of Swedish mothers with children under age seven are in the labor force, while the young homemaker has become virtually extinct. Volunteerism, the product of neighborhoods filled with housewives and home-centered women, has also vanished. Rationalism dominates Swedish sexuality; even Swedish teenagers have finally proven to be effective contraceptors. While the average age of first intercourse by Swedish girls pushes toward fourteen, Sweden is also the only Western country to have shown a significant decline in its teenage abortion rate in recent years.[21]

The Myrdals must rest content, for once the family gloss is pealed away, their population program aimed at the world in which the Swedes now live. Only the ability of the Swedes to reproduce in a postfamily order still remains in question, but even this may have been only a nostalgic quirk of Gunnar's: momentarily useful, but never really shared by his spouse or critical to their authentic vision.

While it is true that the Myrdals drew their interpretations, policy ideas, and even overarching schemes largely from others, they were the necessary actors in an important historical drama. Their creative acts were to draw these concepts together into a unified vision, to sell the program and tactics to the Social Democratic party, and to create and dominate the institutions that would over time bring the vision to fruition.

Some commentators would see Sweden as merely the lead nation in a civilizationwide lurch toward a "post–nuclear family order" and the Myrdals as extraordinarily far-seeing social analysts, reading the path of social evolution better than any of their contemporaries and correctly siding with the victorious sweep of history.[22] It is more accurate, though, to view them as bright and effective ideologues and publicists, who recognized the powerful political potential to be found in the selective use of social science and who led the Swedish people to make choices that produced the world in which their descendants now live.

Coming full circle, the Swedish vision now flows back to the United States. Ideas born through contact with progressive American writers in 1929–30 have evolved into the model society now celebrated by the American political left. The Swedish regime based on state-protected gender equality, social parenting, individualized morality, central guidance, and collectivized housing is held up in the United States today as the solution to the work-family conundrums posed by modern postindustrial life. Some advocates even label their proposed federal program of state day care, paid parental leave, gender-role engineering, and socially conscious housing a "family policy" and urge its adoption on behalf of "society's children." Social scientists, too, join in support of the Swedish model, mobilizing numbers and facts to show that American customs are antiquated, the homemaker an unnecessary relic, the single-family dwelling both inefficient and destabilizing, marriage unnecessary, and the working mother "a social fact." Even public commissions, from 1979's White House Conference on Families to 1989's National Commission on Children, bear the familiar marks of the older experiment. In short, the Myrdals' influence remains active in our day, still defining and fueling the fundamental domestic policy contest of the twentieth century.

Notes

1. The Myrdals' missionary work outside of Sweden is described, in detail, in my "The Roles of Alva and Gunnar Myrdal in the Development of a Social Democratic Response to Europe's Population Crisis, 1929–1938" (doctoral diss., Ohio University, 1978), pp. 415–68.
2. Åke Elmér, *Svensk socialpolitik* (Lund: Liber-Läromedel, 1975), p. 99; and Halvor Gille, *Svensk befolkningspolitik* (Copenhagen: Socialt Tidsskrift, 1949).
3. Ann Katrin Hatje, *Befolkningsfrågan och välfärden: Debatten om familjepolitik och nativitetsökning under 1930-och 1940-talen* (Stockholm: Allmänna Förlaget, 1974), pp. 121–35, 226–32, and 239.
4. Ann-Sofie Kälvemark, *More Children of Better Quality?: Aspects of Swedish Population Policy in the 1930s* (Uppsala: Historishka Institutionen, 1980), pp. 81, 102, 132–39.
5. On these points see Michael Teitelbaum and Jay Winter, *The Fear of Population Decline* (New York: Academic Press, 1985).
6. See the extensive contemporary critique of the Myrdals' work in Anders Byttner, *Vetenskap och politik i befolkningsfrågan* (Stockholm: Centrum-Information AB, 1939).
7. Quotation from Kälvemark, *More Children of Better Quality?*, p. 95.
8. Ibid., p. 86.
9. See my *Family Questions: Reflections on the American Social Crisis*

(New Brunswick, N.J.: Transaction Books, 1988), pp. 171-94; and David Poponoe, *Disturbing the Nest: Family Change and Decline in Modern Society* (New York: Aldine de Gruyter, 1988), pp. 141, 146, and 274–75.

10. Hatje, *Befolkningsfrågan och välfärden*, pp. 47–86.
11. *Handbook on Sex Instruction in Swedish Schools* (Stockholm: National Board of Education, 1956, 1968), pp. 13–15.
12. Alva Myrdal and Viola Klein, *Women's Two Roles: Home and Work* (London: Routledge and Kegan Paul, 1956).
13. Eva Moberg, *Kvinnor och människor* (Stockholm: Bonniers, 1962).
14. Edmund Dahlstrom, "Analysis of the Debate on Sex Roles," in Edmund Dahlstrom, ed., *The Changing Role of Men and Women*, trans. Gunilla and Steven Aulerman (Boston: Beacon, 1962), pp. 106–107.
15. Alva Myrdal, *Towards Equality: The Alva Myrdal Report to the Swedish Social Democratic Party* (1969; reprint, Stockholm: Prisma, 1971), pp. 82–84.
16. Annika Baude and Per Holmberg, "The Positions of Men and Women in the Labour Market," in Dahlstrom, *The Changing Roles of Men and Women*, p. 124.
17. Annika Baude, "Public Policy and Changing Family Patterns in Sweden, 1930–1977," In Jean Lipman-Blumen and Jessie Bernard, eds., *Sex Roles and Social Policy: A Complex Social Science Equation* (New York: SAGE Studies in International Sociology, 1979), pp. 145–72.
18. *Instruction Concerning Interpersonal Relations* (Stockholm: National Swedish Board of Education, 1977), p. 11; and Poponoe, *Disturbing the Nest*, pp. 148–55.
19. See Monica Boethius, "The Working Family," *Social Change in Sweden* 30 (May 1984): 5; "Equality Between Men and Women in Sweden," *Fact Sheets Published by the Swedish Institute*, December 1983, pp. 1–2; and Berit Rollén, "The Working Family: Work and Family Patterns," paper presented at the seminar "The Working Family: Perspective and Prospects in the U.S. and Sweden," sponsored by the Swedish Information Service and the Swedish Embassy, Washington, D.C., May 1984, pp. 1–2.
20. The latest upsurge in concern came in the 1976–78 period. See Erland Hofsten, *Flera Barn i Sverige?: Om befolkningsutvecklingen förr, nu, och i framtiden* (Stockholm: P. A. Norstedt and Söner, 1978/1983), pp. 67–77 and 124–150.
21. A fine description of the sociology of contemporary Sweden is found in Poponoe, *Disturbing the Nest*, pp. 167–77. Also: Elise F. Jones et al., "Teenage Pregnancy in Developed Countries: Determinants and Policy Implications," *Family Planning Perspectives* 17 (March/April 1985): 53–62.
22. While careful to leave open the possibility of reversal, Poponoe's *Disturbing the Nest* leans toward this interpretation; see pp. 187–214 and 305.

Select Bibliography

I. Unpublished Sources

Arbetarrörelsens Arkiv (Labor Movement Archive, Stockholm)
    Alva and Gunnar Myrdal Clipping Collection (AGMC)
    Alva Myrdal Archive (AMA)
    Alva Myrdal Archive Letter Collection (AMAL)
    Ernst Wigforss Colection (EW)
    Eva Wigforss Collection (EVW)
    Gunnar Myrdal Archive (GMA)
    Gunnar Myrdal Archive Letter Collection (GMAL)
    Gustav Möller Archive (GMÖA)
    Per Albin Hansson Collection (PAH)
Preliminär förteckning över Alva och Gunnar Myrdal arkiv (1976)
Socialdemokratiska arbetarparti arkiv (SAP: Social Democratic Labor
    Party Archive, Stockholm)
    Partistyrelsens protokoll, 1934–38
    Verkställande utskottets protokoll, 1934–38
    Verkställande utskottets bilagor, 1934–36
Socialdemokratiska riksdagsgrupp (Social Democratic Parliamentary
    Group, Stockholm)
    Socialdemokratiska riksdagsgruppens förtroenderådets protokoll,
    1935–37
    Socialdemokratiska riksdagsgruppens protokoll, 1935–37
Riksarkivet (National Archives, Stockholm)
    Papers of the 1933 Bostadssociala Utredningen (Social Housing In-
    vestigation), *RA* Komm Nr. 1423 (*RA* 1423), vol. F:1
    Papers of the 1935 Befolkningskommissionen (Population Commis-
    sion), *RA* Komm. Nr. 542 (*RA* 542), vols. 1–13.

Note from Alva Myrdal to the author, 23 July 1977

II. Published Primary Documents

Protokoll från Sverges socialdemokratiska arbetarpartis 15:e Kongress (Stockholm, 3–9 April 1936). Stockholm: Tryckerietaktiebolaget Tiden, 1937.
Riksdagens protokoll: Protokoll vid lagtima Riksdagsmötet och bihang till Riksdagens protokoll. 1931, 1935–39.

III. Interviews by the Author

Gunnar Myrdal, 8 March 1976 (Philadelphia)
Alva and Gunnar Myrdal, 20 July 1976 (Stockholm)
Gunnar Myrdal, 26 July 1976 (Stockholm)
Gunnar Myrdal, 30 July 1976 (Stockholm)
Alva Myrdal, 7 July 1977 (Stockholm)
Alva and Gunnar Myrdal, 29 July 1977 (Stockholm)
Alf Johansson and Brita Åkerman, 26 July 1976 (Stockholm)
Richard Sterner, 29 June 1977 (Stockholm)

IV. Other Interviews (Published and Unpublished)

"Duktiga kvinnor," *Folket*, 2 May 1936.
Herz, Ulrich. "Intervju med Alva och Gunnar Myrdal [Geneva, July 1970]." *I fredens tjänst*, pp. 109–46. Stockholm: Rabén and Sjögren, 1971.
"Myrdals vill ej ha många barn." *Vecko-Journalen*, 5 April 1936.
Nyhlén, Eric. Interview with Gunnar Myrdal (1973–?) *GMA 96.2.1.*
Pehrsson, Kajsa. "Samtal med Alf Johansson." *Att bo*, June 1973, pp. 8–13.

V. Government Documents and Publications

Following Swedish practice, Statens Offentliga Utredningen (SOU) publications are listed here by issue sequence, rather than alphabetically or by author.
Radiotjänst. *Acta och facta i befolkningsfrågan.* Stockholm: Aktiebolaget Radiotjänst, 1935.

————. *Prospekt för radiotjänsts kurs i befolkningsfrågan, 1935–36.* Stockholm: Aktiebolaget Radiotjänst, 1935.

————. *Studiebrev nrs. 1–11 i serien 'befolkningsfrågan.'* Stockholm: Aktiebolaget Radiotjänst, 1935–36.

SOU 1933: 14. *Bostadsfrågan såsom socialt planläganingsproblem: Under krisen och på längre sikt. En undersökning rörande behovet av en utvidgning av bostadsstatistik jämte vissa därmed förbunden socialpolitiska frågor.* Stockholm, 1933.

SOU 1934: 2. *Finanspolitikens ekonomiska verkningar.* Arbetslöshetsutredningen. Stockholm, 1934.

SOU 1935: 2. *Betänkande med förslag rörande lån och årliga bidrag av statsmedel för främjande av bostadsförsörjning för mindre bemedlade barnrika familjer.* Bostadssociala Utredningen. Stockholm, 1935.

SOU 1935: 49. *Betänkande med förslag rörande ändringar i vissa delar av hälsovårdsstadgen samt anordande av förbättrad bostadsinspektion i städer och stadsliknande samhällen m.m.* Bostadssociala Utredningen. Stockholm, 1935.

SOU 1936: 12. *Betänkande angående förlossningsvården och barnmorskeväsendet samt förebyggande mödra- och barnavård.* Befolkningskommissionen. Stockholm, 1936.

SOU 1936: 13. *Betänkande angående familjebeskattningen.* Befolkningskommissionen. Stockholm, 1936.

SOU 1936: 14. *Betänkande angående dels plannmässigt sparande och dels statliga bosättningslån.* Befolkningskommissionen. Stockholm, 1936.

SOU 1936: 15. *Betänkande angående moderskapspenning och mödrahjälp.* Befolkningskommissionen. Stockholm, 1936.

SOU 1936: 46. *Betänkande angående sterilisering.* Befolkningskommissionen. Stockholm, 1936.

SOU 1936: 51. *Yttrande angående revision av 18 kap. 13 strafflagen m.m.* Befolkningskommissionen. Stockholm, 1936.

SOU 1936: 59. *Betänkande i sexualfrågan.* Befolkningskommissionen. Stockholm, 1936.

SOU 1937: 6. *Yttrande i abortfrågan.* Befolkningskommissionen. Stockholm, 1937.

SOU 1937: 43. *Betänkande med förslag rörande lån och bidrag av statsmedel till främjande av bostadsförsörjning för mindre be-*

medlade barnrika familjer, egnahem m.m. Bostadssociala Utredningen. Stockholm, 1937.

SOU 1938: 6. *Betänkande i näringsfrågan.* Befolkningskommissionen. Stockholm, 1938.

SOU 1938: 7. *Betänkande angående barnbekladnadsbidrag, m.m.* Befolkningskommissionen. Stockholm, 1938.

SOU 1938: 13. *Betänkande angående förvärvsarbetande kvinnors rättsliga ställning vid äktenskap och barnsbörd.* Befolkningskommissionen. Stockholm, 1938.

SOU 1938: 15. *Betänkande angående "landsbygdens avfolkning."* Befolkningskommissionen. Stockholm, 1938.

SOU 1938: 19. *Yttrande med socialetiska synpunkter på befolkningsfrågan.* Befolkningskommissionen. Stockholm, 1938.

SOU 1938: 20. *Betänkande angående barnkrubbor och sommarkolonier m.m.* Befolkningskommissionen. Stockholm, 1938.

SOU 1938: 24. *Betänkande med vissa demografiska utredningar.* Befolkningskommissionen. Stockholm, 1938.

SOU 1938: 47. *Betänkande angående gift kvinnas förvärvsarbete, m.m.* Kvinnoarbetskommitten. Stockholm, 1938.

SOU 1938: 57. *Slutbetänkande.* Befolkningskommissionen. Stockholm, 1938.

Statistiska Centralbyrån. *Särskilda folkräkningen 1935/36. VI. Partiella folkräkningen i mars 1936: barnantal och döda barn i äktenskapen.* Stockholm, 1939.

VI. Works by Alva and Gunnar Myrdal

Jointly Authored by Alva and Gunnar Myrdal

Kontakt med Amerika. Stockholm: Albert Bonniers Förlag, 1941.
Kris i befolkningsfrågan. Stockholm: Albert Bonniers Förlag, 1934.

Authored by Alva Myrdal

"A Programme for Family Security in Sweden," *International Labour Review* 36 (June 1939): 723–63.
"Barnförsörjningen, I, II, III." *Tidevarvet*, nos. 34–36 (August–September 1933).

"Befolkningsfrågan skall lösas genom ett rikare liv och bättre bostäder." *Nya Samhället*, 20 April 1936.

"Befolkningskommissionens arbet, 1935–1938." *Social Årsbok 1939*. Stockholm, 1939.

"Bygg en stad i arbete, hälsa och skönhet." *Morgonbris*, March 1935.

"Can Sweden Evolve a Population Policy?" *American-Scandinavian Review* 25 (Summer 1937): 114–18.

"Den återuppväckte befolkningsfrågan." *Social-Demokraten* (Stockholm), 28 March 1941.

"Den nyere tids revolution i kvindens stilling," In Kirsten Gloerfelt-Tarp, ed., *Kvinden i Samfundet*. Copenhagen: Martins Forlag, 1937.

"Den tomma sidan i befolkningspolitiken," *Morgånbris*, March 1936.

"Det er blitt moderne å ha många barn!" *Morgonbladet* (Oslo), 24 October 1935.

(With Eva Wigforss and Edit Sköld) "Ett ord i rättan tid!" *Vi*, 29 January 1938.

"Fackföreningsfolket och befolkningspolitiken," *Fackföreningsrörelsen*, 21 February 1936, pp. 296–99.

"Familjen göres om." *Morgonbris*, 13 July 1933, pp. 13–15.

"Familjen och krisen." *Vi*, 22 February 1941.

"Familjens framtid—folkets framtid." *Den 20 september* (1936) (A campaign brochure).

Familj och lön. Stockholm: Tryckeriaktiebolaget, 1937.

Föräldrarfostrans socialpedagogiska uppgifter och organisation. Stockholm: Marcus Boktryckeri, 1938.

"Hemmadöttrar." *Yrkeskvinnor*, May 1937.

"Hurdan är den gifta lärarinnan?" *Idun*, 9 May 1936.

"Keeping Together and Looking Forward." *Yrkeskvinnor*, 1 June 1937.

"Kollektiv bostadsform." *Tiden* 24 (December 1932): 601–607.

"Kollektivhuset." *Hertha*, January 1933, pp. 9–11.

(With Eva Wigforss, Signe Höjer, Andrea Andreen, and Carin Boalt) *Kvinnan, familjen och samhället*. Stockholm: Kooperativa Förbundets Bokförlag, 1938.

"Kvinnliga präster, landshövdingar och mera sådant." *Yrkeskvinnor*, March 1938.

"Medborgarkunskap efter kön." *Morgonbris*, June 1937.

Nation and Family: The Swedish Experiment in Democratic Family and Population Policy. New York: Harper and Brothers, 1941.

"Ofrånkomlig kvalitetsvärd av den nya generationen." *Tidevarvet*, 6 April 1935.

"Pojkar och flickor." *Morgonbris*, March 1937.

"Population Trends in Densely Populated Areas." *Proceedings of the American Philosophical Society* 95 (13 February 1951): 1–7.

Riktiga leksaker. Stockholm: Kooperativa Förbundets Bokförlag, 1936.

"Sexualfrågan under offentlig utredning." *SAP Information*, February 1937, pp. 49–53.

Småbarnfostran. Stockholm: Kooperativa Förbundets Bokförlag, 1937.

Stadsbarn: En bok om deras fostran i storbarnkammare. Stockholm: Kooperativa Förbundets Bokförlag, 1935.

The Swedish Approach to Population Policies: Balancing Quantitative and Qualitative Population Philosophies in a Democracy." *Journal of Heredity* 30 (March 1939): 111–15.

"Swedish Women in Industry and at Home." *Annals of the American Academy of Political and Social Science* 197 (May 1938): 216–31.

"3000 barn dö årligen i onödan: Skillnaden i levnadsstandard ännu förförande stor i landet." *Social-Demokraten* (Stockholm), 19 September 1936.

Towards Equality: The Alva Myrdal Report to the Swedish Social Democratic Party. Stockholm: Prisma, 1971.

"Uppfostran till 'Äkta Quinnlighet.'" *Idun*, 25 February 1934, pp. 190–202.

"Vart tar pappa vägen?" *Idun*, 10 September 1938.

"Vem har råd att bli intellektuell?" *Morgonbris*, January 1937.

"Vem skall försörja barnen?" *Tidevarvet*, no. 31, August 1933.

"Vi föräldrar måste fostra oss." *Idun*, 4 July 1936.

(With Viola Klein) *Women's Two Roles: Home and Work.* London: Routledge and Kegan Paul, 1956.

"Yrkeskvinnans barn." *Yrkeskvinnor klubbnytt*, February 1933, p. 63.

Authored by Gunnar Myrdal

Against the Stream: Critical Essays on Economics. New York: Pantheon, 1972, 1973.

"Aktuella beskattningsproblem" *Nationalekonomiska föreningens förhand lingar* 8 (1936): 89–105.

"Allmänna och ekonomiska synpunkter på befolkningsutvecklingen." Stenographic record in *Nordisk Försäkringstidskrift: Årgången, 1936 (16).* Stockholm: Paul Bergholm, 1936.

"A Worried America." Address given to the Tenth Annual Meeting of the Lutheran Council in the U.S.A., Philadelphia, Pa. 11 March 1976.

Befolkningsproblemet i Sverge. Stockholm: Arbetarnas Bildningsförbunds Centralbyrå, 1935.

(With Gunnar Lange, Bengt Helger, Alf Johansson, Sune Lindström, Sven Wallander). *Bostaden och vår ekonomi.* Stockholm: Hyresgästernas Förlag, 1934.

(With Uno Åhrén) *Bostadsfrågan såsom socialt planläggningsproblem under krisen och på längre sikt; en undersökning rörande behovet av en utvidgning av bostadsstatistiken jämte vissa därmed förbundna socialpolitiska frågor.* Stockholm: Kooperativa Förbundets Bokförlag, 1933.

"Bostadssociala preludier." Reprint from *Bostadspolitik och samhällsplanering: Hyllningsskrift till Alf Johansson.* Stockholm: n.p., 1968.

"Den förändrade världsbilden i nom nationalekomien," In Gunnar Myrdal and Herbert Tingsten, *Samhällskrisen och Socialvetenskaperna.* Stockholm: Kooperativa Förbundets Bokförlag, 1935.

Det svenska jordbrukets läge i världskrisen. Föredrag vid landtbruks veckans allmänna sammanträde, 14 March 1932. Stockholm: Norrtelje, 1932.

"Familjesynpunkten på bostaden." *Andra allmänna Svenska bostadskongressen. Stockholm, den 29–30 November 1935: Föredrag, förhandlingar och beslut stenografiskt protokoll.* Stockholm: Hyresgästernas riksförbunds, 1936.

"Industrialization and population." *Economic Essays in Honour of Gustav Cassel.* London: George Allen and Unwin, 1933.

"Jordbrukspolitikens svårigheter." *Nationalekonomiska föreningens förhandlingar* (1938): 57–98.

Jordbrukspolitiken under omläggning. Stockholm: Kooperativa Förbundets Bokförlag, 1938.

"Jordbrukspolitik—planmässig och på längre sikt," *Konsumentbladet* 22 (1935): 3f.

Konjunktur och offentlig hushållning: En utredning. Stockholm: Kooperativa Förbundets Bokförlag, 1933.

"Kontant eller in natura i socialpolitiken." *Nationalekonomisk Tidskrift* 76 (1938): 69–91.

"Kosta sociala reformer pengar?" *Arkitektur och samhälle.* Stockholm: Bröderna Lagerström, 1932.

Krise i befolkningsspørsmålet. Oslo: n.p., 1935.

"Lantbrukets bristande räntabilitet", *Svensk Tidskrift* 18 (1928): 463–76.

The Political Element in the Development of Economic Theory (*Vetenskap och politik*). London: Routledge and Kegan, 1953.

Population: A Problem for Democracy. Cambridge: Harvard University Press, 1940.

"Population Problems and Policies," *Annals of the American Academy of Political and Social Science* 197 (May 1938): 200–215.

Prisbildningsproblemet och föränderligheten. Uppsala: Almqvist and Wiksell, 1927.

"Socialpolitikens dilemma, I," and "Socialpolitikens dilemma, II," *Spektrum* 2, no. 3 (1932): 1–13; 2, no. 4 (1932): 13–31.

"Socialpolitik in natura," *Första Maj* (1938), pp. 31–32. SAP party brochure.

Sveriges väg genom penningkrisen. Stockholm: Natur och kultur, 1931.

Vad gäller striden i befolkningsfrågan? Stockholm: Frihets Förlag, 1936.

"Våra sociala syftlinjer." *Frihet,* 1 September 1936.

"Vår losen är: hemmet, familjen." *Hus och Härd,* September 1936.

(With Karl Arvid Edin, Rut Grubb, and Arvid Runestam) *Vårt folks framtid.* Stockholm: C. E. Fritzes Bokförlag, 1935.

"With Dictators as Neighbors." *Survey Graphic* 28 (May 1939): 351–57.

VII. Memoirs

Erlander, Tage. *1940–49.* Stockholm: Tidens Förlag, 1973.

Ohlin, Bertil. *Memoarer: Ung man blir politiker.* Stockholm: Bonniers Förlag, 1972.
Wallander, Sven. *Minnen. Del I: HSB:s öden från 1920-talet till 1957.* Stockholm: HSB:s Riksförbund, 1965.
Wigforss, Ernst. *Minnen III: 1932–1949.* Stockholm: Tidens Förlag, 1954.

VIII. Primary Published Sources

A. Books and Pamphlets

Alegård, Gustaf. *Befolkningsfrågan genom tiderna.* (Studentföreningen verdandis småskrifter 301.) Stockholm: Albert Bonniers Förlag, 1926.
Andersson, John. *Barnalsstringsfrågan och arbetarklassen.* Gothenburg: John Andersson Förlag, 1916.
Asplund, Gunnar, Walter Gahn, Sven Markelius, Gregor Paulsson, Eskil Sundahl, and Uno Åhrén. *Acceptera.* Stockholm: Tidens Förlag, 1931.
Bergegren, Hinke. *Kärlek utan barn.* Stockholm: Ungsocialistiska Partiets Förlag, 1910.
Biorck, G. *Vårt folk och vår framtid.* Stockholm: Meden, 1940.
Bohlin, Torsten. *Äktenskapets kris och förnyelse.* Stockholm: Kooperativa Förbundets Bokförlag, 1933.
Borg, Folke. *Ett döende folk: Synpunkter i befolkningsfrågan.* Stockholm: Hugo Gebers Förlag, 1935.
Byttner, Anders. *Vetenskap och politik i befolkningsfrågan.* Stockholm: Centrum-Information AB, 1939.
Cassel, Gustav. *Liv eller död.* Stockholm: Albert Bonniers Förlag, 1935.
Dahlberg, Gunnar. *Sverges befolkningsproblem.* Special imprint by *Tiden*, no. 5. Stockholm: Tidens Förlag, 1930.
Debatt i befolkningsfrågan. Stockholm: n.p., 1935.
Edin, Karl Arvid, and Edward P. Hutchinson. *Studies of Differential Fertility in Sweden.* London: P. S. King and Son, 1935.
Ett genombrott. Den svenska socialpolitiken: utvecklingslinjer och framtidsmål. Stockholm: Tidens Förlag, 1944.
Guinchard, J., and G. Silén. *En befolkningsgenerations reproduktions förmåga.* Stockholm: K. L. Beckmans Boktryckeri, 1929.

Hofsten, Nils von. *Ärftlighetslärans grunder II: Manniskan.* Stockholm: Albert Bonniers Förlag, 1931.

——. *Steriliseringsfrågan från rasbiologisk synpunkt.* Stockholm: Svenska Föreningens för Pyskisk Hälsovård, 1933.

Hyrenius, Hannes. *Livsvilja eller folkdöd.* Lund: Sundqvist and Emond, 1941.

Karleby, Nils. *Socialism inför verligheten: Studie över socialdemokratisk åskådning och nutidspolitik.* Stockholm: Tidens Förlag, 1926.

Kooperativa förbundet. *Befolknings—och familjerfrågor: Handledning för de kooperativa gruppernas och gillenas diskussioner.* Stockholm: Kooperativa Förbundets Bokförlag, 1935.

Linders, F. J. *Vårt befolkningsproblem.* Stockholm: P. A. Norstedt and Söner, 1930.

Lundborg, H. *Befolkningsfrågan ur rashygiensk synpunkt: Den svenska bondeklassens betydelse.* Sala: Sala-Postens Boktryckeri, 1928.

——. *Västerlandet i fara: Befolkningsfrågor i biologisk och rahsygienisk betydsning.* Gothenburg: Ernst V. Hansson Förlag, 1934.

Nyström, Anton. *Fattigdom och barnalstring.* Stockholm: Björck and Börjesson, 1911.

Öhrvall, Hjalmar. *I vår befolkningsfråga.* Stockholm: Albert Bonniers Förlag, 1917.

Ruben-Wolf, Martha. *Fösterfördrivning eller förebyggande åtgärder.* Stockholm: Förlagsaktiebolaget Arbetarkultur, 1931.

Sandler, Rickard. *Samhället sådant det är.* Stockholm: Frams Förlag, 1911.

Silverstolpe, G. Westin. *Folkmängd och välstånd.* Stockholm: Bokförlaget Brand, 1926.

Sommarin, Emil. *Befolkningsfrågan och jordbruket.* Lund: Gleerup, 1935.

Ström, Tord. *Nu gäller det livet!* Stockholm: Diakonistyrelsens Förlag, 1935.

Sundbärg, Gustav. *Bevolkerungsstatistik Schwedens, 1750–1900: Einige hauptresultate.* Stockholm: P. A. Norstedt och Söner, 1907.

Tonndorf, H. G. *Befolkningsstagnation och kapitalbildning.* Finanstidning reprint no. 6, 1936.

Trägårdh, Ivar. *Civilisations dilemma och andra biologiska skisser.* Stockholm: Holger Schildts Förlag, 1934.

Welinder, P. J. *Fattigdom och folkökning*. Gothenburg: Arbetare-kurirens Förlag, 1928.

Wicksell, Knut. *Barnalstringsfrågan: Föredrag, hållet vid nymalthu-sianska sällskapet*. Stockholm: Federatives Förlag, 1925.

——. *De sexual frågorna: Granskning af hrr Emil Svensens, Björnst-jerne Björnsons samt professor Seved Ribbings brochyrer*. Stockholm: Kungsholms Bokhandel, 1890.

——. *Läran om befolkningen*. Uppsala: Verdandi, 1880.

——. *Några ord om samhällsolyckornas vigtigäste orsak och boteme-del med särskilt afseende på dryckenskapen*. Uppsala: n.p., 1880.

Wicksell, Sven. *Ur befolkningsläran*. Stockholm: Albert Bonniers Förlag, 1931.

Wigforss, Eva. *Arbetsinkomst och familjeförsörjning*. Stockholm: P. A. Norstedt and Söner, 1929.

——. *Familjeförsörjning för industrinsarbetare*. Fack-föreningsrorelsen pamphlet no. 25, 1925.

B. *Select Articles*

Alegård, Gustaf. "Befolkningsförhållandena i olika lander." *Tiden* 19 (November 1927): 407–17, (December 1927): 464–75.

——. "Folkräkning och familjestatistik." *Tiden* 23 (September 1931): 420–25.

——. "Folkökning och krigsfara." *Tiden* 20 (March 1928): 104–14.

——. "Tysklands nativitetsfråga." *Tiden* 22 (December 1930): 611–17.

Aspegren, Gillis. "Befolkningsteorin: Historisk." *Tiden* 18 (1926): 155–67.

Bonnevie, Margarete. "Familje lön eller 'barnetrygd.' " *Tidevarvet*, no. 33 (August 1933).

Edin, Karl Arvid. "Födelsekontrollens inträgande hos de breda län-gren." *Ekonomisk Tidskrift* 31 (1929): 123–52.

——. "Vårt moderna befolkningsproblem." In *Social Hygiene*, pp. 80–83. Uppsala: Almqvist and Wiksell, 1927.

Gårdlund, Torsten. "Befolkningsfrågan i dagens politik." *Tiden* 29 (January 1937).

——. "Plannmässig socialpolitik." *Clarté*, April 1937.

Grimlund, Otto. "Några ord i befolkningsfrågan." *Tiden* 4 (1912): 272–77.

Hofsten, Erland von. "Kontant eller natura i socialpolitiken," *Clarté*, April 1938.

Höjer, Axel. "Den s.k. preventivlagens otidsentlighet." *Tiden* 19 (March 1927): 79–84.

Jerneman, Tor. "Arbetsmarknaden och vår befolkningsfråga, II." *Fackföreningsrörelsen*, 7 March 1936.

Johansson, Alf. "Bostadsbehov och bostadsproduktion." *Tiden* 22 (February 1930): 70–84.

———. "Vad betala vi för bostaden?" In Gunnar Lange, Bengt Helger, Alf Johansson, Sune Lindström, Gunnar Myrdal, and Sven Wallander. *Bostaden och vår ekonomi*. Stockholm, Hyresgästernas Förlag, 1934.

Markelius, Sven. "Kollektivhuset." In *Arkitektur och samhälle*. Stockholm: Bröderna Lagerström, 1932.

Mogård, Bertil. "Folkökning och försörjning." *Tiden* 19 (June 1927): 218–23.

Montgomery, Arthur. "Befolkningskommissionen och befolkningsfrågan." *Ekonomisk Tidskrift* 41 (September 1939): 200–21.

Paulsson, Gregor. "Arkitektur och politik." In *Arkitektur och samhälle*. Stockholm: Bröderna Lagerström, 1932.

Rehn, Gösta. "Dit befolkningsfrågan hunnit." *Clarté*, June 1936, pp. 17–22.

———. "Socialpolitik 1937–II." *Metallarbetaren*, October 1937.

Severin, Frans. "Fackföreningsrörelsen och befolkningsfrågan." *Tiden* 19 (June 1927): 204–17.

Silverstolpe, G. Westin. "Malthus och nutidens nationalekonomi." *Tiden* 19 (January 1927): 11–20.

Wicksell, Knut. "Befolkningsfrågans nuvarande läge." *Tiden* 16 (June 1924): 193–208.

Wicksell, Sven D. "Folkmängden och dess förändringar." *Tiden* 18 (December 1926): 321–34.

———. "Sveriges framtida befolkning under olika förutsättningar." *Ekonomisk Tidskrift* 28, no. 4–5, (1926): 91–123.

Wigforss, Enrst. "Provisorisk löneförbättring och familjeförsörjning." *SAP Information*, March 1937, pp. 65–69.

IX. Secondary Sources

Ahlberg, Gösta. *Befolkningsutvecklingen och urbaniseringen i Sverige, 1911–1950.* Stockholm: Stockholms Kommunalförvaltning, 1953.

Åkerman, Brita. "For ett bättre boende." *FORM* 66, no. 6–7, (1970): 296–99.

————. "Goda grännar på 1920-talet—och på 70-talet." *Att bo*, June 1973, pp. 18–23.

Alva och Gunnar Myrdal: I fredens tjänst. Stockholm: Rabén and Sjögren, 1971.

Borgström, Georg. *Malthus om befolkningsfrågan.* Stockholm: LTs Förlag, 1969.

Braatoy, Bjärne. *The New Sweden: A Vindication of Democracy.* London: Thomas Nelson and Sons, 1939.

Carlsson, Gösta. "The Decline of Fertility: Innovation or Adjustment?" *Population Studies* 20 (February 1966): 149–74.

Cervin, Ulf. "Kris i befolkningsfrågan." *1900-talet. Vår tids historia i ord och bild*, pp. 45–50. Helsingborg: Bokfrämjandet, 1975.

Dahlstrom, Edmund, ed. *The Changing Role of Men and Women.* Trans. Gunnilla and Steven Aulerman. Boston: Beacon, 1962.

Det gäller vårt liv. Stockholm: Folkhuset, 1976.

Elmér, Åke. *Från fattigsverige till välfärdsstaten.* Stockholm: Bokförlaget Aldus/Bonniers, 1963.

————. *Svensk socialpolitik.* Lund: Liber-Läromedel, 1975.

Eriksson, Ingrid, and John Rogers. *Rural Labor and Population Change: Social and Demographic Developments in East-Central Sweden During the Nineteenth Century.* Stockholm: Almqvist and Wiksell, 1978.

Furniss, Norman, and Timothy Tilton. *The Political Theory of the Welfare State.* Bloomington: Indiana University Press, 1977.

Gårdlund, Torsten. *Knut Wicksell: Rebell i det nya riket.* Stockholm: Albert Bonniers Förlag, 1956.

Gille, Halvor. *Svensk befolkningspolitik.* Copenhagen: Socialt Tidsskrift, 1949.

Glass, D. V. *Population Policies and Movements in Europe*. Oxford: Clarendon Press, 1940.

Glesinger, Egon. "Gunnar Myrdal." Mimeographed biography presented to Gunnar Myrdal on his fiftieth birthday, 6 December 1948.

Grönlund, Otto. *Översikt av befolkningsrörelsen i Sverige under 200 år*. Stockholm: P. A. Norstedt och Söner, 1949.

Gustafsson, Göran. *Religionen i Sverige: Ett sociologiskt perspektiv*. Stockholm: Norstedts Tryckeri, 1981.

Hadenius, Stig, Bjorn Molin, and Hans Wieslandeder. *Sverige efter 1900: En modern politik historia*. Stockholm: Bokförlaget Aldus/Bonniers, 1967.

Hagård, Birger. *Nils Wohlin: Konservativ Centerpolitiker*. Linkoping: AB Sahlströms Bokhandel, 1976.

Hatje, Ann Katrin. *Befolkningsfrågan och välfärden: debatten om familjepolitik och nativitetsökning under 1930- och 1940-talen*. Stockholm: Allmänna Förlaget, 1974.

Heckscher, Eli F. *Svenskt arbete och liv: Från medeltiden till nutiden*. Stockholm: Albert Bonniers Förlag, 1941.

Hellstrom, Gunnar. *Jordbrukspolitik i industrisamhället med tyngdpunket på 1920- och 30-talen*. Stockholm: LTs Förlag, 1976.

Herz, Ulrich. "Två livs öden i vår tid." *I fredens tjänst*, pp. 23–51. Stockholm: Rabén and Sjögren, 1971.

Hofsten, Erland. *Flera Barn i Sverige? Om befolkning sutvecklingen förr, nu, och i framtiden*. Stockholm: P. A. Norstedt and Söner, 1979/1983.

Hofsten, Erland, and Hans Lundström. *Swedish Population History: Main Trends from 1750 to 1970*. Stockholm: National Central Bureau of Statistics, 1976.

Höijer, Ernst J. *Sveriges befolkningsutveckling genom tiderna*. Stockholm: Svenska Bokförlaget, 1959.

Höök, Erik. *Befolkningsutveckling och arbetskraftsförsörjning*. Stockholm: Victor Pettersons Bokindustriaktiebolag, 1952.

Hyrenius, Hannes. *Befolkning och samhälle*. Stockholm: Tidens Förlag, 1951.

Iverus, Ivar. *Versuch einer Darstellung der Zusammenhanges zwischen Bevölkerungsentwicklung, Familienpolitik und öffentlichen Meinung in Schweden*. Helsinki: Kir Japaino o.y. Sana, 1953.

Janson, Florence Edith. *The Background of Swedish Immigration,*

1830–1930. 1934 Reprint. New York: Arno Press and the *New York Times*, 1970.

Kälvemark, Ann-Sofie. *More Children of Better Quality?: Aspects of Swedish Population Policy in the 1930's.* Uppsala: Historiska Institutionen, 1980.

———. *Swedish Marriage Loans: A Means of Increasing Population? A Preliminary Report.* Uppsala: n.p., 1976.

Kirk, Dudley. *Europe's Population in the Interwar Years.* Princeton, N.J.: League of Nations, 1946.

Koblik, Steven. *Sweden's Development from Poverty to Affluence, 1750–1970.* Minneapolis: University of Minnesota Press, 1975.

Koch, Karin. "Nymalthusianismens genombrott i Sverige." *Studier i ekonomi och historia tillägnade Eli F. Heckscher på 65-årsdagen den 24 november 1944*, pp. 73–88. Uppsala: Almqvist and Wiksell, 1945.

Lewin, Leif. *Planhushållningsdebatten.* Uppsala: Political Science Association, 1967.

Lind, Ingela. "Hemutställningen 1917." *FORM* 66, no. 6–7 (1970): 273–80.

Lindhagen, Jan. *Socialdemokratins program. I rörelsens tid 1890–1930.* Stockholm: Tidens Förlag, 1972.

Lipman-Blumen, Jean, and Jessie Bernard, eds. *Sex Roles and Social Policy: A Complex Social Science Equation.* New York: SAGE Studies in International Sociology, 1979.

Lundkvist, Sven. *Folkrörelserna i det svenska samhället, 1850–1920.* Stockholm: Almqvist and Wiksell, 1977.

McCleary, G. F. "Pre-war European population policies." *Milbank Memorial Fund Quarterly* 19 (April 1941): 105–20.

Micklewright, F. H. Amphlett. "The Rise and Decline of English Malthusianism." *Population Studies* 15, no. 1 (1961–62): 32–51.

Moberg, Eva. *Kvinnor och människor.* Stockholm: Bonniers, 1962.

Nyman, Olle. *Svensk Parlamentarism, 1932–36: från minoritets parlamentarism till majoritetskoalition.* Uppsala: Almqvist and Wiksell, 1947.

Öhman, Berndt. *Svensk arbetsmarknadspolitik, 1900–1947.* Stockholm: Bokförlaget Prisma, 1970.

Overbeek, J. *History of Population Theories.* Rotterdam: Rotterdam University Press, 1974.

Poponoe, David. *Disturbing the Nest: Family Change and Decline in Modern Society*. New York: Aldine de Gruyter, 1988.

Quensel, Carl-Erik. *Den äktenskapliga fruktsamheten i Sveriges städer 1911–1953 efter äktenskapets varaktighet och hustruns ålder*. Lund: Statistiska Institutionen, 1956.

Råberg, Per-Göran. "Stockholmsutställningen 1930." *FORM* 66, no. 6–7 (1970): 286–93.

Severin, Frans. *The Ideological Development of Swedish Social Democracy*. Stockholm: SAP, 1956.

Sjöstrand, Johannes. *Den äktenskapliga fruktsamheten i Sverige*. Stockholm: Isaac Marcus Boktryckeri, 1940.

Sodersten, Bo. "Per Albin och den socialistiska reformismen." In Gunnar Frederickson, Dieter Strand, and Bo Södersten. *Per Albin linjen*. Stockholm: Bokförlaget PAN/Norstedts, 1970.

Teitelbaum, Michael, and Jay Winter. *The Fear of Population Decline*. New York: Academic Press, 1985.

Thomas, David Johnson. "Swedish Social Democracy, 1932–1960: A Study of Ideology." Doctoral diss., Harvard University, 1968.

Thomas, Dorothy Swaine. *Social and Economic Aspects of Swedish Population Movements, 1750–1933*. New York: Macmillan, 1941.

Thulstrup, Åke. *Svensk politik, 1905–1939: från unionsupplosningen till andra världskriget*. Stockholm: Albert Bonniers Förlag, 1968.

Tingsten, Herbert. *The Swedish Social Democrats: Their Ideological Development*. Trans. Greta Frankel and Patricia Howard Rosen. Totowa, N.J.: Bedminster Press, 1973.

Wahlund, Sten. *Andras ungar*. Stockholm: Wahlström and Widstrand, 1948.

Wärenstam, Eric. *Fascismen och nazismen i Sverige, 1920–1940*. Stockholm: Almqvist and Wiksell, 1970.

Widemar, Ingrid Garde. "I politiken." In *Kerstin Hasselgren. En Vänstudie*. Stockholm: P. A. Norstedt och Söner, 1968.

Widman, Dag. "20-talet—på gränsen till en ny tid." *FORM* 66, no. 6–7 (1970): 281–85.

Willers, Uno. "Alva och Gunnar Myrdal." *I fredens tjänst*, pp. 13–22. Stockholm: Rabén and Sjogren, 1971.

Index